Studies in Economic Reform and Social Justice

After the Crash

Designing a Depression-Free Economy

Mason Gaffney

Edited and with an Introduction by
Clifford W. Cobb

WILEY-BLACKWELL

The Series
Studies in Economic Reform and Social Justice

Laurence S. Moss, Series Editor

Robert V. Andelson, ed.
Land Value Taxation Around the World, 3rd edition

Critics of Henry George, 2nd edition, Volume 1 (2003)
Critics of Henry George, 2nd edition, volume 2 (2004)

J.A. Giacalone and C. W. Cobb, eds.
The Path to Justice: Following in the Footsteps of Henry George

Christopher K. Ryan
Harry Gunnison Brown
An Orthodox Economist and His Contributions

Philip Day
Land: The Elusive Quest for Social Justice, Taxation Reform
and a Sustainable Planetary Environment

Laurence S. Moss, ed.
Natural Resources, Taxation, and Regulation:
Unusual Perspectives on a Classic Topic

Laurence S. Moss, ed.
Henry George: Political Ideologue, Social Philosopher
and Economics Theorist

Clifford W. Cobb, ed.
Selected Works of Mason Gaffney
After the Crash: Designing a Depression-free Economy

Studies in Economic Reform and Social Justice

After the Crash

Designing a Depression-Free Economy

Mason Gaffney

Edited and with an Introduction by
Clifford W. Cobb

Blackwell Publishing was acquired by John Wiley & Sons in February 2007. Blackwell's publishing program has been merged with Wiley's global Scientific, Technical, and Medical business to form Wiley-Blackwell.

Registered Office
John Wiley & Sons Ltd, The Atrium, Southern Gate, Chichester, West Sussex, PO19 8SQ, United Kingdom

Editorial Offices
350 Main Street, Malden, MA 02148-5020, USA
9600 Garsington Road, Oxford, OX4 2DQ, UK
The Atrium, Southern Gate, Chichester, West Sussex, PO19 8SQ, UK

For details of our global editorial offices, for customer services, and for information about how to apply for permission to reuse the copyright material in this book, please see our website at www.wiley.com/wiley-blackwell.

Wiley also publishes its books in a variety of electronic formats. Some content that appears in print may not be available in electronic books.

Designations used by companies to distinguish their products are often claimed as trademarks. All brand names and product names used in this book are trade names, service marks, trademarks, or registered trademarks of their respective owners. The publisher is not associated with any product or vendor mentioned in this book. This publication is designed to provide accurate and authoritative information in regard to the subject matter covered. It is sold on the understanding that the publisher is not engaged in rendering professional services. If professional advice or other expert assistance is required, the services of a competent professional should be sought.

Library of Congress Cataloging-in-Publication Data

Gaffney, Mason.
    Studies in economic reform and social justice : after the crash : designing a depression-free economy / Mason Gaffney ; edited and with an introduction by Clifford W. Cobb.
        p. cm.
        Includes index.
        ISBN 978-1-4443-3358-9 (hardcover)—ISBN 978-1-4443-3307-7 (pbk.) 1. Real property tax. 2. Business cycles. I. Cobb, Clifford W. II. Title.

    HJ4165.G34 2009
    330—dc22
                                                                                    2009030447

A catalogue record for this book is available from the Library of Congress.

Set in 10 on 13pt Garamond Light by Toppan Best-set Premedia Limited
Printed in Singapore by KHL Printing Co Pte Ltd.

01—2009

Dedication

To the memory of Laurence S. Moss, the past editor of the *American Journal of Economics and Sociology,* who first conceived of the idea of publishing a book supplement on Mason Gaffney's selected works ("Best of Mase") on Henry George. This was Larry's way of paying tribute to Professor Gaffney's many contributions to our understanding of the ideas of Henry George.

Acknowledgments

The second essay in this volume, entitled "A New Framework for Macroeconomics" is a substantially revised, edited, and updated version of "Toward Full Employment with Limited Land and Capital," pp. 99–166, in *Property Taxation, Land Use, and Public Policy*, edited by Arthur D. Lynn, Jr. ©1976 by the Board of Regents of the University of Wisconsin System. Reprinted by permission of the University of Wisconsin Press.

The editor would like to thank the following for assistance during the preparation of this manuscript: Pat Aller, Kris Feder, David Giesen, Suzanne Murphy, and the staff of the California State Library.

Contents

Frontispiece Portrait of Mason Gaffney ix

Editor's Introduction—*Clifford W. Cobb*. 1

1. The Role of Land Markets in Economic Crises—
   Mason Gaffney. 27

2. A New Framework for Macroeconomics: Achieving Full
   Employment by Increasing Capital Turnover—
   Mason Gaffney. 61

3. Money, Credit, and Crisis—*Mason Gaffney* 155

Index 211

Mason Gaffney 1998

Editor's Introduction

By CLIFFORD W. COBB*

The current economic crisis appears to be a vortex without any bottom. As of May 2009, the $700 billion bailout of financial institutions (the Troubled Asset Rescue Plan) may have forestalled a total collapse of the U.S. economy. However, nothing has stemmed the flood of foreclosures, the tightening of bank credit, the depression in home construction, the bankruptcies of small business, and the rising rate of unemployment. To avoid the total collapse of the economy, advocates of an unrestrained free market have been forced to accept the partial federal ownership of some major banks, General Motors, and other corporations (but not "nationalization," which would entail government management). Nevertheless, the current crisis has shaken confidence in the ability of capitalism to function as a self-regulating system.

Throughout a long career, Professor Mason Gaffney has identified the endogenous sources of instability in capitalist economies and has shown precisely how capitalism can become a more self-correcting system. The three essays in this volume, based mostly on his earlier writings, examine the theoretical and policy errors that permitted the current crisis to arise. He laments that those same errors have also fostered chronic underemployment of labor, wasteful use of urban and suburban land, military adventurism, and other pathologies. All of those errors stem from undifferentiated capital investment strategies in both the private and public sectors. The persistent problems of modern economies (including the current crisis) are not a function of "capitalism" per se, but rather of flawed models that have distorted markets in systematic ways. In particular, Gaffney points to biases in the relationship between land and capital (the boom-bust cycle

*Clifford Cobb has worked for the Robert Schalkenbach Foundation and Redefining Progress; e-mail: cliff.cobb@gmail.com. He is author of *Responsive Schools, Renewed Communities*, co-author with John Cobb of *The Green National Product*, and co-editor of *The Path to Justice: Following in the Footsteps of Henry George*, another volume in the Wiley-Blackwell series "Studies in Economic Reform and Social Justice."

American Journal of Economics and Sociology, Vol. 68, No. 4 (October, 2009).

of rising and falling land prices, complemented by wasteful capital investment that loses its value in the downturn), between land and labor (the underemployment of labor caused by excessive investment on marginal land), and between labor and capital (the displacement of labor by capital because of overinvestment in capital of long maturity).

Gaffney unites diverse economic traditions (institutionalist, Austrian, Georgist, and others) to produce a novel conceptual understanding of how economies generate their own pathologies, including periodic contraction and loss of liquidity. From that framework, he offers solutions that mainstream macroeconomists ignore because of their focus on monetary variables (including deficit spending). The most distinctive feature of Gaffney's approach is his insistence on taking seriously the real factors of production that lie behind the abstractions of modern economics. By differentiating among various types of capital investment, instead of treating it as a uniform variable, Gaffney shows that policies encouraging excessive investment in land and slow-maturing capital bear prime responsibility for a range of economic ailments. Based on that analysis, it becomes evident why Keynesian, socialist, and Reaganite policies all fail. As long as the current tax system is allowed to bias the location, intensity, and durability of capital investment, the problems attributed to capitalism will recur.

The essays in this volume go behind the headlines and the superficial descriptions of current events. They offer an in-depth look at the causes of recent events through the lens of insights gleaned from patterns that have persisted for hundreds of years. In contrast to economists who treat recessions and depressions as natural calamities that cannot be avoided or as punishment for the sin of overconsumption, Gaffney shows that economic downturns are the result of specific policies and that they can be avoided. He offers an analysis that enables us to understand how the crisis arose and what must be done to prevent a recurrence of this catastrophe.

Before explaining the significance of Gaffney's methods and findings, I will first set the stage with a few words about the present crisis and then discuss some current theories of the crisis and what is wrong with them. That will enable the reader to appreciate the importance of Gaffney's contributions.

I

Brief Summary of the Present Crisis

THE CURRENT GLOBAL ECONOMIC CRISIS consists of a collapse of credit markets that are essential for the functioning of a modern market economy. Faced with a loss of equity capital, banks are reluctant to make ordinary business loans. Without credit, many businesses are facing bankruptcy and liquidation. That means a rising rate of unemployment, reduced personal spending levels, and declining business revenues. All of the factors that normally work together to create a vibrant economy (expanding credit, capital formation, rising incomes, and increased employment) have been working in reverse, causing a downward spiral of reduced capital investment and increases in business failure, personal bankruptcy, unemployment, poverty, and homelessness. On a collective level, we are facing the same problem as an individual who is "house-poor"—owning an asset that is not liquid, but unable to pay for daily needs. On a much larger scale, the nation and the world find themselves in that situation today.

The people to whom we turn as experts on economic matters have failed us, not because they have personal shortcomings, but because their theories do not provide the means of analyzing the sources of the present crisis adequately.

Most economists believe that a market economy is a self-correcting system, but they also assume it sometimes needs government assistance in recovering from a shock and regaining equilibrium. The only remedies most economists learned in the past century to correct disequilibrium were monetary (cutting interest rates to stimulate investment) and fiscal (running a government deficit to inject money into the economy directly). Those types of policies deal only with symptoms. To use a common hydraulic metaphor, the monetary and fiscal policy instruments favored by most economists are the equivalent of pumping more water through clogged pipes, without much interest in what caused them to clog in the first place. Because economists are largely indifferent to what causes economic flows to become restricted, they lack models about how to respond if conventional measures are ineffective—if the blast of water does not break up the obstruction, so to speak. Thus, when we encounter a depression of the sort that now looms over us, the silence of most economists is deafening.

Economists commonly look for external events ("shocks") to explain the cause of sudden economic crises. In this case, however, the shock has come from inside the system. A financial bubble formed as investors bid up the price of U.S. housing by 73 percent from 1999 through 2006 (Federal Housing Finance Agency 2009: 48–50).[1] (There was considerable regional variation. In the Pacific region, prices climbed 143 percent over the same period, and much of the resulting crisis emerged from the Pacific.) Even as prices neared their peak in 2005, there were respected economists (Lereah 2005; Mandel 2004, 2005) who imagined that those prices could never come down. As Mandel (2005), chief economist at *Business Week*, put it, "the expected rise in housing prices makes housing investment effectively free (or even better)." As recently as September 2007, Christina Romer (2007: 2), the new chair of the Council of Economic Advisers, claimed that "better policy, particularly on the part of the Federal Reserve, is directly responsible for the low inflation and the *virtual disappearance of the business cycle* in the last 25 years" (emphasis added). Since Romer has been on the Business Cycle Dating Committee of the National Bureau of Economic Research, her dismissive attitude toward the present downturn reveals an amazing degree of myopia.

There is some confusion about what a real estate price bubble means. When real estate prices rise and fall, that actually represents a change in the price of the *land*, not the associated buildings. Unlike a building, land has no cost of reproduction, does not physically wear out, and is priced solely according to demand. The equilibrium price of any parcel of land is based on the discounted flow of net revenue in its highest and best use, but, as recent experience attests, prices in a bubble can rise above that level based on expectations, and they can fall below that level in the period of retrenchment. Preventing these bubbles and the reduction in productive activity they cause in their aftermath is (or should be) one of the aims of economic policy.

Since the 1970s, mortgages have been increasingly bundled and securitized—turned into derivatives called mortgage-backed securities (MBSs) or collateralized mortgage obligations, which can be combined into standardized units and sold as bonds. As of 2008, $6.6

trillion in mortgages were held in the form of MBSs and only $4.4 trillion were held by banks, savings and loans, and other institutions that held the mortgages on their own books (Board of Governors of the Federal Reserve System 2009: Table L.218). Originating lenders thought they had nothing to worry about. They passed along the risk to others—the investment banks on Wall Street. The investment bankers thought they were secured against defaults because they bought insurance called credit default swaps. The giant insurance company, AIG, was the primary issuer of credit default swaps. Based on those assurances, brokers were able to sell these derivatives to banks around the world.

What few noticed was that the whole securitization process was like an inverted pyramid: a large network of financial transactions resting on a small base of mortgages (small in the sense that the derived instruments were highly leveraged). The derivatives turned "toxic" for two reasons: (1) because, in many parts of the country, *all* real estate was becoming overpriced (high ratio of price to imputed cashflow) in a growing bubble; and (2) because the rising price of housing induced banks to issue mortgages with faulty underlying fundamentals. The whole system of real estate lending rested on unrealistic future ex-pectations that households could pay off adjustable rate mortgages (ARMs) when interest rates rose or that they could refinance when a balloon payment came due. According to the Mortgage Bankers Association (2007), subprime loans, which were issued to households that did not meet normal banking standards for ability to pay, were a disproportionate share of subsequent defaults, about 7 percent of mortgage loans outstanding, but 43 percent of the foreclosures started in late 2007. The delinquency rate on subprime ARMs rose from less than 6 percent in 2005 to 25 percent in May 2008 (Bernanke 2007, 2008).

It is, however, a mistake to blame the bubble on subprime lending. The expansion of subprime lending took place mostly in 2005 and 2006, *after* five or more years of dramatic residential price increases, so it was merely a magnifier, not a primary cause, of the mortgage crisis (Federal Housing Finance Agency 2009: 48ff). According to Harvard's Joint Center for Housing Studies (2008: 39, Table A-6), the share of mortgage originations that were subprime rose from less than 8 percent in 2001–2003 to 20 percent in 2005 and 2006. The explosion of subprime loans occurred *after* the homeownership rate had peaked in 2004 and was starting to decline (Joint Center 2008: 4).

The primary cause of the bubble was the allure of speculative gain—the fantastic idea, which periodically grips entire societies for a few years, that it is indefinitely possible to create wealth out of nothing by simply buying land (plus associated buildings) and then reselling for a higher price. Speculative bubbles, by their nature, cannot be sustained because they produce no new value. Cash drains and a fear of rising interest rates eventually cause land prices to grow more slowly and then level off, followed by a steep decline, leaving late buyers with negative equity—property worth less than the loan.

In the current cycle, the air began leaking from the bubble at the end of 2005 or early 2006.[2] As housing prices fell and balloon payments came due on loans worth more than the property, a trickle of defaults turned into a flood, rising from 1.2 percent in 2006, to 2.0 percent in 2007, to 3.3 percent in 2008.[3]

The rise of foreclosures and the decline in housing prices set in motion a cascade of financial calamities. Investment banks were highly leveraged. From 1997 until 2004 (and again after August 2008), their leverage (debt to liquid asset ratio) was limited to 15 to 1. But in April 2004, the Securities and Exchange Commission authorized large investment banks to set leverage ratios according to their own risk management models (Spaulding 2008). The ratio at Bear Stearns rose to 33 to 1 before it became insolvent and its assets were transferred in March 2008 to JPMorgan. With that sort of leverage, a loss of only 4 percent caused them to become insolvent. Merrill Lynch and Lehman Brothers also failed in September 2008, as did Fannie Mae and Freddie Mac, the two largest holders of mortgage-backed securities. As the dominos fell, the self-corrective elements of the economy were not in sight.

Although the media have focused on the financial sector and the dangers of insolvency, the fallout from the mortgage meltdown has been felt throughout the economy. The unemployment rate has increased by 75 percent, from a decade average of 4.9 percent (1998–2007) (U.S. Council of Economic Advisers 2009: Table B-42) to 8.6 percent in April 2009 (U.S. Department of Labor, Bureau of Labor Statistics 2009). Housing starts have declined by 79 percent, from an average of 375,000 in each of the first quarters of 2005 and 2006 to

78,000 in the first quarter of 2009 (U.S. Department of Commerce, Bureau of the Census 2009). The suicide of David Kellermann, the acting CFO of Freddie Mac, on April 22, 2009, was a shocking reminder of the potential rise in similar deaths during the current economic crisis (Desmon and Calvert 2009).[4] The suicide rate during the 1930s Depression climbed about 25 percent above the level of the 1920s (U.S. Department of Commerce, Bureau of the Census 1975: Series B-166).

The entire economy, not only in the United States but in much of the world, has been pulled into the vortex of tightening credit as a result of mortgage delinquencies and foreclosures and the corresponding loss of bank assets. The most astonishing feature of the crisis is how localized its sources were. Just four states—Nevada, California, Arizona, and Florida—accounted for 47 percent of foreclosure filings and 42 percent of foreclosure starts in the first quarter of 2008 (Rismedia 2008). Those four states also accounted for 89 percent of the increase in foreclosures in the second quarter of 2008, according to the Mortgage Bankers Association (York and Vintner 2008).[5] More than half of the foreclosures in 2008 took place in just 35 counties, with just eight counties in four states accounting for 25 percent of all foreclosure filings (Cutts 2009). The land speculation mania was not a uniform national problem. Yet it has affected the entire world through its influence on the banking system.

The same real estate speculation that has weakened the U.S. economy has operated in many other countries as well. It has affected most industrial countries, except Japan and Germany (Montagu-Pollock 2009).[6] In 13 countries, house-price appreciation from 2000 through 2007 was 40–70 percent. In nine countries, the rise was 75–100 percent. In four countries, house prices rose from 140–300 percent. Including bubbles that started in the 1990s, there were eight additional countries in which house-price appreciation exceed 100 percent. In Ireland, for example, house prices rose 314 percent from 1996 to 2007 (about 100 percent from 2000 to 2007) (Duffy 2009).[7] From 1997 through 2005, house prices rose about 150 percent in England and Wales (Academetrics 2009). This global experience should alert analysts in the United States that this phenomenon cannot be explained in terms of particular events in the United States, such as subprime mortgages or changing demographics.

One gloomy factor on the horizon, which has received very little attention during the present crisis, is that land or real estate booms often consist of two waves, the second one peaking about two years after the first one. In this case, gross investment in residential construction began to fall after the fourth quarter of 2005, and it has declined about 52 percent from then until the first quarter of 2009 (U.S. Department of Commerce, Bureau of Economic Analysis 2009: Table 5.3.6, line 18). But gross investment in *nonresidential* construction (representing the second wave) continued growing 14 percent after January 2006, until it peaked in the second and third quarters of 2008, then fell 6 percent in the third quarter of 2008 and another 11 percent in the fourth quarter (U.S. Department of Commerce, Bureau of Economic Analysis 2009: Table 5.3.6, line 2).[8] Private business inventories also rose until the third quarter of 2006, remained constant until the first quarter of 2008, then fell by 3 percent by the first quarter of 2009 (U.S. Department of Commerce, Bureau of Economic Analysis 2009: Table 5.7.6b, line 1). In short, the consequences of the collapsing housing market were partially masked by sustained nonresidential investment and constant inventories in 2007 and part of 2008. Now that other investment is also falling rapidly, the crisis in 2009 and 2010 will be larger than the changes in the housing market alone would have indicated.

II

Inadequate Explanations of the Crisis

IT IS REMARKABLE that land price bubbles have been ignored by economists, who are certainly aware of them from both personal experience and anecdotal observation. Because land remains an obscure and insignificant feature in mainstream economic theories (which focus exclusively on labor and capital), those same theories cannot analytically account for recessions or depressions caused by real estate bubbles. As a result, when speculation does play a decisive role in economic events, the behavior of land markets is treated as an exogenous variable—an external shock that could not have been anticipated.

Shiller (2005, 2007) has come closer than other well-known economists to incorporating real estate speculation into a story of recent economic events. Shiller's observations do not, however, amount to a theory. In the middle of a housing price bubble, he recognized it and foresaw that it would eventually come to an end. By contrast, David Lereah (2005), chief economist of the National Association of Realtors, wrote that the housing market would remain strong for a decade. Shiller's refutation of that idea was based on nothing more than the fact that historically all bubbles have burst.

Economists, thus, have no theory about the source of the crisis. Popular sentiment has blamed imprudent borrowing by low-income households, subprime mortgages, deregulation, the securitization of mortgages, high-risk lending by banks, financial fraud, exotic derivatives (such as credit default swaps), low interest rates from 2001 to 2004, and many other features of the current crisis that have been in the news. However, all of these explanations are ad hoc, not based on theory.

If economists and political leaders are ever to devise policies that will avoid severe contractions, they will need a predictive model, not ex post observations about the features of the immediate crisis. Until such a theory of how land bubbles form is developed, historical patterns will have to serve as the best guide. Shiller (2005) criticizes ad hoc explanations of the current housing price boom and bust, such as demographic pressure, low interest rates, and deregulation, by pointing out that those factors have existed at various times without causing a land price bubble. Yet Shiller's own analysis is ahistorical. He exhibits no familiarity with the literature of the 1930s on how real estate speculation and bank lending practices created the conditions for the Great Depression.[9] Nor does Shiller show any awareness of a more recent literature (Foldvary 1997, 1998, 2007; Harrison 1983, 1997, 2005) based in part on the work of Henry George ([1879] 1979: 263–281), who provided a conceptual framework more than a century ago for understanding the main cause of depressions in terms of land speculation.[10] That Shiller neglects George's contribution comes as no surprise, since Shiller's method is to look for the psychological roots of economic behavior rather than structural causes. When Shiller (2008) considers methods of preventing future bubbles, his solutions all lie in the domain of psychology and education—training households to be better shoppers. He asserts that prevention lies in better consumer education to help home buyers make better decisions. He does not analyze the kinds of faulty incentives that might bring about systemic failure.

III

Excessive Reliance on Financial Analysis of Crises

ALTHOUGH ROBERT SHILLER has offered no structural analysis of the patterns associated with speculative bubbles in real estate, he has at least recognized that land plays a powerful role in shaping economic conditions. That is preferable to the many economic studies that treat economic crises as the result solely of financial transactions.[11]

In recent decades, when developed nations have had relatively stable economies, economists have focused their attention on the crises affecting developing countries or regions such as Mexico, Brazil, and Southeast Asia. The standard explanation for all of these crises has been framed in terms of capital flows and exchange rates. According to this conventional understanding, financial liberalization has allowed capital to flow freely into a country such as Mexico or Thailand. The sudden increase in capital produces a "financial" bubble, with rising "asset" values. When the bubble bursts, asset prices fall, bankruptcies proliferate, and the invested capital quickly flows out, causing currency depreciation, and rising import costs. The result is a recession or depression.

Both Joseph Stiglitz and Paul Krugman have written extensively about economic crises in developing nations and have hinted that real estate bubbles could be a significant part of this highly disruptive process, but neither has made that point explicitly. Each prefers to trace the origins of economic disasters to financial deregulation, moral hazard, and flaws in international finance.[12] In so doing, these activist scholars have overlooked the semi-autonomous role of land speculation as a systemic source of financial instability. For example, Stiglitz and Uy (1996: 259), in an article examining the sources of "financial crises" in East Asia, make reference to real estate lending or speculation as one element in their list of recent crises. (In the case of Japan in 1991, they refer to the primary cause as "[e]xcessive exposure to real estate lending (90 percent of bad loans), and a steep decline in real estate prices.") This factor appears to be merely anecdotal, of no analytic significance for them. In another article, Stiglitz (1996: 157) recognizes that banking regulations should limit lending for real estate: "[Discouraging] the allocation of capital to areas such as real estate meant that more capital was available for areas with higher technological benefits, such as plants and equipment." But a passing comment such as that does not translate into a recognition of the role of real estate in propagating the financial crises. Instead, Stiglitz's analytic variables are all financial.

Paul Krugman (1998) similarly recognizes that land prices are the stuff of which "asset price" bubbles are formed, but he insists that the cause lies in the banking system. Referring to the 1997 Asian crisis, he says:

> The first act was the story of the bubble. It began, we now think, with bad banking. . . . All those irresponsible loans created a boom in real estate and stock markets, which made the balance sheets of banks and their clients look much healthier than they were.

Krugman does not explore the obvious possibility that the bubble begins with real estate and entices banks to expand their balance sheets. In that alternative story, money flows into a country precisely because a real estate boom already exists, and investors are hoping to profit from it. For Krugman, causality always begins with banking and runs toward real transactions, not the other way around.

A more sustained recognition by a finance-oriented economist of land's role in economic crises is an exploration by Gabriel Palma (2000) of regional economic crises in the 1990s. Since the paper is on the need for capital controls, the problem of land price bubbles is a secondary or tertiary issue. Nevertheless, Palma provides detailed evidence of a connection between real estate bubbles and subsequent economic collapse in Chile, Mexico, and Malaysia. In Mexico, before the 1994 crisis, there was a 600 percent increase in real estate prices and a 100 percent increase in residential construction over five years, while investments in machinery, equipment, and infrastructure fell by over 50 percent (Palma 2000: 19, 21). In Chile, there was a 900 percent increase in a real estate price index in six years (Palma 2000: 41). In Malaysia, there was a 350 percent increase in real estate prices from 1992 to 1997 (Palma 2000: 47–48). In each case, the rapid climb in land prices was followed by a precipitous fall that left banks with nonperforming loans and "toxic assets" (to use the term popularized in the United States). The fact that Palma does not integrate these facts into the analysis is perhaps less important than the evidence he provides that real estate bubbles are in some way linked to crises.

IV

Do Monetary and Fiscal Remedies Still Work?

BECAUSE ECONOMISTS TREAT rapid changes in real estate prices as an epiphenomenon, not a causal factor in economic crises, their remedies do not take land speculation into account. Instead, they concentrate exclusively on solutions that are aimed at changing financial flows. Ultimately, their ideas can all be traced back to hydraulic metaphors. When an economy slows down, conventional economic wisdom says that something is clogging the pipes. The remedy lies in blasting water (money) through the pipes to enable them to flow freely again. The conventional responses to crisis by mainstream macroeconomists are (1) to cut interest rates to promote investment or (2) to run a fiscal deficit.

Recently, however, the economists who favor these conventional therapies are having doubts. In the wake of the Asian financial crisis of 1997–1998, Paul Krugman (1999) concluded that traditional fiscal and monetary policies were no longer effective in fighting economic contraction in the wake of speculative attacks against a currency.[13] When developing nations (such as Mexico or Thailand) are forced to devalue their currencies by a small amount, the predicted result is an inflow of capital to buy the devalued currency. However, in recent experience, the result has been a continuous fall in the value of that currency. Even as a nation slips into recession, it may be forced to defend its currency by raising interest rates to extremely high levels (50 to 70 percent in some cases). That prevents the use of monetary policy to fight deflation. At the same time, capital flight prevents the use of deficit spending to "prime the pump." Deflationary policies destroy small businesses and increase unemployment rates during the recession. This experience has raised serious questions about the efficacy of demand management tools. As Krugman (1999: 58) himself observes:

> The truth is that the world economy poses more dangers than we had imagined. Problems we thought we knew how to cure have once again become intractable, like temporarily suppressed bacteria that eventually evolve a resistance to antibiotics. More specifically, the problem of aggregate demand, of getting people to spend enough to employ the economy's productive capacity, is not, as we might have thought, always a problem with an easy solution.

The limits of demand management in dealing with economic instability apply also to mature economies. Japan has found itself in a liquidity trap since 1991. (A liquidity trap means that the central bank is lending at a near-zero interest rate, and yet that fails to stimulate investment. In other words, monetary policy is powerless.) Fiscal policy has also provided no relief. "Japan's experience shows how hard it can be, once in such a trap, to get out again" (Krugman 1999: 70). Japan may not be a special case. Krugman (1999: 69) suggests that other nations face the same threat:

> Are other advanced countries at any risk of finding themselves in the same situation? The conventional answer is no, that Japan's problems are uniquely severe. But ten or even five years ago few economists would have taken seriously the possibility that Japan could be in its present predicament, and thus the emergence of liquidity traps elsewhere is no longer inconceivable. Indeed, in the early 1990s some economists worried that the United States might be approaching liquidity-trap territory.

The early 1990s in the United States was a period much like the present one—a recession following a prolonged period of real estate speculation, in which housing prices climbed 33 percent from 1985 to 1989. (During a comparable length of time in the present boom and bust, from 2002 through 2006, housing prices rose 46 percent (Federal Housing Finance Agency 2009: 48ff).) In 1990–1991, the United States avoided a liquidity trap and recovered, perhaps because real estate prices merely leveled off for a few years before climbing again.[14] Because his economic models do not take variations in land prices into account, Krugman (1999: 69) attributed the 1990–1991 recession to "a slump in consumer spending together with financial difficulties in the banking sector," completely ignoring the rise and flattening of home prices that preceded the slump.

Standard remedies have failed to restore economies going through "financial crises" for one fundamental reason: they do not deal with the sources of the crisis in the real economy. When investment flows into land speculation, and investment in productive business activity slows as a consequence, no amount of financial manipulation can compensate for that misallocation of resources.

V

Taking Real Estate (Land) Seriously

DEMAND MANAGEMENT—whether monetary or fiscal—has lost much of its efficacy, at least during crises. By the admission of Paul Krugman, one leading proponent of demand management, economies are not responding to the old medicine the way they are supposed to. Having said that, he does not tell us where else to turn.

The search for a theory that would explain the causal mechanisms behind periodic economic crises must take real estate seriously. (By "real estate," I mean the land or sites that rise in value with increased demand, and only secondarily the buildings on them.) Since economists such as Shiller, Krugman, and Stiglitz have already included real estate as an intermediate factor in booms followed by destructive busts, the key question is not whether real estate is involved in economic crises. The question that needs to be addressed is whether real estate speculation is the *central cause* of those crises. In simplified form, the issue is whether causality flows primarily from real estate bubbles to banking or vice versa. They almost certainly interact, but, for economists, the question should be where the core of the problem lies. For policymakers, the issue is whether bank regulation or land-value taxation is the more effective means of limiting speculative bubbles.

This is not the place to present the evidence on those questions. For the sake of brevity, I would simply point out that capital inflows were not a necessary or sufficient condition for 19th-century land booms, which were also followed by bank panics and depressions. In addition, there are current cases in which real estate bubbles developed independently of an unusual influx of foreign capital, such as Mumbai, Ireland, and Spain in recent years.[15] The banking system must always be complicit in land price bubbles, but the international flow of "hot money" in pursuit of real estate investment opportunities is merely an accident of present circumstances, not a general feature of the enduring pattern of bubbles. The problems created by booms and busts in real estate must be directly addressed with policies related to land prices and the association of capital investment with land speculation. The instability created by those investment patterns will never be adequately addressed through reform of the financial system alone.

VI

The Distinctive Contributions of Mason Gaffney

THE ESSAYS IN THIS VOLUME by Mason Gaffney offer a way of understanding the roots of instability in capitalist economies from a new vantage point. Rather than starting his analysis with recorded financial transactions as the most basic elements of macroeconomics, Gaffney begins with overlooked distinctions among actual transactions, some of which enhance productivity, while others diminish it. By differentiating land from capital, and durable capital from working capital, Gaffney shows how these elementary distinctions can be used to reframe the organization of economic life.

In Chapter 1, Gaffney argues that the current economic crisis is not new. He observes that the current crisis arose through a cycle similar to one that has been repeated many times in the past.[16] He builds on the insights of Henry George, who attributed depressions to land speculation, but Gaffney goes beyond George by adding a capital theory. Gaffney reveals why land speculation is a necessary, but not sufficient, explanation of how credit-based economies suddenly seize up.

Chapter 1 lays out the steps by which land speculation biases capital investment by encouraging premature development and excessive public spending on infrastructure, leading to collapse.[17] During the inevitable contraction phase, when land prices decline, many banks that lent money for real estate during the upswing become insolvent or at least unable to lend money, even for prudent projects. The resulting severe contraction of credit leads to higher unemployment and a period of negative growth (recession or depression).

This process of overexpansion followed by calamitous contraction—which Gaffney reminds us occurs on an approximately

18-year cycle—is not a fact of nature that must be endured.[18] Instead, Gaffney argues the cycle can be mitigated, or avoided entirely, with one simple expedient—by making effective use of the property tax. Part of the remedy lies in shifting the primary burden of the property tax to the portion that falls on land values. Unlike capital, land can be taxed without reducing the amount produced. In fact, a tax on land increases the efficiency of land use by improving the intensity, timing, and location of development. Gaffney explores the reasons for those nonrevenue benefits of taxing land in great detail. However, as he discusses further, the benefits of the property tax in defusing real estate price bubbles are limited by the frequency and accuracy of property assessment. Unless the assessor keeps pace with the speculator, this policy instrument is of little avail for avoiding wild swings in economic output.

In the second chapter, Gaffney extends his analysis to the more general problem of misallocation of capital. As the pattern unfolds, we can now see that the disequilibrium that produces booms and busts is a special case of a more pervasive pattern that weakens market economies. Gaffney reintroduces the concept, derived from Wicksell, of the "valence" of capital, a term that refers to the frequency with which capital turns over and interacts with labor. The rate of turnover of capital, the inverse of its payout period, is a measure of how hard capital works, somewhat like the concept of "velocity" applied to money.

Chapter 2 lays the groundwork for a new framework in macroeconomics. In this framework, the quantity of capital investment, so important in other aggregate economic models, is of limited relevance. Since about 75 percent of gross investment is required to offset depreciation in the stock of capital, the restraint shown by households and businesses by saving (i.e., not consuming) adds only about 2–3 percent to the net stock of capital.[19] The truly dynamic quality of capital lies in its capacity to employ labor, and that is related primarily to its turnover, not to the stock of capital or to net additions to the stock. Using capital turnover as the key to macroeconomic health, Gaffney shows how taxes on labor (and favoritism to capital in the tax code) send the wrong economic signals. They unintentionally encourage investment in durable capital with very slow turnover. Investments with long maturity have the unintended consequence of reducing demand for labor and lowering wages and employment opportunities. Correcting the anti-labor biases in the tax system could thus resolve a number of macroeconomic problems.

Finally, in Chapter 3, Gaffney addresses the role of banking in the success or failure of an economy. A primary function of banks is to create liquidity—by effectively breaking large, lumpy investments into smaller units that can facilitate economic transactions. But borrowing short and lending long makes banks inherently vulnerable to loss of confidence by the public, particularly after booms in which banks have lent heavily for land and long-term projects. To prevent the conditions that lead banks to the brink of insolvency (and force central banks or governments to bail out the banking system), Gaffney proposes a simple remedy: restrict collateral to assets with short maturity, and avoid land as collateral. This conclusion follows directly from his analysis of capital turnover in Chapter 2. In Chapter 3, he applies the same logic to the banking system and shows how lending on inflated land values and premature construction led directly to the crash of 1929 and the Great Depression (as well as lesser-known economic crises).

VII

Conclusion

IN THE FOLLOWING ESSAYS, Mason Gaffney arrives at analytic and policy conclusions at variance with most other members of the economics profession. He directs attention to differences between land and capital, between different maturities of capital, and between quantitative and qualitative controls over banking. Applying those differences, he recommends solutions that are completely absent from the normal instruments of macroeconomic management: (1) a tax on land values (combined with improved assessment) heavy enough to remove the incentive to speculate on them; (2) a reduction of taxes on labor and an end to favorable tax treatment of capital, both to avoid distortions in the use of labor and capital in production; and (3) regulation of banking to eliminate the use of land as collateral for loans. Together, those policies would effectively put an end to real estate bubbles and the resulting painful contractions.

As important as those conclusions are, they are perhaps not as significant as the method by which they were reached. The most fundamental difference between Gaffney's approach throughout his career and mainstream views on macroeconomics is that Gaffney begins his analysis with real transactions and real costs. That is radically at odds with the idea that one can manage economies simply by manipulating monetary aggregates, without any reference to the realities behind them. Unlike most other economists, Gaffney does not presume that all forms of capital are instantaneously interchangeable just because they are represented by the same mathematical symbol in models of economic behavior. Instead, he gives priority to understanding actual relationships in the world and their consequences. He does not deny the value of abstraction or even of mathematical formalism, but he does not allow them to become ends in themselves. Gaffney reminds us that we need to test those abstractions by their ability to improve social conditions. For if economists cannot help us solve real problems, of what use are they?

Notes

1. The House Price Index of Federal Housing Finance Agency (FHFA) was previously published by the Office of Federal Housing Enterprise Oversight (OFHEO).

2. There are three housing prices indices one may consider. (1) National Association of Realtors or NAR (Christie 2006). The NAR index showed that "from the fourth quarter of 2005 to the first quarter of 2006, median prices nationwide fell from $225,300 to $217,900, a drop of 3.3 percent. . . . [I]n the fourth quarter of 2005, prices fell 1 percent from the third quarter." (2) S&P/Case-Shiller (Standard and Poor's 2006). As late as July 25, 2006, the S&P/Case-Shiller Index said that U.S. home prices were still trending upward as of May 2006. On August 5, 2006 (a year after NAR showed a decline), the S&P indicated that there was no change in S&P/Case-Shiller Composite Index from May to June of 2006, meaning that house prices had stopped rising. (3) The FHFA House Price Index (HPI) (Federal Housing Finance Agency 2009) peaked in April 2007 and fell continuously through December 2008 (from a peak of 224.5 to 199). However, "[t]he [FHFA] index tracks home values on mortgages that were guaranteed or funded by Fannie Mae and Freddie Mac. Therefore, it is missing the entire subprime mortgage market, and lots of falling home values" (Wilder 2009).

Conclusion: I judge the turning point as the end of 2005 based on the (more comprehensive) NAR index *and* on the fact that *the rate of increase* in housing prices fell in the FHFA Index the fourth quarter of 2005 and even more in the first quarter of 2006.

3. There is more than one way of counting foreclosures. The Mortgage Bankers Association National Deliquency Survey of bank foreclosure inventories gives higher estimates than RealtyTrac's estimate of housing units that received at least one foreclosure filing. I have used the higher numbers for 2006–2008 from MBA (2008, 2009), rather than the corresponding estimates of 0.6 percent, 1.0 percent, and 1.8 percent from RealtyTrac Staff (2008, 2009), because the MBA survey appears to be more comprehensive.

4. Historian David M. Kennedy (1999: 174), referring to the way Americans experienced the Great Depression, has explained why financial trauma can lead to suicide: "Contempt for the Depression's victims, ironically enough, often lodged most deeply in the hearts and minds of the victims themselves. Social investigators in the 1930s repeatedly encountered feelings of guilt and self-recrimination among the unemployed, despite the transparent reality that their plight owed to a systemic economic breakdown, not to their own personal shortcomings. The Depression thus revealed one of the perverse implications of American society's vaunted celebration of individualism. In a culture that ascribed all success to individual striving, it seemed to follow axiomatically that failure was due to individual inadequacy."

5. "The problems in California, Florida, Arizona and Nevada are somewhat atypical of the rest of the country. These four states were responsible for 62 percent of all foreclosures started on prime ARMs and 84 percent of the increase in prime ARM foreclosures. These states also accounted for 49 percent of subprime ARM foreclosures started during the first quarter [of 2008] and were responsible for 93 percent of the increase in subprime ARM foreclosures. In addition, these four states accounted for 60 percent of the increase in foreclosures on prime fixed-rate mortgages and 53 percent of the increase in subprime fixed-rate mortgages" (York and Vintner 2008).

6. Several dozen nations (or generally a few major cities within each nation) experienced recent real estate bubbles. The following list (with house-price appreciation from 2000–2002 to 2006–2008 in parentheses, or with alternative dates) is derived from Montagu-Pollock (2009). The data were presented originally in graphic form, not in tables, so there is approximately a 5–10 percent margin of error just from the way the data were presented. Argentina (40 percent), Australia (70 percent), Canada (50 percent from 2000 to 2007), China (Shanghai only, 150 percent), Colombia (80 percent), Croatia (60 percent), Cyprus (40 percent), Denmark (>200 percent from 1993 to 2007), Finland (100 percent from 1997 to 2008), France (Paris, 160 percent from 1998 to 2008), Greece (225 percent from 1993 to 2007), Hong Kong (175 percent), Hungary (80 percent from 2000 to 2006), Iceland (>60 percent), Indonesia

(100 percent from 2000 to 2008), Ireland (320 percent from 1996 to 2007), Italy (100 percent), Malta (45 percent in 2004–2005), New Zealand (>50 percent), Norway (240 percent from 1994 to 2007), Philippines (40 percent), Poland (>75 percent), Serbia (300 percent), Singapore (40 percent), Slovak Republic (100 percent), Slovenia (100 percent), South Africa (>90 percent), South Korea (70 percent from 1999 to 2008), Spain (100 percent), Sweden (150 percent from 1998 to 2008), Thailand (45 percent), Ukraine (140 percent), the United Kingdom (>50 percent), the United States (100 percent from 1996 to 2006), Uruguay (55 percent).

7. Duffy (2009) shows the average house price in Ireland peaked at 311,078 euros in January and February 2007. The index began measuring house prices in Ireland in March 1996, when the average house sold for 75,169 euros.

8. *Net* investment would be a better metric, but the latest figures from the Commerce Department were from 2007. The rate of capital consumption rises during a recession, as existing capital structures and equipment lose some of their value due to rising interest rates. On that basis, one would expect net declines in capital to be even more dramatic than gross declines.

9. See references in Gaffney's first and third essays in this volume to Hoyt, Simpson, Vanderblue, Maverick, and Fisher, and to the 1972 dissertation by Holland.

10. George ([1879] 1979: 277–278) argued that the causes of a depression can be traced back, step by step, from high involuntary unemployment, to a build-up of commercial inventories, to a sudden contraction of credit, and finally to the ultimate cause: "the speculative advance of rent or land values" (i.e., the speculative increase in land prices). Where George merely hinted at the myriad processes by which land speculation is translated into a credit freeze, Gaffney in this volume spells out the connections.

11. The classic work on this subject is Kindleberger ([1978] 2005). Until the fifth edition of this book, in 2005, he did not deal with real estate bubbles in any significant way, and even then, that category did not enter deeply into his analysis.

12. Moral hazard in this context refers to policies that insure banks and their depositors against loss but allows banks to make risky loans. In brief, it means combining deregulation with insurance.

13. Krugman (1999: 56–74). Krugman explains that each nation has three macroeconomic goals in international finance: (1) capital mobility (free movement of investment funds across national boundaries); (2) autonomous control of national monetary policy (to regulate prices and employment levels); and (3) stability of exchange rate (price stability in international exchange). However, "the iron law of international finance is that countries can achieve at most two of the three" (Krugman 1999: 61). Most nations in recent decades have chosen to give up the third goal (exchange rate stability) to achieve the first two. But recent experience has shown that capital mobility

may prevent both exchange rate stability and management of the domestic economy.

14. House prices in California declined 15 percent from 1990 to 1994, at which point they remained depressed until 1997. However, during that period, other parts of the country did not follow the same pattern (Federal Housing Finance Agency 2009: 54–55).

15. The case of Mumbai (formerly Bombay) and other Indian cities from 1990 to 1996 is discussed by Nijman (2000). The author questions the glib assertion that capital inflows were primarily responsible for making Mumbai the most expensive city in the world in the mid-1990s. If liberalized capital flows and banking regulations were the source of instability in real estate, how can that be reconciled with the fact that "in 1998, it was estimated that less than 8 percent of real estate transactions involved a financial institution. The bulk of existing real estate therefore is the full property of the owner and carries no costs such as mortgage interest" (Nijman 2000: 579). Without denying some role for foreign investors, Nijman (2000: 581) insists that "[t]he most active players in the residential and commercial market were the real estate businesses and property developers. These were almost all Indian (domestic) and local companies, some with a long history in the Mumbai region."

16. As Gaffney (2009) has pointed out in a review of Anderson (2008), in addition to five crashes tied to real estate in the United States during the 19th century, there was also one in 1797–1798 on both sides of the Atlantic: "It was 1797 when the [Bank of England] suspended cash payments, when Pitt imposed the first income tax to raise funds to fight Napoleon, when English capital was diverted on a grand scale from America to subsidizing Napoleon's enemies, when Robert Morris, financier of the American Revolution, lost 200,000 acres and went to debtor's prison, when Andrew Jackson lost his lands and conceived his hatred of banks. This was a major crash, and the likely reason John Adams lasted only one term, Hamilton lost favor, and Jefferson became president."

Going back further, one find examples of the boom-bust cycle in real estate in "the Mississippi Bubble of 1720, the Tulip Bubble of the 1630s, which Eichholtz and Shiller showed to have been a land bubble, the end of the Great Migration to New England after 1630, the Florentine and Medici banking collapse of 1494; and so on. M. E. Levasseur has traced such cycles back to the year 1200."

17. The land speculation process affects the economy in the following manner. First, a period of land speculation (residential, then nonresidential) is set in motion by rising future expectations, fueled by various factors. Rising land prices increase the cost of buying existing homes. To satisfy the apparent increase in demand for housing, homebuilders initiate new developments, some in marginal locations, while cities subdivide new land and pour money into infrastructure for the new acreage. Before the peak of

this land-buying and home-building frenzy is reached, investors initiate construction of new offices and commercial buildings. This second wave of construction delays the looming contraction by a year or two (which is why the Great Crash took place in 1929, not 1927 at the end of the housing boom of the 1920s). Eventually, the price of buildable land peaks and then falls—rapidly.

18. In principle, that which can be predicted can often be managed or prevented. Gaffney (2009) explains that there are leading indicators that anticipate the final rise in the boom phase of a cycle before the collapse: "Some reliable indicators of a forthcoming peak are: A, unusually high land prices and price/rent ratios; B, a rash of extra-tall buildings; C, a boom in copper prices; and D, an inverted yield curve."

19. A simple example might help. If the stock of private, nonresidential capital in the United States is about $12 trillion in capital, and gross investment in that form of capital is $1.2 trillion each year, growth of 10 percent per year might seem quite significant. But if *net* investment is only $300 billion (25 percent of gross), then net investment adds only 2.5 percent to the stock (300/12,000). Gaffney insists that turnover of capital is more important than additions to the stock.

References

Academetrics. (2009). "House Price Index." Available online at: http://www. acadametrics.co.uk/ftHousePrices.php

Anderson, Phillip J. (2008). *The Secret Life of Real Estate.* London: Shepheard-Walwyn.

Bernanke, Ben S. (2007, October 10). "The Recent Financial Turmoil and Its Economic and Policy Consequences." Speech at the Economic Club of New York, New York. Available online at: http://www.federalreserve. gov/newsevents/speech/bernanke20071015a.htm

———. (2008, May 5). "Mortgage Delinquencies and Foreclosures." Speech at the Columbia Business School's 32nd Annual Dinner, New York. Available online at: http://www.federalreserve.gov/newsevents/speech/ Bernanke20080505a.htm#f1

Board of Governors of the Federal Reserve System. (2009, March 12). "Table Z.1, Flow of Funds Accounts of the United States." Washington, DC: Federal Reserve System.

Christie, Les. (2006, May 16). "Real Estate Cools Down." CNNMoney.com. Available online at: http://money.cnn.com/2006/05/15/real_estate/NAR_ firstQ2005_home_prices/index.htm

Cutts, John. (2009, March 19). "35 Counties Push Up Foreclosures by State Rankings." Available online at: http://www.realestateproarticles.com/Art/ 6310/265/35-Counties-Push-Up-Foreclosures-by-State-Rankings.html

Desmon, Stephanie, and Scott Calvert. (2009). "As Economic Crisis Goes On, Financial Fears Can Push Some Over the Edge." *Baltimore Sun* (April 23). Available online at: http://www.baltimoresun.com/news/local/bal-te.md. strain23apr23,0,453118.story

Duffy, David. (2009, April 25). "ESRI House Price Index." Economic and Social Research Institute. Available online at: http://www.esri.ie/irish_economy/ permanent_tsbesri_house_p/hpi_tables_March_2009.pdf

Federal Housing Finance Agency. (2009, February 24). "Record Home Price Declines in Fourth Quarter; Isolated Pockets of Strength." News release. Available online at: http://www.fhfa.gov/webfiles/1282/4q08hpi.pdf

Foldvary, Fred. (1997). "The Business Cycle: A Georgist-Austrian Synthesis." *American Journal of Economics and Sociology* 56(4): 521–541.

———. (1998). "Market-Hampering Land Speculation: Fiscal and Monetary Origins and Remedies." *American Journal of Economics and Sociology* 57(4): 615–637.

———. (2007). *The Depression of 2008.* Berkeley, CA: Gutenberg Press.

Gaffney, Mason. (2009, May 7). "Review of *The Secret Life of Real Estate.*" Earthsharing Australia. Available online at: http://www.earthsharing.org. au/2009/05/07/review-the-secret-life-of-real-estate/

George, Henry. ([1879] 1979). *Progress and Poverty: An Inquiry into the Cause of Industrial Depressions and of Increase of Want with Increase of Wealth—The Remedy.* New York: Robert Schalkenbach Foundation.

Harrison, Fred. (1983). *The Power in the Land.* New York: Universe Books.

———. (1997). "The Coming 'Housing' Crash." In Jones, F. J., and Fred Harrison, *The Chaos Makers.* London: Othila Press.

———. (2005). *Boom Bust.* London: Shepheard-Walwyn.

Joint Center for Housing Studies. (2008). *The State of the Nation's Housing: 2008.* Cambridge: Graduate School of Design, Harvard Kennedy School.

Kennedy, David M. (1999). *Freedom from Fear: The American People in Depression and War, 1929–1945.* New York: Oxford University Press.

Kindleberger, Charles. ([1978] 2005). *Manias, Panics, and Crashes: A History of Financial Crises*, 5th ed. Hoboken, NJ: John Wiley & Sons.

Krugman, Paul. (1998, March 2). "Asia: What Went Wrong." *Fortune.* Available online at: http://money.cnn.com/magazines/fortune/fortune_archive/ 1998/03/02/238550/index.htm

———. (1999). "The Return of Depression Economics." *Foreign Affairs* 78(1): 56–74.

Lereah, David. (2005). *Are You Missing the Real Estate Boom? Why Home Values and Other Real Estate Investments Will Climb Through the End of the Decade—And How to Profit from Them.* New York: Broadway Business. Rpt. (2006) as *Why the Real Estate Boom Will Not Bust—And How You Can Profit from It: How to Build Wealth in Today's Expanding Real Estate Market.* New York: Broadway Business.

Mandel, Michael J. (2004). *Rational Exuberance: Silencing the Enemies of Growth and Why the Future Is Better Than You Think.* New York: HarperBusiness.

———. (2005, June 24). "Housing Versus Business Investment." *Business Week.* Available online at: http://www.businessweek.com/the_thread/economicsunbound/archives/2005/06/housing_versus.html

Montagu-Pollock, Matthew. (2009). "House Price Time Series." Global Property Guide. Available online at: http://www.globalpropertyguide.com/real-estate-house-prices/A

Mortgage Bankers Association. (2007). "Delinquencies and Foreclosures Increase in Latest MBA National Delinquency Survey." Press release. Available online at: http://www.mbaa.org/NewsandMedia/PressCenter/58758.htm

———. (2008). *National Delinquency Survey Q4 07.* Washington, DC: Mortgage Bankers Association. Available online at: http://media.mcclatchydc.com/smedia/2008/03/06/18/Hall-NDS-Q407.source.prod_affiliate.91.pdf

———. (2009, March 5). "Delinquencies Continue to Climb in Latest MBA National Delinquency Survey." Press release. Available online at: http://www.mbaa.org/NewsandMedia/PressCenter/68008.htm

Nijman, Jan. (2000). "Mumbai's Real Estate Market in 1990s: De-Regulation, Global Money and Casino Capitalism." *Economic and Political Weekly* 35(7): 575–582.

Palma, Gabriel. (2000, November). *The Three Routes to Financial Crises: The Need for Capital Controls.* CEPA Working Paper Series III, Working Paper No. 18. New York: New School for Social Research. Available online at: www.newschool.edu/cepa/publications/workingpapers/archive/cepa0318.pdf

RealtyTrac Staff. (2008, January 29). "U.S. Foreclosure Activity Increases 75 Percent in 2007." Press release. Available online at: www.realtytrac.com/ContentManagement/pressrelease.aspx?ChannelID=9&ItemID=3988&accnt=64847

———. (2009, January 15). "Foreclosure Activity Increases 81 Percent in 2008." Press release. Available online at: www.realtytrac.com/ContentManagement/pressrelease.aspx?ChannelID=9&ItemID=5681&accnt=64847. Accessed March 28, 2009.

RISMedia. (2008, June 10). "RealtyTrac Report and MBA National Delinquency Survey Closely Mirrored." Available online at: http://rismedia.com/2008-06-09/realtytrac-report-and-mba-national-delinquency-survey-closely-mirrored/

Romer, Christina. (2007). "Macroeconomic Policy in the 1960s: The Causes and Consequences of a Mistaken Revolution." Paper presented at the Economic History Annual Meeting, September 7, 2007. Available online at: http://elsa.berkeley.edu/~cromer/MacroPolicy.pdf

Shiller, Robert J. (2005). *Irrational Exuberance*, 2nd ed. Princeton: Princeton University Press.

———. (2007, June). *Historic Turning Points in Real Estate*. Cowles Foundation Discussion Paper No. 1610. New Haven, CT: Cowles Foundation for Research in Economics, Yale University. Available online at: http://cowles.econ.yale.edu/P/cd/d16a/d1610.pdf

———. (2008). *The Subprime Solution: How Today's Global Financial Crisis Happened, and What to Do About It.* Princeton: Princeton University Press.

Spaulding, William C. (2008, August 29). "Net Capital Requirement." Available online at: http://thismatter.com/money/terms/n/net-capital-requirement.htm

Standard and Poor's. (2006, August 29). "Slowing Gains Evident from the S&P/Case-Shiller Home Price Indices." Press release. Available online at: http://www2.standardandpoors.com/spf/pdf/index/082906_homeprice.pdf

Stiglitz, Joseph E. (1996). "Some Lessons from the East Asian Miracle." *World Bank Research Observer* 11(2): 151–177.

Stiglitz, Joseph E., and Marilou Uy. (1996). "Financial Markets, Public Policy, and the East Asian Miracle." *World Bank Research Observer* 11(2): 249–276.

U.S. Council of Economic Advisers. (2009). *Economic Report of the President, 2009 Spreadsheet Tables.* Available online at: http://www.gpoaccess.gov/eop/tables09.html

U.S. Department of Commerce, Bureau of Economic Analysis. (2009). "Table 5.3.6, Real Private Fixed Investment," and "Table 5.7.6B. Real Private Inventories and Real Domestic Final Sales by Industry." In *National Income and Product Accounts.* Washington, DC: U.S. Government Printing Office. Available online at: http://bea.doc.gov/national/nipaweb/SelectTable.asp?Selected=N. Accessed on May 22, 2009.

U.S. Department of Commerce, Bureau of the Census. (1975). "Vital Statistics and Health and Medical Care." In *Historical Statistics of the United States: Bicentennial Edition, Colonial Times to 1970, Vol. 1.* Washington, DC: U.S. Government Printing Office. Available online at: http://www2.census.gov/prod2/statcomp/documents/CT1970p1-03.pdf

———. (2009, April). "Quarterly Starts and Completions by Purpose and Design." *New Residential Construction Index.* Available online at: www.census.gov/const/www/newresconstindex.html

U.S. Department of Labor, Bureau of Labor Statistics. (2009, April). "Table A-13: Employment Status of the Civilian Noninstitutional Population by Age, Sex, and Race." *Labor Force Statistics from the Current Population Survey.* Available online at: ftp://ftp.bls.gov/pub/suppl/empsit.cpseea13.txt

Wilder, Rebecca. (2009, March 24). "OFHEO Says Home Values Rose in January?" News in Economics. Available online at: http://www. newsneconomics.com/2009/03/ofheo-says-home-values-rose-in-january.html

York, Adam, and Mark Vintner. (2008, June 13). "*Housing Chartbook: June 2008.*" FXStreet.com. Available online at: http://www.fxstreet.com/fundamental/analysis-reports/special-commentary/2008-06-13.html

1
The Role of Land Markets in Economic Crises

By Mason Gaffney*

ABSTRACT. It is widely recognized that the economic crisis of 2009 was caused by unsound lending for real estate. Largely ignored, however, is that this contraction was easily predicted on the basis of a well-established pattern of land speculation, premature subdivision, and excessive building on marginal land that recurs approximately once every 18 years. Capital locked up in projects that are started during a land bubble is effectively lost during the downturn, leaving the nation without sufficient capital to finance ordinary business operations during the recovery period. The best instrument for avoiding this boom-bust cycle is the property tax and, more specifically, the portion that falls on land. We explore here the ways in which the property tax influences the intensity, timing, and location of development. We also examine why frequent and accurate assessment are essential to make the property tax an effective method of preventing speculative real estate bubbles.

I

Boom and Bust in Real Estate

WE HAVE FALLEN INTO an economic disaster, probably the worst since the 1930s. Here is some of the evidence:

- The unemployment rate rose 78 percent from April 2008 to April 2009 (from 5 percent to 8.9 percent), an unusually rapid increase in joblessness (U.S. Bureau of Labor Statistics 2009a).

*Mason Gaffney has been a Professor of Economics at the University of California, Riverside for 33 years; e-mail: m.gaffney@dslextreme.com. He is the author of *The Corruption of Economics*, an explanation of how land became excluded from neoclassical economic models. He has also written extensively on various aspects of resource economics, urban economics, tax policy, and capital theory.

American Journal of Economics and Sociology, Vol. 68, No. 4 (October, 2009).

- Nearly 12 percent of all Americans with a mortgage—a record 5.4 million homeowners—were at least one month late or in foreclosure at the end of 2008, according to the Mortgage Bankers Association (CBS News 2009).
- In addition to the 1 million households that have been hit with foreclosure since 2006, it is likely that almost 6 million further households will face that situation by 2013 (Grow, Epstein, and Berner 2009).
- The net worth of American households fell by 31 percent (annualized rate) during the fourth quarter of 2008, the largest rate of decrease in 50 years (Board of Governors of the Federal Reserve System 2009). Losses by unincorporated business were almost as great (a 29 percent drop). (Since household consumption has remained steady, there has been a huge drop in savings.)
- Corporate profits from current operations declined by $250 billion or almost 17 percent in the fourth quarter of 2008, the largest percentage drop since 1953. That does not include losses in the financial sector from mortgage defaults (Nutting 2009). Since most new investment comes from corporate profits, this bodes ill for the possibility that corporate investment will recover quickly.
- Job losses in the fourth quarter of 2008 rose to 0.9 percent, the second largest loss in 50 years. So far, 2009 has been far worse in terms of rising unemployment. Mass layoffs in February 2009 were 150 percent above the average for the period from January 2005 to October 2007 and 28 percent above the last quarter of 2008 and January 2009 (U.S. Bureau of Labor Statistics 2009b). According to Milne and Sakoui (2008), twice as many companies will declare bankruptcy in 2009 as in 2007: "The U.S. will see 62,000 companies go bust next year, compared with 42,000 this year and 28,000 last year, says a report by Euler Hermes, part of German insurer Allianz."

We probably have not yet hit the bottom, the equivalent of 1893 or 1933, so the full severity of this crisis is not visible. But based on those signs, this turn of the wheel is likely to be as damaging as those two depressions.

We have seen economic overexpansion followed by a severe contraction many times before. The peak of each cycle has recurred roughly every 18 years. Major wars and plagues have broken the rhythm, but the cycle has persisted over the last 800 years.

Understanding the cause of this cycle is imperative if we are ever to learn to tame it and avoid the catastrophe that it brings. We need a better understanding of the conditions that have repeatedly debilitated the financial system and crippled the national (and international) economy.

The place to begin looking for answers is not inside the financial system, where attention has been focused lately. Instead, to understand the cause of the current economic malaise, we need to examine the way the boom led to a bust. Our hypothesis has nothing to do with the "hangover hypothesis," a moralizing approach that proclaims suffering today as the wages of sinful overconsumption in the past. There was in fact overconsumption, but what we are looking for are the causes of that behavior outside of personal motivation. We want to understand the structural conditions that created the binge of 2002 to 2006, which led to the current contraction.

The proximate cause is plain if we will but look. The boom and bust of the land market represents a pattern of land speculation that has preceded many similar episodes in the past. Hence, we start by examining the record of how land speculation precedes economic crises.

A. Hoyt's Land Cycle Research

In his 1933 work on cycles in land values, Homer Hoyt covered in fine detail the five major cycles that crested and crashed in 1837, 1857, 1873, 1893, and 1926–1929 (Hoyt 1933). At the end he generalized "the Chicago Real Estate Cycle," a regular rhythm of boom and bust with the same features in the same sequence. The boom sets us up for the bust (Hoyt 1960: 7).

At the same time that Hoyt was publishing his work, Ernest Fisher (1928, 1933) showed that the rise and fall of suburban platting activity in a number of cities related closely to national economic phases of expansion and contraction. Fisher (1933: 153) determined that, starting in 1850:

The most pronounced peaks in [platting] closely coincide . . . with the peaks in general business activity; and the most abrupt declines in platting activity have occurred at the time of our severest business depressions. For example, platting activity in the Cleveland metropolitan area reached great peaks in 1856, 1873, 1891, 1903, and 1926; it fell to the lowest points in 1861, 1878, 1896, and 1930.

Fisher discovered the same pattern in Chicago, Milwaukee, Toledo, San Francisco, Detroit, and Grand Rapids. In short, the phenomenon analyzed by Hoyt was not unique to Chicago.

It is uncanny how the latest boom from 2002 to 2007 tracks the events that Hoyt recorded and generalized. There was "an increase in rents, building, . . . and subdivision, . . . each of which was carried in turn to speculative excess, and each of which interacted upon the others and upon land values to generate and maintain the boom psychology." The cycle, Hoyt (1933: 369) continued, is "the composite effect . . . of a series of forces that . . . communicate impulses to each other in a time sequence, . . . in a definite order."

He breaks the major events down into 20 elements (Hoyt 1933: 373–403). We can consolidate a few to simplify, but the cycle is not so simple: if it were, mankind would have mastered it long ago, instead of constantly repeating it. Rather, I add a few events that others than Hoyt have noted—an asterisk (*) precedes each of these non-Hoyt elements below.

- Population grows.
- Building rents rise.
- Values of standing buildings rise.
- New building rises.
- Easy credit comes forth to builders, land buyers, and subdividers.
- Nationally, people moving to new areas raise total need for buildings because migrants leave their old homes behind them.
- * Construction itself makes jobs, with demand for more buildings.
- * Outside money flows into growth areas, taking as security liens on new buildings and on lands. As to the local balance of payments, this has the same *temporary* effect as exporting the buildings and lands: unearned increments become part of the local economic base. However, this is a trap: it evolves into debt

service, an outflow of funds that, over time, exceeds the original inflow.

- Easy credit evolves into "shoestring financing" (the 1933 expression for today's "subprime lending").
- New buildings absorb vacant land; land prices boom and spread outward.
- Governments spend freely, on borrowed money, for street improvements and public works to boost land sales.
- Population growth rate slows, but "authoritative" forecasts come forth of more population growth—today's "irrational exuberance," which Hoyt calls a "mania."
- * "Builders' Illusion" sets in, where builders conflate the rise of land prices with a return on their building investment, boosting the incentive to build above what the actual return on building per se would justify. This is because building, however legitimate, entails buying and selling land, a form of "flipping." Unearned increment becomes, for some parties, part of the incentive to build. Ditto for "flipper-remodelers": it's fun to remodel or just redecorate on a rising market. This illusion may be most extreme in large, self-contained, integrated developments, where each building is expected, even in a steady market, to pay for itself in part by raising the value of adjoining parcels. The big developer, being human, may credit himself for the rising tide of the market in general. Such illusions, widely shared, can result in overproduction of new buildings relative to the basic demand.
- Land subdivision and development (or partial development) for urban use goes to greater excess than any other variable in the cycle.[1] The quantity of land is fixed, but people spread out over more and more land. Call it bringing more land into the market, or bringing the market to more land, the effect is the same: a growing overhang of ripening land.[2]
- * "Expert" appraisals of land are based on sales of comparables, and upward price trends. These sales, in turn, were influenced by appraisers who based their opinions on earlier comparables and upward trends, and so on. This is because there is no cost of production to check excesses. Thus a herd mentality can take over, divorcing prices from reality: "irrational exuberance."

- * Rising debt service overtakes inflow of new capital.
- * Corruption and graft that inevitably accompany easy money come to light, eroding and then cracking confidence in markets and banks and the "high, wide, and handsome" libertine boomtime philosophy that has papered over coven and fraud.
- * Lenders' loan turnover has to slow down as they turn from short-term trade credit or commercial loans to long-term loans based on land collateral. A bank that is all loaned out, no matter how sound its balance sheet, cannot make new loans much faster than its debtors pay back the old ones.
- * A rise of land prices cannot simply flatten out at a high plateau because the increment has become part of the expected return that buyers are paying for, and lenders are relying on. So prices that cannot rise further have to drop: there is no equilibrium level at the inflated prices of the boom.
- At the crest, asking prices almost always drop more slowly than bid prices. This makes sales (deeds recorded) drop sharply, even as recorded prices hold steady.
- Subprime borrowers face foreclosure; their distress sales force prices down, in a cumulative spiral.
- Banks, whose capital and surplus is always a small fraction of their liabilities, lose much of their capital and surplus when many debtors default. They are always vulnerable, since they borrow short and lend long, so they have to stop making new loans. Some or many fail. Depositors may panic.
- * Lending slows faster than recorded interest rates rise because banks cut off subprime borrowers. (Professor Ben Bernanke, in calmer days, developed this thesis for the 1930s.)
- * Self-financed firms fare better than bank customers, but their capital returns more slowly than before, or not at all, cutting their rate of reinvesting.
- * Building stops; workers starve or emigrate; chaos reigns, and the economy hits bottom.
- * Governments and leading gurus blame the crash on falling land values, bend their efforts to bailing out big banks and sustaining land values, prolonging the depression. In the process, most

actors lose sight of the original cause, speculation in rising land values, and the stage is set to begin the next cycle.

In conclusion, the boom is initiated by rapid growth of construction and land prices interacting in a rising spiral, and the cycle is completed with an equally rapid fall, first in land values, then in construction activity. The land market is thus closely connected to the instability of the market and the financial system. As we shall see in a later chapter, this cycle also does serious damage to the banking system, causing it to freeze and stop functioning as a source of liquidity.

On the basis of Hoyt's 18-year cycle, Harrison (1997: 27) predicted the present crisis:

> By 2007, Britain and most of the other industrially advanced economies will be in the throes of frenzied activity in the land market to equal what happened in 1988/89. Land prices will be near their 18-year peak, driven by an exponential growth rate, on the verge of the collapse that will presage the global depression of 2010.

Foldvary (1997: 538) made a similar prediction:

> The 18-year cycle in the U.S. and similar cycles in other countries give the geo-Austrian cycle theory predictive power: the next major bust, 18 years after the 1990 downturn, will be around 2008 . . . .

B. Elements of the Land Cycle

Writing in the years after the crash of 1873, American economist Henry George sought to understand the cause of these periodic "paroxysms" that cause the economy to expand and contract suddenly. He believed the origin of the problem lay with "land speculation," which meant holding land off the market waiting for a rise. He likened it to an unconscious "combination" (a cartel) of landowners creating an artificial scarcity. He attributed industrial depressions to inexorably rising rents and land prices that progressively squeezed labor and investors off the land and into the unemployment lines. It was too simple. A good explanation must account for land value collapses, like today's, playing a key role in the crash.

So, let us now consider how the rising price of land enters into investment decisions that trigger a downturn, which can lead to recession or depression. The following steps occur during the cycle of overexpansion and contraction. They do not necessarily follow this order, which is why I have called them "elements" rather than "steps."

- Element 1: From prosperity to overpricing of land. We begin with prosperity generated by normal forces of economic growth: investment of capital in the production of goods and services, which raise incomes and land values. The optimism generated by prosperity carries the seed of its own destruction because it encourages landowners to demand too much, to overprice their land and its rent. Unlike other products, land can remain overpriced for several years because it does not trigger the production of more land.
- Element 2: Overpriced land induces sprawl. Land ownership shares some features that are like a cartel. Like all cartels, the unconscious combination of land speculators creates a price umbrella under which new resources enter the market. This "price umbrella syndrome" periodically creates an artificial surplus of land. The price of marginal land is bid up high enough to bring it into use. Thus, while overpricing prevents construction on better building sites, construction continues on marginal land of lower quality and distant location, resulting in lower rates of return, and in sprawl. The significance of sprawl here is not esthetic or environmental. From an economic perspective, sprawl is harmful because it scatters economic activity over the landscape in ways that raise costs of interaction. Even in the Internet age, a great deal of economic exchange still requires movement of people and goods across space, and those costs increase as travel distances rise. When the land market encourages scattered development, it reduces the overall efficiency of economic exchange.
- Element 3: Inflated land prices reduce profitability of productive investment. Overpricing land and rents means a larger share of the pie goes to landowners as such. That necessarily leaves less of the pie for true social investors, that is, those who hire workers and create incomes to build new capital. Rising rents

squeeze tenants. They use less space, leaving vacancies. Others retreat toward cheaper, marginal land, where they are less productive and earn less income. This, in turn, lowers the marginal rate of return on investing and dramatically lowers profits (since a 10 percent drop in sales may cause a 60 percent drop in profits). Since reinvestment of working capital comes from those profits, it lowers the inducement to invest. This creates a self-reinforcing cycle during the upswing. When the marginal rate of return falls on productive investment, that makes land look more attractive as an alternative, causing land prices to be bid up further, which reduces returns on productive investments, and so on. Higher land prices lower some marginal returns still more, especially in the construction industry, which causes builders to overinvest in land purchases in advance of construction. Rising land prices evoke "rent-leading" land improvements (building in excess capacity in expectation of rising rents). At best, the added capital invested in new buildings, far ahead of market demand for them, means capital will be locked up in a long-term project, with little prospect of yielding income in the near future that can be reinvested. At worst, that capital is lost forever.

- Element 4: Land-price appreciation induces destruction of capital. After land has appreciated, those who sell appreciated land regard their gains as personal income. Most personal income is consumed. Yet there is no social production corresponding to this higher consumption. Therefore, it must draw down existing stocks of capital. Land buyers pay for the land from new savings or from recovery of old capital. There is less capital overall, because sellers have consumed what they got. Owners of income property consume their inventory and depreciation allowances. It is as though grocers ate up part of their own wares, instead of selling and replacing them, leaving some shelves empty. The normal and healthy flow of investing consists of refilling shelves as the goods go out. Now, that flow drops.[3]

- Element 5: Overpriced land misguides investing. The high price of land leads investors to substitute capital for land, at the margin. In general, the market favors substitution of low-priced inputs for high-priced inputs, but when the price of land rises through temporary pressures, that causes distortions. In particular, the kind of capital that substitutes for land is mostly fixed capital, which turns over much slower than average. (For example, the capital stored in an office building turns over about once every 50 years. The capital stored in the inventory of a convenience store turns over several times a year.) Forms of capital that turn over slowly include: (1) land-saving capital (tall buildings, farm machinery used in the field); (2) land-enhancing capital (all investments that develop property to a higher use, such as houses on farmland or stores replacing houses); (3) land-linking capital (railroads, water pipes, electrical cable, and other connective infrastructure); (4) claim-staking capital (exploratory drilling, research and development, lobbying for special privilege, and other rent-seeking actions); and (5) rent-leading capital (excess capacity built in expectation of rising demand and rents). All of these forms of capital tie up funds for long periods and remove capital from forms that create more jobs. The details of how this works will be discussed in the next chapter of this volume.

- Element 6: Lending for overpriced land weakens banks. One might hope that banks and other financial intermediaries would show restraint and prudence by refusing to lend against overvalued property during the period of rising land prices. That is never the case. Bankers fuel the frenzy by overlending to land buyers and refinancers, with inflated appraisals. When the price of land eventually stops rising and buyers default, many financial intermediaries are criticized for being corrupt and/or mismanaged. While that may be true, attributing the negative results solely to bankers distracts us from the larger pattern that causes crises. The relationship between land speculation, excess durable capital investment, and banking crises is the subject of the final chapter of this volume.

- Element 7: Overpricing land reduces real saving, which leads to collapse. The unrealistic inflation of land prices cannot continue forever. Shifting investments to land and from short-term to long-term capital investments has real consequences that cannot be ignored. Banks expand their balance sheets for a while, but as capital turnover slows down and capital markets lose some of their liquidity, interest rates must rise. Interest rates also increase because landowners treat their unearned gains as current income and raise their consumption, thus lowering their real saving. The upsurge of interest rates should ideally be equilibrating, calling forth more capital. In the circumstances, with much capital trapped unrecoverably in fixed forms, the high interest rate fails to evoke more funds, but worsens the capital shortage by tightening the trap.

- Element 8: Land remains overpriced, even after the economy collapses. When overpricing meets resistance, it is followed by holdout over a long period of attrition. Land has more holdout power than labor (which starves) and capital (which wastes). The holdout of land is aggravated by monopoly tendencies that are inherent in the land market. As the price of property falls below the amount owed by borrowers in their mortgage (i.e., they have negative equity), borrowers abandon their property to the lender. Also, credit contraction increases the unemployment rate, leading to a higher rate of foreclosures. Once banks hold the overvalued assets on their books, they face a choice between writing down the value to the new market value (thereby taking a loss) or holding the property until it can be sold at or near the old price. The latter choice is common, which freezes credit markets for months, years, or even decades. See Gaffney (1994: Appendices 2, 3, and 4).

Austrian cycle theorists have dwelt on this tilting of what they call "the structure of production," with too much capital getting sunk irrecoverably in what they call "higher-order" goods. Well and good, but unfortunately they find its cause solely in "forced saving" from bank expansion, with no reference at all to its geographical roots, and the role of inflated land collateral enabling bank expansion.

Banks should be regulated away from lending on land collateral. Logically, there is a powerful reason to regulate banks of deposit. This is because they are always technically insolvent, never able to meet their short-term liabilities from their long-term assets. A related reform might be to make mortgage notes part of the property tax base. This idea is so deeply radical that I only hint at it here, without claiming to have thought it through. We will discuss the problems of land as collateral in bank expansion in the third chapter of this volume.

In the remainder of this chapter, I wish to examine two issues: (1) the factors that influence real estate decisions, including holding land and construction of improvements—specifically the location, timing, and intensity of those uses, and (2) how an unbalanced rise in land prices can be avoided, thereby preventing economic crises from occurring. This can be achieved with the property tax and particularly by frequent assessment of property values, so that rising taxes can prevent land price bubbles before they get under way.

The key mechanism for controlling swings in land prices is the property tax. To understand how the property tax performs that service, we will first examine the secondary effects of the property tax on the land use and distribution of ownership.

The elements of the proposed remedy involve improved administration of the property tax. The first remedy is better assessment, including up-to-date assessment. The second remedy involves shifting the property tax increasingly away from taxation of buildings and toward taxation of land.

Later chapters will consider remedies involving changes in the income tax and in bank regulations. In this chapter, I will focus exclusively on instruments that can regulate land price appreciation. The aim is not to prevent the increase in the *value* of land, which is one of the best indicators of the overall health of the economy. However, sharing the value of land and its increments between private owners and the public fisc will have the salutary effect of dampening economic cycles and promoting positive forms of development.

II

Factors Affecting Land Use (Intensity, Timing, Location)[4]

PROPERTY TAXES AFFECT several aspects of land use: (1) intensity, (2) frequency of demolition and renewal, (3) size of parcel, (4) choice of location of improvements, and (5) the time when land is ripe for higher use. It is the last function of affecting the timing of development that is most crucial in avoiding steep speculative increases in land prices followed by precipitous declines. However, all aspects of the way the property tax influences development play some role in shaping the land use decisions that affect economic cycles. In short, the property tax affects land use and investment decisions.

The property tax is at least three taxes: one on land, one on buildings, and one on personal property (in practice, business inventories). Each has its distinctive effects. I treat the first two separately, and omit the last, which is the smallest, in the interest of brevity.

The effect of property taxes depends among other things on how high the real tax rate is. A rough national mean today might be about 1–2 percent with a wide dispersion about the mean. At these levels, the tax rate may not seem very high next to mortgage interest rates of 6 percent or so, and annual inflation at 4 percent or so. But subtracting 4 percent inflation from 6 percent makes the real interest rate only 2 percent, down in the same range as the property tax rate. Also, the effect of the tax rate may outweigh the effect of interest at an equal rate if the interest is only forgone interest on equity because the tax is a cash outgo.

A. Intensity of Use

1. Taxes on Buildings

The property tax on buildings is a percentage of their value and is therefore something like an increase in the real interest rate. The cost of a building consists of three independent parts. First, there is the visible cost of the materials and labor that go into making the building. When a builder borrows to construct a building, that cost is the principal of the loan. The second part of the building cost is interest on the loan. The third cost is the property tax, an annual charge against the value of the building over its life of 50 to 100 years. I have not listed those costs in order of importance. Interest is the largest cost by far in building, as it is with all very durable goods. The property tax added is the second largest cost, unless rates are uncommonly low. Finally, the principal on the loan, the cost of the building construction itself, is the third largest cost of a building.

The effect of raising building costs (interest, taxes, labor, or materials) is to reduce construction.[5] And when one does build under conditions of higher costs, everything about a building that is marginal is made submarginal. Every individual site, considered in isolation, is less intensively improved. Chopped off are marginal increments to quality, durability, height, and all aspects of intensity (excepting lot coverage, discussed separately). In essence, one applies less capital per unit of land. It is a matter of diminishing returns of capital applied to land.

What is marginal to the owner is of more than marginal value to the health of neighborhoods, so the loss of marginal increments to one owner's capital is a collective loss of consequence. In some jurisdictions it has been found that building owners neglect exterior appearance specifically and selectively because they believe it influences assessors.

Taxing buildings makes capital more expensive, just as interest on the building loan does. A 3 percent annual property tax on a building is approximately equivalent to a 50 percent one-time excise tax on the construction of the building.[6] In other words, the building tax portion of the property tax adds 20–60 percent onto the cost of construction, depending on the tax rate. That motivates people to substitute land for capital, and encourages horizontal spread. Vertical rise meets increasing capital costs per square foot, whereas horizontal spread enjoys decreasing capital costs per square foot, up to a point, and saves on capital by consuming more land.

This produces the anomaly that taxing buildings, although it lowers intensity, acts to increase lot coverage. By putting a premium on horizontal spread, it encourages the building to invade the yard. This might be overcome by enlarging the lot, but here one runs directly into one's neighbor trying to do the same thing. A corollary is artificially forced demand for land, and higher land prices. In time this also leads to urban expansion and larger lots. (This is a reiteration of Element 2 above: Overpriced land promotes sprawl.)

A high-rise building is sometimes painted as a desperate expedient of poverty, but it is more accurately seen as a luxury that lets us enjoy the benefits of closer living without walling off all open space. The luxury is available when capital is cheap. Taxing buildings makes capital artificially dear and prices this luxury out of the market.

2. Taxation of Land Value

Because the land portion of the property tax cannot be passed forward or backward, it falls exclusively on the owner.[7] The land tax affects the selling price of land in much the same way the interest rate does. (A higher interest rate or tax rate on land lowers the selling price of land. Lower interest and tax rates raise the selling price.)[8] In theory, the tax on land should be neutral in its effect on land use. However, that is true only under the simplifying but unreal assumption that there is a perfect market for capital. In fact, interest rates vary among people. They are regressive—the poor have lower credit ratings and thus pay higher interest rates. By contrast, tax rates on land are uniform. They are not higher on the poor than on the rich. Substituting taxes for interest therefore undoes the effect of regressive interest rates. Raising the tax rate on land hits the rich owner harder than the poor.[9] This is what gives the land tax a progressive quality. It increases the bidding power of the poor for land, causing them to encroach on lands held by the rich. This occurs through subdivision of large holdings, accelerated release of ripening land to higher uses, consolidation of very small holdings, and sales of land from the rich to the poor.

The effect of land taxes on intensity of land use is therefore not a simple plus or minus. The effect is equalizing as among classes. Land taxes let the poor, who live crowded on poor land, live less crowded and move to better land. They lower density for the poor by raising it for the rich, who own most of the land.

That is not widely understood. It is often advanced that land taxes "force land into use," and result in higher density. This simplicity is catchy and will not easily give way. But it is misleading. Land taxes crowd the rich, but open up more land for the poor. Only from the standpoint of the wealthy are land taxes simply intensifying. Rather, the land tax is redistributive. Nevertheless, to the extent that the rich are able to hold land idle, particularly land with high potential for productivity, a tax on land value will tend to transfer ownership to those who will use it productively, which is likely to increase overall production.

Land taxes tend to lower intensity of land use in fringe areas, otherwise known as sprawl. This has the opposite effect of the portion of the property tax that falls on buildings. As we saw, the building tax encourages substitution of land for capital, thus promoting demand for marginal land. By raising the cash-flow demands on those who hold high-value land in low-value uses, the land tax promotes development that will meet the demand for land in central, rather than peripheral, locations. This weakens outthrusting demand for marginal land.

B. Timing of Demolition and Renewal

1. Short-Run Effects

When a building is old, the effect of building taxes is probably to lengthen its life, and certainly to defer the renewal of its site. It is not the taxes on the old building itself that lengthen its tenure. On the contrary, they may cause premature demolition and replacement by a parking lot or a vacant lot if the owner can count on the assessor then lowering the valuation, a point on which local practice varies. Renewal is deferred beyond the optimal year of renewal because of the threat of taxes on the successor building.

Because of neighborhood effects, which are mutually reinforcing, what defers renewal of the individual site for 25 years may defer renewal of neighborhoods and cities for 50 years or, in some cases, forever. The city may die. Some cities are dying in this way. Perfectly good land is abandoned, rendered unrenewable by the cumulative neighborhood effects of counterproductive tax policy. This condition contributes to national economic malaise, particularly because the death of cities has neighborhood effects on other cities in the region, as trade falls off among them. This factor is not related to the sudden rise of land prices that causes eventual contraction and economic crisis, but it contributes to the difficulty recovering from such a catastrophe.

Land taxes are more neutral than building taxes in the renewal decision, and in perfect capital markets they might be completely so. In practice, they accelerate renewal because they drain cash from owners of derelict buildings on good locations who are waiting for high bids from potential builders on that site. In this way, land taxes affect behavior not so much through substitution effects (changing relative prices) but through wealth and liquidity effects. Raising the tax rate on land changes relative wealth and holdout power and credit ratings. The effect of a cash drain on a holdout lowers her wealth and liquidity. The cash drain of land taxes also conveys information to many owners who are only vaguely aware that they are holding a resource of high salvage value to society. Land taxes build a fire under sleeping owners. Anyone who talks with owners of ripening land soon learns that many who are not in debt perceive their holding costs in terms of taxes more than forgone potential revenues, even though the latter are five to ten times higher than the tax bill.

2. Long-Run Effects

Taxes also affect the *planned* life of buildings. Because they act like higher interest rates, they discourage durability, which may be perceived as substituting capital for labor. From this, it is easy to infer that building taxes act to shorten planned life. Easy, but wrong, for the taxes also force substituting land for capital. In the discussion of intensity of use, that meant spreading out in space. Here it means spreading out in time, letting structures stand a long time before demolition.

So we seem to have two contrary forces at work. Building taxes cause us to build less durable structures, but then to defer demolition. These two forces are consistent in that each helps save on capital. They are at odds in that the first appears to shorten life, the second to lengthen it. The matter is resolved by distinguishing service life from carcass life of buildings. Service life is a measure of how many years of useful service is provided by the building. This can be lengthened not only by the use of better building materials up front, but also by investments in maintenance during the life of the building. Carcass life is how long a building occupies a site, which it may do for years after anyone is able to use it. Taxing buildings makes us shorten service life, but lengthen carcass life, thus creating a geriatric afterlife of buildings during which they occupy space without doing much good. Houses are built for faster recovery of capital but slower recovery of site, so that the shells of old structures, the ghosts of departed values, stand to haunt us after they have been drained of most of their serviceability. Taxing buildings defers demolition by weakening the profit motive to rebuild and increase supply. It also lengthens the dead period between buildings when land is held out of service.

Land taxes are neutral in respect to marginal incentives, but they have a definite wealth effect, especially in contrast to the taxation of buildings. Taxing buildings drains wealth from builders and creates a liquidity crisis for them. Taxing land serves the same discipline to nonbuilders and to the holders of obsolete and inadequate improvements. By this mechanism, land taxes affect the market sharply by encouraging new development. Particularly in the recovery period after an economic downturn, when credit is tight, a tax on land could help to free up financing to redevelop cities.

C. Choice of Location

The effect of taxing buildings is not merely incremental in the manner treated so far. It changes the relative bidding power of different uses, and changes the structure of cities.

In a perfect market, uses needing high accessibility cluster around a center of maximum access. Access is mutual, so the presence of those seeking access is a net benefit to others seeking access, and clustering is self-reinforcing, up to a point. Likewise, uses needing specific mutual access, or access to the same people or things, cluster in specialized neighborhoods and districts. Aggregate transportation needs are minimized, for any level of linkage. There is a logic to market decisions—the "highest and best" use in the market sense also has a good claim to approximating highest and best use in a more ultimate sense of social good (Gaffney 1970b, 1972). So it is a social cost of moment to deny the market allocation of land without some good reason like a playground, minipark, or street.

Two rival uses compete on equal terms for land, and represent equally high and good use, when they have the same imputed site value, S:

$$S = PVR - C, \tag{1}$$

where PVR is the present value of revenues (net, discounted), and C is cost of construction. It is the difference between PVR and C that makes site value, not the absolute size of either. Thus a gas station can sometimes compete with an apartment; though present value of revenues is less, so is construction cost. But the effect of building taxes varies with C, the tax base. As between two uses equally high and good, that is, with an equal difference of PVR and C, the building tax intercedes in favor of the one of lower construction cost (C). Although its revenue is less, the gas station outbids the apartment because the apartment would have paid more building taxes.

This is a matter of leverage. A given percentage increase in cost cuts deeper into the residual land value afforded by the more intensive use because its cost is higher relative to the land value. Let us give that some precision and generality.

We begin by converting the stream of future building taxes to a lump sum, their present value (PV). "Present value" of the stream means if you borrowed PV and paid it off on the installment plan over the life of the building, your annual payment would be the amount of your building tax. The PV of an annual payment of $1 over 60 years is a lump sum of around $14 (discounting future dollars at 7 percent per year compounded). So a property tax rate of 1 percent of building cost is equivalent to a present value of 14 percent of building cost. (In an earlier example, we used a discount rate of 5 percent, for a present value of about 19 percent of building cost for each 1 percent of tax on the building. Below, we will compare the two.)

The present value of future tax payments comes out of what a builder can bid for land. For every 1 percent added to the tax rate, he reduces his bid by 14 percent of the cost of the planned building (C). The higher is C, the more the disadvantage the high-intensity use has compared with the low-intensity use. Let us couch this in terms of the percentage drop in what competing uses can bid for a site. The absolute drop, for each 1 percent of tax rate, is:

$$-\Delta S = 0.14C. \qquad (2)$$

That drop as a percentage of site value is:

$$-\Delta S/S = 0.14\,C/S. \qquad (3)$$

The ratio of building costs to site value (C/S) for a high-rise structure might run 8/1. Since $8 \times 0.14 = 112$ percent, the tax reduces the bid by more than 100 percent and so wipes out the site value. In other words, the person who plans to build a high-rise will be able to build only if the site is provided at no cost. The builder cannot afford to pay even $1 for the site because the building tax has sterilized it for that intensive use. (At a lower discount rate, such as 5 percent, the building tax would wipe out the site value at a C/S ratio of only about 5/1, a less intensive use of the site.)

By contrast, the C/S ratio for a gas station might be only 1/2. (That would be true for a $70,000 gas station on a $140,000 hot corner.) Since $1/2 \times 0.14 = 7$ percent, the oil company can outbid the high-rise competitor. The oil company would need to reduce the bid on the site only 7 percent below the bid it would have made if there were no taxes. The effect of building taxes is to give the less intensive use a comparative advantage over the more intensive.

That does not mean the total abolition of high-rise buildings everywhere. This is not the way the world works. It means gas stations get more land, and better land. (They also spread out.) Apartments get less land, and worse. (They also are built shorter.) Gas stations move into the center; apartments move outward to the urban periphery. This helps account for the anomaly of intensive uses popping up on poor land and mixed in with much lower uses, while low uses preempt much of the central land. In general, there is a poorer matching of buildings and uses with sites.

The bias against uses with a high ratio of building costs to site value is a bias against the poor, who live at much higher density (higher capital/land ratio) than the rich and on land of lower unit value as a rule. I noted earlier that the tax on buildings affected incentives somewhat as would a rise of interest rates. Here we reach the limits of that parallel. The building tax is more specifically targeted against intensive use than is the interest rate. In the extreme, on an unpaved parking lot yielding income with no building, the building tax does not lower its value a bit, while a higher interest rate would lower the value. More generally, remembering that site value (S) is equal to the present value of revenues (PVR) less building cost (C), building taxes are proportional to C, while higher interest rates have an effect that is proportional to PVR. Thus the artificial scarcity of capital caused by the building tax is more disruptive to the integrity of urban linkages than is a natural scarcity of capital reflected in high interest rates. Indeed, high interest rates would also make roads and allied infra-structure costlier, raising horizontal transportation costs and raising the premium on central location.

D. Ripening of Land for Higher Use

Under dynamic conditions, land is often in transit from one use to another and usually higher use. In anticipation of a move, it develops an "expectation value," or speculative value, that is higher than income from the current best use will support. When should the owner take the quantum jump and initiate the higher use? When is the land ripe for the change?

The choice of ripeness date (D) is difficult because a durable building, indivisible in construction, must be placed on the land to shift its use. As demand for the site grows with each succeeding year, the hypothetical optimal improvement that one would put up if he were going to build in that year changes. Each succeeding year's optimal building yields a higher revenue stream relative to the build-ing cost and thus more net present value to the land.

To avoid premature, preclusive underimprovement or other irre-versible error, one postpones building. D-date (ripeness) arrives when the value imputed to the site by each succeeding year's hypothetical optimal building stops rising faster than the interest rate. (Gaffney (1969) treats the effect on ripeness of later generations of use, a point omitted here.) If the site value is appreciating faster than the interest rate, then the owner will postpone development. When the site appreciates more slowly than the interest rate (or other investments), then the owner will sell the site and put the money into an alternative investment. (Premature development, while the site value was increas-ing rapidly, would produce a use that is less intensive than optimal.)

Taxing buildings affects ripeness. We have seen that taxing build-ings applies leverage against intensive building. It follows that taxing buildings affects the growth rate of site values, assuming that the optimal C/S changes with ripening. The effect of a building tax is to retard ripeness by reducing the rate of growth of the building cost relative to the growth rate of the site value. The nationwide effect of having buildings taxed in all jurisdictions is to lower the level of interest rates that investors require land to earn, thus allowing more land to lie idle at any given time. The net effect of the building tax is that landowners build less and build later. This is another way in which building taxes contribute to slow recovery from a recession.

Since buildings on fully ripened land tend to be capital intensive, it might seem that delaying ripeness would lead to more intensive use of space and less sprawl. That is not the case.[10] The main effect is to delay construction of any kind. Part of ripening is not waiting so much for greater demand but for greater certainty. Certainty means waiting for neighbors to commit themselves. Land speculators wait for neighbors to develop their property. Whoever leads off ripens his neighbor's land and shortens the sterile downtime of land between major improvements. Building taxes that retard the improvement of one site thus retard the ripeness of neighboring complementary sites by generating uncertainty. Uncertainty of this kind is an external nuisance every bit as noxious as odors and noises.

Land taxes speed up ripening, but not by adding to carrying costs, as is commonly believed. Instead, land taxes hasten ripening because buildable land is mostly held by wealthy interests whose comparative advantage lies in holding assets where the main cost is forgoing a return on equity. Hastening the ripening of such land is simply an aspect of the transfer from rich to poor discussed earlier. Nevertheless, this is a real effect. Whereas building taxes delay development, land taxes speed up the process, counteracting some of the negative effects of building taxes. It might seem that land taxes would lead to premature development if not offset by building taxes, but that is not true. Anyone who prematurely develops land because of the pressure of land taxes will lose money in the long run by foregoing future development opportunities. Because developers are quite capable of making the necessary calculations, the substitution effect of the land tax is neutral. Meanwhile, the wealth effect of the land tax is better than neutral because it removes the market distortion that is otherwise caused by differential access to credit.

Frequently, the date of ripeness is outside the owner's direct control and depends on when public works are extended. Today, in many suburban areas, sewer hookups are controlling. Here, land taxes cannot speed ripening until sewer hookups are available. But they can then speed private building to match public sewer extensions and effect great savings on public capital of all kinds. It is traditional to blame premature building and sprawl on ad valorem assessment of ripening land. Premature extension of public works is guiltier, coupled with postmature conversion of ripe land close in, made unripe or submarginal by taxes on building or by preferential rationing of limited sewer hookups to influential speculators in peripheral lands.

III

Avoiding the Real Estate Cycle

WE HAVE NOW SEEN that the property tax—a combination of a tax on land value and a tax on building value—has complex impacts on the intensity, timing, and location of land use.

In this section, we will briefly recapitulate some of the findings of Section II, as they relate to the general issue of land price bubbles.

A. Property Tax Slows Speculation

1. Land Taxes

The basic principle is simple: an increase in the tax on land values raises the cost of holding land, particularly on those who hold land idle. As a result, it spurs development on a continuous and orderly basis, not on the manic and speculative basis of the real estate cycle.

Prospective buyers are less prone to buy real estate for speculative purposes if the tax on land values is high enough to reduce the capital value of the land and if the assessment is up to date (an issue considered below). Land taxation contains a built-in contra-cyclical factor. When a land boom reaches its manic phase, growth expectations rise so high that they offset interest costs: people think they are holding land with no net carrying cost. They expect their homes not just to shelter them but also to pay off their own mortgages, upkeep, and maintenance by appreciating. In this phase, the land tax can serve as an equilibrating force. If land is quickly reassessed at market value, the rising tax on land during these episodes imposes a sobering cash drain on the participants (Gaffney 1993).

To be effective as a brake on periodic land booms, the tax on land values must be high enough to offset the expected growth of land values, which is the basis for rising prices in the market. If potential buyers expect land prices to rise by 10 percent per year (as they have done during some years in some cities), then the combination of taxes and interest would need to be higher than that to send the signal that the price rise cannot be sustained. Even at a lower rate, the tax on land raises carrying costs and slows down price appreciation during a bubble.

2. Building Taxes

As discussed earlier, the property tax on buildings encourages substitution of land for capital, thus promoting demand for marginal land. Since new subdivision development is part of the activity that occurs at a frenzied pace during the upswing of the real estate cycle, the building tax generally adds fuel to the fire. At the same time, the building tax may serve to overcome the tendency during a building boom to construct extravagant high-rise buildings that will not be occupied for many years following the downswing of the cycle. It seems likely that these two effects offset each other to some extent. On the whole, we should look to the taxation of land values as the key to damping the wide oscillations in the real estate cycle.

B. The Importance of Assessment

Unfortunately, the property tax *as it is currently administered* is prevented from serving as an effective antidote to sudden surges in subdivision, excessive construction, and land price increases that outrun realistic expectations of future cash flow or service value. If the property tax is to serve its proper role in splashing cold water on the overheated real estate market, the assessment process needs to be accurate and to keep up with the rising price of land. In a rising market, the frequency of assessment is of utmost importance, although it is rarely achieved by local tax authorities. The best way to solve that problem would be to eliminate the tax on buildings and to adopt a computerized mass appraisal (CMA) system at the state level, which would enable assessments to be updated continuously.

1. Accuracy of Assessment

If assessments are not accurate, tax policy is hindered in its ability to send the right signals to potential buyers and speculators in real estate. Vertical inequity is a common problem. Assessments are regressive if lower-valued properties are assessed at a higher proportion of their market value than higher-valued properties.[11] Horizontal inequity is also a problem. In a single city, one property might be assessed at $300,000, and a property of equal value might be assessed at $500,000. Both vertical and horizontal inequity in assessment practices create the sense that the assessment is random, which reduces the power of the property tax to function as a policy tool. Bringing the assessment ratio (assessed value divided by market value) into greater uniformity will rationalize the property market within a jurisdiction, to some extent.

Actually, the situation is worse than the typical study of assessment bias reveals. The assessment/sales ratio understates actual discrimination by not considering properties that do not sell frequently. Turnover is lower among larger holdings, which are the most likely to be underassessed. Thus, it is possible to maintain a high assessment/sales ratio alongside considerable vertical inequity within a jurisdiction as long as low-value property with high turnover is assessed accurately. That is because the high-value property does not show up very often in the calculation of the ratio.

If that hidden bias is true of residential land, it is even more true of other urban land that tends to escape notice, such as old railyards, utility rights of way, and the like. The quinquennial Census of Governments at one time provided valuable evidence of assessment ratios.[12] However, real business property was excluded from the survey before the 1967 report, so subsequent reports failed to show the underassessment of industrial property. In addition, the survey from the beginning failed to include unsubdivided acreage inside standard metropolitan statistical areas (SMSAs). Much of that land is held for speculative purposes, and much is in estates held by the super-rich or as industrial acreage (Gaffney 1973). My own research in Milwaukee in the 1960s found that industrial land there was assessed at anywhere from 5 percent to 40 percent of the market value (Gaffney 1970a: 169).

In addition, the assessment/sales ratio provides no information about the underassessment of land under existing buildings and corresponding overassessment of buildings. This practice is so widespread as to be viewed as normal and thus escape the attention of most researchers. Property owners want the share of building value in their official assessment to be overstated (and for land value to be correspondingly understated) because buildings are depreciable on the federal income tax, and land is not. The IRS is independent of local assessors de jure, but in fact it authorizes building owners to use locally assessed values as evidence to determine what fraction of their real estate is in the depreciable building. To the local jurisdiction, which collects the same tax rate on land and buildings, this might seem like a harmless bias. However, it is a major factor in the failure of assessors to capture the true growth of land value, which is the source of the recurrent folly of the land cycle.

To observe the extent of underassessment of land, there is no simple corrective calculation. To achieve an accurate understanding of land value, one must conduct a detailed reassessment using the building-residual method of valuation, as the great Alfred Marshall insisted, by valuing the land first, as though it were vacant, based on highest and best use (Marshall [1890] 1920: V, Ch. XI, para. 4): "The aggregate site value of any piece of building land is that which it would have if cleared of buildings and sold in a free market." The land value is then subtracted from the current market value of the land-building combination, leaving the building value as the residual. This is a forward-looking method of assessment. In contrast to the methods often used by assessors, who are swayed in their valuations by current or past use of each location, this method defines land value as reuse value, looking always to the future, not the past. Using that method in Milwaukee in 1965, I found that taxable land value was $2.4 billion, or 3.2 times as much the official (equalized) assessed value of land of $748 million (Gaffney 1970a: 170). Since that sort of underassessment of land relative to buildings remains standard practice in the United States today, one of the first reforms necessary to avoid catastrophic binges of land speculation is to adopt the building-residual method of assessment. If that were done, the true value of land would be reflected in tax bills (and official records), and tax assessors could readily douse the flames of land speculation by rapid reassessment.

Because land is underassessed and buildings are overassessed, an improved system of assessment that corrects those biases would have an effect quite similar to shifting the tax rate from buildings to land. All of the features of a tax on land that are superior to a tax on buildings, including the damping of "irrational exuberance" associated with land booms, would be achieved simply by improving the system of assessment in most jurisdictions. Since the health of the national and international economy depends on this, there may be a need for a higher authority to step in and resolve the problem of systematic bias in current assessments.

2. Frequency of Assessment

Accuracy of property assessment is of little avail in preventing land price bubbles if the assessments are not kept up to date. If land prices double every five years in some areas during a boom, an assessment frozen at some level prior to the mania will have no influence on the behavior of buyers and sellers "flipping" property in the hopes of a quick gain. In theory, assessment occurs every year or every three years in most jurisdictions, but there are so many exceptions that the theory bears little resemblance to the practice. As an extreme example, one county in Pennsylvania was reassessed in 2000 for the first time since 1958 (Junker 2002). During the interim 42 years, the county relied on "base-year assessment," in which the assessment is marked up slightly from the previous year. That method, which has been widely used, ignores changes in the real estate market and mismeasures the true value of properties.

For all of its faults, at least Pennsylvania allows all property to be reassessed at market value, even though the new assessments cannot raise the average property tax bill by more than 5 percent over the previous tax year, no matter how much property values rise. In that sense, frequent reassessment would do little to prevent or slow down land price mania.

The biggest problem with assessment lies in California, Florida, and similar states that have adopted legislation that puts a cap on how much assessed value is allowed to rise each year. Proposition 13 in California limited assessment growth to 2 percent or the change in the Consumer Price Index (CPI), whichever is less. Florida's Amendment 10, adopted by voters in November 1992, limits the growth of assessment of residences to 3 percent or the CPI, whichever is less. A number of states set limits on assessment increases: Alabama, Arizona, Arkansas, California, Florida, Georgia, Illinois, Iowa, Maryland, Michigan, Nevada, New Jersey, New York, Oklahoma, Oregon, South Carolina, Texas, and Washington (Mikhailov and Kolman 2002).

It is interesting to compare that list with the January 2009 list of foreclosures by state. The top eight states, ranked in terms of foreclosure activity per household (Nevada, California, Arizona, Florida, Oregon, Illinois, Georgia, and Michigan), were all states with assessment limits (RealtyTrac Staff 2009). That does not prove causation, and the data are not stable from month to month, but they confirm a plausible connection between assessment limits and land price bubbles. In states where assessments are legally limited and cannot climb the steep path of rising real estate prices, the tax on land cannot fulfill its potential as an equilibrating force. Limiting assessments has a strong political appeal to long-time residents of a state because it protects them from rising taxes as their location becomes more desirable. The downside is that that seemingly small privilege has consequences that reach around the globe. The U.S. financial debacle has crippled the economies of many other countries, and most of the damage in the United States was done in a handful of states. Those states, particularly California and Florida, allowed land prices to soar by failing to tax real estate at anything near full market value.

IV

Conclusion

THE CURRENT ECONOMIC DISTRESS that afflicts the United States and the world is the continuation of a long historical pattern. The pattern consists of a cycle of rising land prices, overinvestment in capital affixed to land, and widespread purchase of economically marginal land, followed by a rapid reversal of land prices, defaults on loans, and stranded assets that yield no cash flow.

Homer Hoyt identified a cycle that recurred at approximately 18-year intervals in Chicago in the 19th century. Instead of drawing conclusions about the kinds of policies that could prevent the human cost of those cycles in real estate, Hoyt used his knowledge to time his real estate investments, so as to make a fortune.

Nevertheless, Hoyt's data, along with Henry George's theory of periodic depressions caused by land speculation, have provided the origins for my own forays into an understanding of how land and capital interact to cause such deep crises during the downswing of the real estate cycle. That is what I have offered in this chapter.

I have provided considerable detail about how the pricing and taxing of land relates to investment decisions—their timing, intensity, and location. These relationships are important because they demonstrate that there is a connection between local decisions regarding the geographic expansion of the metropolis and national or even global consequences regarding the fate of the economy. The central message, which will continue in the following essays, is this: if economic policy encourages (or fails to discourage) the periodic overpricing of land and the concomitant investment in buildings on marginal land, the effect will be to tie up capital in marginal uses and paralyze the economy. What is perhaps surprising is how few cities, engaged in such periodic manias of overextension, can bring a national economy to its knees. This demonstrates just how sensitive the national economy is to local land markets.

If the reader takes away only one lesson from this essay, it will have been successful. That lesson is simple: the real economy matters. As I will stress in subsequent essays, the theories of Keynes and other schools of economic thought have focused far too much attention on questions of money and finance, as if an economy could be well-managed on the basis of correct monetary policies alone. What I hope I have begun to make clear is that monetary policy is a refinement. It will fail if the basics, involving land and capital, are not attended to. The basics have, however, been neglected for several generations.

Although the current economic crisis is causing great hardship to millions of people, it could perhaps turn out to be of some social value. Since this crisis has begun to reveal how little wisdom contemporary economists have on questions about basic economic stability, this could be the occasion for serious reformulation of economic theory. If this crisis can serve to put economists, political leaders, and the public on the path to a healthier economy in the long run, all of the suffering that families will go through may not have been in vain.

Notes

1. According to Fisher (1933: 157, 160): "In Cleveland, in 1926, there were 20 [recorded lots] per hundred in use." For other cities the percentages of subdivided lots in use were: Grand Rapids, Michigan, 24 percent; Chicago, 54 percent; Detroit, 25 percent; Milwaukee, 23 percent; Birmingham, Alabama, 25 percent. Because of this wasteful use of land, "capital expended in the installation of streets, sidewalks, and public utilities lies idle and is rapidly disappearing, while only the miles of decaying sidewalks and reeling lamp posts remain to bear mute testimony to the speculative folly of both sub-divider and 'investor.'" Also see Cornick (1938).

2. Based on recorded real estate activity in Alameda County, California, Maverick (1932) found that subdivision was the most volatile variable in the real estate cycle. He found cycles in that county of subdivision, deeds recorded, and land values from 1853 to 1929 that corresponded very closely with national cycles in real estate. He concluded that "subdivisions, number of deeds, and values all show major movements at the same times, but that the violence of the movements is great in subdivisions, intermediate in values, and relatively slight in number of deeds." Peaks in the number of lots subdivided were in 1876, 1891, 1907, and 1926, which corresponds closely to national land value peaks, which were followed by recessions. Even after smoothing the data, he found that the number of lots subdivided was 10 times greater in peak years of the cycle than in trough years.

3. In purely monetary, demand-side terms, aggregate spending remains the same at first. Consuming the inventory and depreciation allowance means a flow of investing is replaced by a flow of consumer spending. However, the added consumer spending does not flow through the "grocery store" to hire workers, create incomes, and produce goods. It is offset by "disinvestment." If money spending holds up while production and hiring fall, the result is inflation without full employment (stagflation).

4. This section draws heavily upon Gaffney (1980).

5. Delays in construction raise the interest costs of a particular building, which is why contractors are so sensitive to timing issues. However, we are concerned here only with costs that all construction shares, not with individual projects.

6. This is how that 57 percent figure is derived: using a 5 percent discount rate, a stream of annual $1 taxes for 60 years equals the value of a

$1 annuity over that period, or $18.93. Thus, a 1 percent property tax rate on the building is equivalent to an 18.9 percent excise tax on construction, and a 3 percent property tax rate on the building is approximately equivalent to a 57 percent excise tax. Since the building will depreciate somewhat over those 60 years, we round it down to a 50 percent excise tax equivalent.

7. Taxes can be shifted only to the extent that they influence supply and demand. The tax on land shifts the demand curve downward, but the supply is fixed. The net effect is to lower the price at which it sells.

8. Raising the tax on land reduces its selling price, which reduces the interest cost of buying or holding land. The selling price (V) is approximately equal to the net rent of the land (a) divided by the sum of the interest rate and tax rate, or $V = a / (i + t)$. Since $a = Vi + Vt$ (interest payment plus tax payment), if the property tax on a parcel rises by $500, the interest payment on that parcel will fall by $500. In other words, the tax on land does not raise the cost of holding land. Instead, it displaces the interest cost. More is paid to the tax collector; less is paid to the bank or other mortgage holder.

9. The carrying cost of land (c) is equal to its price or value (V) times the combination of interest (i) and the tax on land value (t). So, $c = V(i + t)$. The poor pay more to carry a given piece of land, because the cost is mostly interest. As t is made larger, V falls, so Vi falls, and the impartial tax cost displaces the regressive interest cost.

10. "Marginal" land connotes low intensity, but the connotation is misleading. Our intuitive sense of intensity is based on a physical or per acre concept (such as capital invested per acre), while economics is concerned with values (capital invested per dollar of revenue or service value). (Since site value [S] equals revenue [R] minus cost [C], or $S = R - C$, then $C = R - S$ and $C/R = [R - S]/R$.) The cost/revenue ratio defines economic marginality. Since a marginal site is one with little site value, that means $(R - S)/R$ (or C/R) rises toward unity on increasingly marginal locations, as less and less revenue is left over to provide site value. In these terms, marginal land, or land with a high cost/revenue ratio, is the most intensively used. Thus, when land ripens, it is used at a lower economic intensity, with higher site value (or economic surplus), as C/R falls.

11. A few recent studies revealing the regressive character of assessment in many jurisdictions are Sirmans, Diskin, and Friday (1995); Goolsby (1997); and Cornia and Slade (2005).

12. The final report on assessments was U.S. Department of Commerce, Bureau of the Census (1982).

References

Board of Governors of the Federal Reserve System. (2009, March 12). "Table B.100 Balance Sheet of Households and Nonprofit Organizations." *Flow of Funds Accounts of the United States, Release Z.1.* Available online at: http://www.federalreserve.gov/releases/z1/Current/

CBS News. (2009, March 9). "12 percent of Homeowners Behind on Mortgages: Numbers Also Include 48 Percent of Subprime Mortgage Holders; Reflect Spreading Recession." Available online at: http://www.cbsnews.com/stories/2009/03/05/business/main4844773.shtml

Cornia, Gary C., and Barrett A. Slade. (2005). "Property Taxation of Multifamily Housing: An Empirical Analysis of Vertical and Horizontal Equity." *Journal of Real Estate Research* 27(January/March): 17–46.

Cornick, Philip H. (1938). *Premature Subdivision and Its Consequences.* New York: Institute of Public Administration, Columbia University.

Fisher, Ernest M. (1928). "Real Estate Subdividing Activity and Population Growth in Nine Urban Areas." *Michigan Business Studies* I(9).

Fisher, Ernest M. (1933). "Speculation in Suburban Lands." *American Economic Review* 23(March): 152–162.

Foldvary, Fred. (1997). "The Business Cycle: A Georgist–Austrian Synthesis." *American Journal of Economics and Sociology* 56(4): 521–541.

Gaffney, Mason. (1969). "Replacement of Individual by Mass System." *Proceedings of American Real Estate and Urban Economics Association* 4: 21–68.

——. (1970a). "Adequacy of Land as a Tax Base." In *The Assessment of Land Value.* Ed. Daniel M. Holland. Madison, WI: University of Wisconsin Press. Available online at: http://www.masongaffney.org/publications/G1Adequacy_of_land.CV.pdf

——. (1970b). "Land Rent, Taxation, and Public Policy." *Papers of the Regional Science Association* 23: 141–153.

——. (1972). "The Sources, Nature, and Functions of Urban Land Rent." *American Journal of Economics and Sociology* 31(July): 241–257.

——. (1973). "An Agenda for Strengthening the Property Tax." In *Property Tax Reform.* Ed. George Peterson. Washington, DC: Urban Institute. Available online at: http://www.masongaffney.org/publications/G4-AgendaforStrengtheningthePropertyTax1.CV.pdf

——. (1980). "Tax Reform to Release Land." In *Compact Cities: A Neglected Way of Conserving Energy: Joint Hearings, Committee on Banking, Finance and Urban Affairs; and Committee on Interstate and Foreign Commerce, U.S. House of Representatives, 96th Congress 1st Sess.* Washington, DC: USGPO. Available online at: http://www.masongaffney.org/publications/E4-TaxReformtoReleaseLand.CV.pdf

——. (1993). "The Taxable Capacity of Land." In *Land Value Taxation: Papers from a Conference Sponsored by the Government Law Center of Albany Law School, Senate Environmental Conservation Committee, and New York State Division of Equalization and Assessment.* Ed. Patricia Salkin. Albany, NY: Government Law Center. Available online at:

http://www.masongaffney.org/publications/G29-TaxableCapacityofLand.CV.pdf

——. (1994). "Land as a Distinctive Factor of Production." Pp. 39–102 in *Land and Taxation*. Ed. Nicolaus Tideman. London: Shepheard-Walwyn.

Goolsby, William C. (1997). "Assessment Error in the Valuation of Owner-Occupied Housing." *Journal of Real Estate Research* 13(1): 33–45.

Grow, Brian, Keith Epstein, and Robert Berner. (2009, February 12). "How Banks Are Worsening the Foreclosure Crisis." *Business Week*. Available online at: http://www.businessweek.com/magazine/content/09_08/b4120034085635.htm

Harrison, Fred. (1997). "The Coming 'Housing' Crash." In *The Chaos Makers*. Eds. F. J. Jones and Fred Harrison. London: Othila Press.

Hoyt, Homer. (1933). *One Hundred Years of Land Values in Chicago: The Relationship of the Growth of Chicago to the Rise in its Land Values, 1830–1933*. Chicago: University of Chicago Press.

——. (1960). "The Urban Real Estate Cycle: Performances and Prospects." *Urban Land Institute Technical Bulletin* 38(7).

Junker, Matthew. (2002). "Fayette Assessment Appeals Exceed Earlier Estimates." *Pittsburgh Tribune-Review* (August 10). Available online at: http://www.pittsburghlive.com/x/pittsburghtrib/s_85597.html

Marshall, Alfred. ([1890] 1920). *Principles of Economics*, 8th ed. London: Macmillan. Available online at: http://www.econlib.org/library/Marshall/marP38.html#Bk.V, Ch.XI

Maverick, Lewis A. (1932). "Cycles in Real Estate Activity." *Journal of Land & Public Utility Economics* 8(May): 191–199.

Mikhailov, Nikolai, and Jason Kolman. (2002). *Types of Property Tax and Assessment Limitations and Tax Relief Programs*. Cambridge, MA: Lincoln Institute of Land Policy. Available online at: http://www.lincolninst.edu/subcenters/property-valuation-and-taxation-library/dl/mikhailov.pdf

Milne, Richard, and Anousha Sakoui. (2008). "Company Crashes Set to Hit Record Next Year." *Financial Times* (December 7). Available online at: http://www.ft.com/cms/s/0/935e5284-c489-11dd-8124-000077b07658.html

Nutting, Rex. (2009, March 26). "Worst Quarter for the Economy Since the 1930s: In Terms of Lost Wealth, Lost Jobs, Falling Output, the Fourth Quarter Stands Out." MarketWatch.com. Available online at: http://www.marketwatch.com/news/story/story.aspx?guid={564b8982-ace7-464c-914e-24c37b5c1b21}

RealtyTrac Staff. (2009, February 2). "Foreclosure Activity Decreases 10 Percent in January." Available online at: http://www.realtytrac.com/ContentManagement/PressRelease.aspx?channelid=9&ItemID=5822

Sirmans, G. Stacy, Barry A. Diskin, and H. Swint Friday. (1995). "Vertical Inequity in the Taxation of Real Property." *National Tax Journal* 49(March): 71–84.

U.S. Bureau of Labor Statistics. (2009a). "Table A-1: Employment Status of the Civilian Noninstitutional Population 16 Years and Over." *Labor Force Statistics from the Current Population Survey.* Washington, DC: USBLS. Available online at: ftp://ftp.bls.gov/pub/suppl/empsit.cpseea1.txt

——. (2009b). "Economic News Release, Table 1: Mass Layoff Events and Initial Claimants, 2005 to 2009." Washington, DC: USBLS. Available online at: http://www.bls.gov/news.release/mmls.t01.htm

U.S. Department of Commerce, Bureau of the Census. (1982). *1982 Census of Governments, Vol. 2: Taxable Property Values and Assessment Sales-Price Ratios.* Washington, DC: U.S. Government Printing Office.

2

A New Framework for Macroeconomics

Achieving Full Employment by Increasing Capital Turnover

By Mason Gaffney*

ABSTRACT.   Most forms of macroeconomics today, whether Keynesian or monetarist, presuppose that problems of economic instability can be treated as errors in financial management. Neither fiscal nor monetary policy recognizes the existence of systemic faults in the real economy that result in overinvestment in durable capital that turns over slowly, in contrast to forms of capital that interact more frequently with land and labor. Only by removing serious distortions in microeconomic relations can macroeconomic problems be resolved. The current global economic crisis exemplifies the limitations of policies that ignore distortions in the rate of turnover of investment capital.

I

Introduction

POLITICAL AND ECONOMIC LEADERS are looking for a quick fix for the current economic crisis. They are unable to find remedies, however, because their models presuppose that the economy is in equilibrium and that any disturbance is caused by an external "shock," which is understood as a random event that could not have been predicted.

*Mason Gaffney has been a Professor of Economics at the University of California, Riverside for 33 years; e-mail: m.gaffney@dslextreme.com. He is the author of *The Corruption of Economics*, an explanation of how land became excluded from neo-classical economic models. He has also written extensively on various aspects of resource economics, urban economics, tax policy, and capital theory. A version of this essay was previously published as "Toward Full Employment with Limited Land and Capital," pp. 99–166, in *Property Taxation, Land Use, and Public Policy*, edited by Arthur D. Lynn, Jr. ©1976 by the Board of Regents of the University of Wisconsin System. Reprinted by permission of the University of Wisconsin Press.

American Journal of Economics and Sociology, Vol. 68, No. 4 (October, 2009).

In this case, the pundits are blaming subprime mortgage lending and other questionable business practices, as if they were foreign objects in an otherwise healthy system.

To solve the current crisis and avoid similar crises in the future, we start with a different premise. The economic problems we face today are not the result of personal foibles or random events. They stem from the misallocation of capital. The consequences of that misallocation have manifested themselves in regular cycles of expansion and contraction, which have recurred approximately once every generation in the United States since 1798 (and perhaps earlier). Of course, every cycle has its peculiar features, including people who engage in sleight-of-hand financial manipulations, but we should not be distracted by personality. The important story lies deeper, at the level of how capital functions in an economy.

The story behind the news is that lending for land and expansionary capital investment has repeatedly created a temporary euphoria of rising prices, only to be followed by a sudden downturn, in which asset prices fall, interest rates rise, and unemployment rises. Mainstream macroeconomists offer no explanation for the cause of this cycle, and their only remedy is to reinflate the bubble, to start the cycle again.

Meanwhile, we find ourselves in a condition aptly described by Henry George more than a century ago: "Though custom has dulled us to it, it is a strange and unnatural thing that men who wish to labor, in order to satisfy their wants, cannot find the opportunity" (George [1879] 1979: 270). The paradox of an economic system that disemploys people who wish to work and whose wants are not satisfied has still not been resolved. After more than 60 years of monetary and fiscal management, we are back at square one, facing a national crisis similar to the depression of the 1870s, when Henry George wrote, or the 1930s, when Keynes wrote.

Federal fiscal and monetary policies, alongside recent bailouts of financial institutions, prove powerless to restore economic activity and soak up surplus labor. Prominent economists seem confused and helpless when faced with the most basic malfunction of the system, that is, shortness of work tied to a contraction of credit. Why cannot these idle persons find work to fill those shortages? If economics cannot solve this elementary but stubborn riddle, it is not good for much.

The thesis of this essay is that contemporary macroeconomics is based on faulty premises, and the policies based on those premises have led us astray. The spending and investment cures that leaders apply in cases of economic contraction are not cures at all. They are the source of the problem, so the harder they try to solve the problem, the worse they make it. That does not mean the classical remedies—increased saving or wage cuts—will solve the problem, either. What is needed is a new approach based on vital distinctions that have been overlooked. Rather than thinking simply in terms of "more" or "less" spending, taxing, or capital investment, we need to re-examine the effects of different kinds of capital investment on employment and the ways in which taxation has discouraged the right kinds of capital investment.

The beginning of wisdom on macroeconomics starts with the recognition that some forms of capital displace workers and other forms enhance employment. It is not necessary for government officials to sort through lists of capital investments to make this determination. The market can do so quite well on its own, if it is coaxed to do so by the right incentives. As we shall see, different kinds of taxes have quite unexpected impacts on the ways in which land and capital are combined with labor. The choice between full employment (with labor-enhancing forms of capital) or financial crisis (with labor-displacing forms of capital) is largely a result of which tax policies are adopted as well as the kinds of direct capital investments made by government agencies. This essay will deal with general principles and with taxes. Methods of selecting appropriate government capital projects are discussed only in passing.

A. Paradox: Idle Labor, Shortages of Capital, and Land

The paradoxical condition of work needing to be done and workers not being allowed to do it cannot be considered in isolation. The problems we now face did not come upon us suddenly. They have been building for years.

Real wage rates in the United States have lost ground since 1973, particularly in relation to the price of housing. The United States used to be the employment mecca of the world, but in the past three decades, an increasing number of jobs have been "outsourced," shifted to other countries. We are unable to absorb the same workforce that was employed a few years ago.

At the same time, the other sinews of production, capital and land, are growing short, and very dear. The price of land for housing was recently bid up to absurd heights before it collapsed and brought down the financial house of cards that was fueled by housing speculation. In the wake of the boom and bust of the housing market, capital financing is particularly hard to obtain.

Materials prices are high, particularly the price of energy. The price of oil in 2009 has fallen from the 2008 peak, but only because of the recession. After spending billions on two wars in Iraq to secure oil supplies, American consumers were still paying between $3 and $4 per gallon for gasoline in 2007 and 2008. In nominal terms, gasoline prices more than doubled between January 2005 and the summer of 2008 (U.S. Department of Energy, Energy Information Administration 2009: Fig. 2).

The required complement of land and capital per worker and consumer has risen sharply for many years, much more quickly than the workforce. So now we are bumping into the ineluctable logic that if we require a vast complement of resources per worker, and require jobs for all, we will chew up lots of resources, and push on the limits of the Earth. We will push up materials prices; we will pollute the environment; and we will provoke our neighbors by coveting their raw materials. We will push on the limits of our capital supply, too, unless it grows faster than it has been growing.

Along with short work, we face a swelling array of secondary evils: crime, protracted apprenticeship periods, soaring welfare and dependency, forced early retirement, imperialism to make jobs and acquire raw materials, pork barrel politics, seniority, suppression of competition, exclusionary local codes and zoning, and rejection of the free market. All these evils have their independent roots, but are inflated by unemployment and the fear of it.

Some unemployment is iatrogenic; that is, caused by the doctor. Critics of welfare point out how welfare payments have boomed into a cause of unemployment. For 25 years since the publication of *Losing Ground* (Murray 1984), conservatives have attacked welfare as the root of most evils in American society. But before anyone blames welfare, we should first analyze why we have been unable to solve the perennial problem of a system that prevents 4 to 8 percent of the population from work (and a much higher percentage in low-income neighborhoods). Since work shortage also serves to rationalize welfare, we have a vicious circle. But there is little doubt which came first, nor is there much doubt that we can solve the problem humanely only by opening more jobs, regardless of the direction of welfare reform.

Each of the secondary evils, like welfare, could be a study in itself. Yet until we face the elemental riddle at the fountainhead of all this trouble, each such study only diverts us from meeting the ultimate challenge for economists that George posed in 1879.

B. Recent History of the Failure of Macroeconomics

By the end of the 1970s, there was a general recognition that fiscal and monetary policy had failed. Instead of "fine-tuning," we had "stagflation." Keynesianism foundered as it steered between the shoals of inflation and the rocks of unemployment and ran onto both at once. The so-called New Economics taught that that would not happen. "Fiscal Policy and Full Employment Without Inflation" was the promise (Samuelson 1955: 336), and the world believed it. Samuelson (1955: 350) wrote of the new "mastery of the modern analysis of income determination," and of the "momentous Employment Act of 1946 . . . to fight mass unemployment and inflation." Inflation could result mainly only from "overfull employment." All that turned to ashes in the crucible of 14 percent inflation in 1979, which was brought under control only by double-digit unemployment. For a couple of decades, in the 1980s and 1990s, it seemed that Keynesianism had died. However, in the past year, it has come into vogue again, in response to the current credit contraction.

Economists of influence seem capable of little but following Pavlovian responses learned in school: in a word, that the way to make jobs is to recycle money faster. Most of what we call macroeconomics today is an embroidery on that one simple theme, the simplicity hidden beneath elegant variations and elaborate circumlocutions that dazzle and boggle and addle without adding much substance.

The "New Economics," when new in the 1950s, was positive and optimistic, and promised a lot. There were free lunches in those days—when you put the idle to work, there is such a thing. The Puritan ethic was the goat, obsolete and absurd, dour and dismal. But by the 1970s, the New Economics had become a New Dismal Science, a science of choice in which all the choices are bad. The pessimism was rooted in the Phillips Curve, an observed tradeoff between unemployment and inflation. Paul Samuelson (1970) summarized the dismal sentiments of that era when he opined: "One must face up to the bitter truth that only so long as the economy is depressed are we likely to be free of inflation." This was not bread, but a stone.

Conservatives offered the same tradeoff in even starker terms. Milton Friedman (1968) and Edmund Phelps (1968) independently reached the same conclusion: that any effort to reduce unemployment and raise real wages through demand management must necessarily lead to a higher rate of inflation and a consequent reduction in real wages. The "natural" rate of unemployment or NAIRU (non-accelerating-inflation rate of unemployment) was the level of unemployment at which the economy would be in equilibrium. They argued that the Keynesian tradeoff between inflation and unemployment was largely a mirage because any reduction in unemployment would be temporary and would simply inject inflationary pressures without any corresponding social benefit. The conservatives could gleefully announce that "this is the best of all possible worlds" and that any efforts at improvement will merely cause greater suffering.

Since conservatives recognized that policy could allow for short-term variations around the long-run equilibrium, policy making after 1968 settled into a grim choice on which conservatives united with liberals. They differed mainly on whether to allow more unemployment or more inflation. There was little challenge to the conceptual framework. Controlling spending was all that mattered. Monetarists debated Keynesians over the most effective way to regulate spending, and were more disposed to favor less of it, and recognize other constraints. Yet neither side much deviated from the premise that spending money is the governor of the economy, the autonomous force that other activity obeys, the key of control. As Otto Eckstein summed up the situation in the 1970s:

> The collective intelligence of the economics profession is unable to fundamentally restructure the intellectual substance of the field. . . . We have a theoretical apparatus that can be used for a wide variety of things. There is no other way, and I do not think we know how to find one. (1974: 56)

The one new idea that entered economic debates in the 1980s was the Laffer Curve, the assertion that tax cuts would solve problems of scarcity by increasing output, as if there was no limit on the "free lunch" offered by Keynesians. In a sense, this was a welcome relief from the debates over the Philips Curve and NAIRU, which imposed a straitjacket on economic policy. At bottom, though, it was more of the same. The Keynesians, the conservatives, and Laffer all agreed that the manipulation of aggregate spending was all that mattered. They all implicitly concurred that the real economy no longer mattered.

II

Why We Need a New Form of Macroeconomics

EVERY VARIATION on the general theme of monetary and fiscal controls has led to disastrous policy results: periods of inflation followed by periods of high unemployment, with high levels of resource consumption in both periods. The problem is that the practical solutions have been based on an intellectual foundation that de-emphasizes causal factors in the real economy that combines land, labor, and capital.

A. The Origins of Macroeconomics

Modern macroeconomics evolved under a different set of problems than we face today, and its founders built into its vitals a number of special premises and limitations. It is geared to assume no or few resource constraints, and has little response for the new challenges of environmental limits and scarce raw materials.

"Growth" is one of its ideals, and simply to make jobs in a stable equilibrium independent of growth is outside its purview. Geared to approve waste, it has nothing for emerging needs to conserve scarce resources. Geared to define the economic problem as how to dispose of surpluses, it ill becomes a world of excess demand and short supplies. Geared to treat capital as a glut, and the central economic problem as how to dispose of excess saving, it is at a loss with capital shortage in the form of either credit constraints or high interest rates.

Geared to treat both resources and capital as cheap, it all too easily lets labor be treated as the only cost of production worth mentioning—a new labor theory of value—and ignores distribution. It plays into the hands of anti-labor interests by picturing inflation in terms of a "wage-price spiral."

Macroeconomics today ignores the possibilities of substituting labor for land and capital. Geared to idealize federal spending, it drifts easily into mercantilism and imperialism, especially in the more idealistic, missionary phases of "economic development." Geared to accept and live with concentration of wealth and economic power, it has little to say about the effects of industrial mergers in substituting capital for labor by putting plants on standby and "outsourcing" jobs. It has no basis for condemning the monumental waste of capital in urban sprawl, or the global sprawl of imperialism, because each inflated need is an investment outlet. On the contrary, continuous territorial expansion and development are its answers to the limited land supply.

A design feature in the apparatus of modern macroeconomics is that the best way to recycle stagnant money is to find investment outlets. Since the rate of profit is always threatening to push zero, such outlets are to be cherished, and we should subsidize and force-feed investment if needed, as by loans at low interest, to keep money recycling. If we stack up layers of capital at low productivity, that is no problem. Seminal investments like roads and water supplies that open new lands are best of all, for they induce ancillary investments that recycle yet more stagnant money.

Boondoggling is all right because it makes jobs, and if it soaks up a disproportionate quota of capital per job, that helps dispose of excess saving. In all of these ways, demand management principles seem designed as the perfect "straw man" for Marxism, which predicts that "capitalism" must fail because of the declining return on capital. In fact, the problem is not so much "capitalism" as particular policies that weaken a market economy by treating every problem as a form of underconsumption.

B. *The Half-Truths of Macroeconomics*

The result of the conventional belief that indiscriminate injections of money or capital investment into a sluggish economy is a panacea has been to let a thousand policies bloom that foster substituting capital for labor. This finds support from some other errors or half-truths, left over from the old economics, that die very hard.

1. Half-Truth #1: Adding Capital to Increase Labor Productivity Raises Wages

One of these half-truths is to define "productivity" along a single dimension, as output per worker. Of course, this is an important measure, since wages are related to this measure of productivity. The premise behind the present focus on labor productivity is that adding energy, land, and capital to each unit of labor will make it more productive—and raise wages. This conserves labor and uses resources and capital. However, real wages have not risen since 1973, despite enormous growth of per capita GDP. That should have made it clear that a one-dimensional approach to productivity fails utterly.

In addition, as a society, we also value the natural world, so the conservation of energy, water, and land are also important. The conventional approach of macroeconomics squanders resources in order to maintain full employment, but that is not necessary. In fact, it is counterproductive. To the extent that resources substitute for labor, resource conservation can raise wages and employment. At present, we reduce wages by allowing resources to be squandered.

Only in the last few decades, with the birth of the concept of total factor productivity, and the new emphasis on energy efficiency, are most economists beginning to escape the limits of a single-minded orientation toward labor productivity, with its built-in bias against use of labor. Substituting capital and land for labor raises "efficiency," so conceived, only by wasting capital and land, and is only efficient in unrealistic models in which land and capital are underpriced or ignored. High labor efficiency then means low land efficiency and low capital efficiency, either directly or at one remove in the form of low energy efficiency, low water efficiency, low feed-grain efficiency, and so on.

Misled by this concept, we have exulted in high output per person as a symbol and measure of national and company "productivity," and accepted an extreme substitution of capital and resources for labor. The well-known displacement of farm labor is not an exception but more like the rule. John Kendrick (1961: 148–149, Table 39) calculated that the ratio of capital to labor for a large group of industries in the United States rose at an average annual rate of 1.3 percent from 1899 to 1953. That means that the capital intensity of labor (the capital/labor ratio) doubled during that period. The growth of capital intensity rose to 1.9 percent per year in the 1950s, to 2.7 percent in the 1960s, 2.3 percent in the 1970s and 1980s, 3.2 percent in the 1990s, and 4.3 percent from 2000 to 2007 (more than three times the rate in the first half of the 20th century). The result was a doubling of capital intensity between 1950 and 1980, and another doubling from 1980 to 2004 (U.S. Bureau of Economic Analysis 2009: Tables 2.1, 2.2; U.S. Council of Economic Advisers 2009: Table B-35). Thus the rate of substitution of capital for labor increased throughout the 20th century, but it succeeded in raising real wages for only the first 70 years.

Private, nonresidential capital was not the only type of capital that grew relative to labor inputs. The standard estimates of capital intensity omit government capital (roads, dams, schools, and other public buildings), the infrastructure into which we have poured so much public treasure at low interest rates. (From 1950 to 2007, government fixed capital per capita grew by about 430 percent, or 3.0 percent per year, a growth rate about 10 percent higher than the growth of private capital per worker.) The figures for private capital also omit housing, which soaks up so much capital per job created. They omit the recreation boom, which requires so much more land and equipment per consumer hour, and per measure of personal joy, than the quiet pleasures of yesteryear. And they omit the swing of consumers toward goods and services like electric power and natural gas, whose production is capital-intensive and whose prices fall relative to labor-intensive products when the capital input is subsidized.

Table 1

Energy Efficiency in Dollars of Value-Added per
Kilowatt-Hour (VA/KWH) for Selected Industrial Groups*

Industry Group	VA/KWH	Industry Group	VA/KWH
Cookies & crackers	0.91	Blast furnaces & steel mills	0.033
Book printing	0.50	Primary copper	0.020
Millwork plants	0.36	Paving mixtures	0.018
Wood furniture	0.28	Paper mills	0.016
Fluid milk	0.13	Pulp mills	0.015
Frozen fruits & vegetables	0.12	Petroleum refining	0.012
Yarn mills	0.12	Sawmills	0.008
Aluminum rolling & drawing	0.048	Brick	0.008
Wool-weaving mills	0.048	Primary aluminum	0.007
		Cement, hydraulic	0.006
		Lime	0.004

*KWH equivalents used where relevant.
Source: Wilson (1974).

Capital was not the only factor applied wastefully in combination
with labor. Producers also used a great deal of energy as inputs to
manufacturing processes. They were particularly heedless of energy
costs prior to the first OPEC oil embargo of 1973. Table 1 shows the
amounts of value-added resulting from energy inputs in various
industrial processes, as of 1967. In general, food processing and other
secondary processes use about 10 percent as much energy per dollar
of value-added as processing of raw materials.

Until 1973, we substituted energy for labor and called it progress
and efficiency. After 1973, industrial and commercial uses of energy
per worker declined to 1950s levels, but energy intensity (energy used
per dollar of value added) in the United States remains about 35
percent higher than in other advanced industrial nations such as
France, Germany, and Japan (U.S. Department of Energy, Energy
Information Administration 2006: Table E-1p).

A comprehensive accounting of our lavish input of capital, energy, and land per worker would reverse the common stereotype that labor unions invented featherbedding. In every sector of our economy, we have been extravagant and wasteful in our use of physical capital and resources.

2. Half-Truth #2: Capital Always Complements Labor

The second supporting ancient half-truth is that capital cannot really displace labor in a vertically integrated whole economy because labor produces capital anyway. In other words, if we think of capital goods as objects produced by labor, then investment in capital necessarily entails an investment in labor as well. According to this logic, it is impossible to displace labor by producing more automated factories because labor is required to build those automated factories. This is the counterpart of the modern macroeconomist's concept that investment employs labor. According to that view, all capital is like a hammer: it enables a worker to perform more effectively by complementing labor and increasing the value of labor. The idea that some forms of capital might substitute for labor and reduce wages and employment does not enter the picture. Either way you perceive it, the meaning is that benefits to capital are passed through to labor.

That is a half-truth, and the untrue half has helped lead us into our present crisis. The problem is that capital can substitute for labor. This poses a problem for two distinct groups: those who favor fiscal policy to create jobs by investing directly in capital projects (public works), and the supply-side tax cutters who want to induce more capital investment by cutting the tax on capital gains.

There is considerable overlap between the two groups. The fiscal managers say investment creates jobs, so they generally favor policies that subsidize investment. Supply-siders tend to oppose direct government investment in capital. Instead, they would remove taxes on capital. But many Keynesians in the 1950s and 1960s also favored lower taxes on the income from capital, using the investment tax credit, expensing of capital investments, accelerated depreciation, and exemption of imputed income of homeowners.

In some respects, Keynesians are similar to Georgists who seek to reduce taxes on capital at the local level by exempting buildings from the property tax. Jack Stockfisch (1957: 38) had the insight to point out years ago that these Keynesian inducements to invest were Georgist ideals applied to the income tax.[1] Both Keynesians and Georgists share the idea that benefits to capital are benefits to labor.

But a great deal of the cash and service flow from capital imputes to capital, as such, as interest. The longer the life of the capital item, generally, the larger share that is. A great deal of interest is internalized and invisible, hence too easily overlooked and forgotten. But a couple of simple examples should make the point.

When one buys a durable good on an installment plan, such as central heating and air conditioning for a home, if the payments were to stretch out beyond 15 or so years, more than half the total is interest. Let us suppose the installed system costs $4,000. A $4,000 loan for 20 years at 10 percent interest will be paid off in yearly payments of $463.21 (11.6 percent of the principal). The total payments will be 20 × $463.21, or $9,264. Since the principal is $4,000, the total interest charge would be $9,264 − $4,000, or $5,264, which is 57 percent of the total payment. Even at 8 percent, the total interest charge would still be slightly over half of the total. At 10 percent interest, the total interest charges could be substantially reduced by paying off the loan more quickly. By liquidating the loan in 10 years instead of 20, the total interest would be only 37 percent of the loan.

This fits with our intuition. If you borrow money from someone, the longer you take to pay it off and the less you pay each time, the larger the amount of principal on which the interest accrues in each loan period, so the more total interest you pay. (At the limit is an interest-only loan, which would last forever because the principal is never paid, and 100 percent of the payments are for interest.)

Since the lessons from this simple example play a significant role in the analysis to follow, I want to dwell on them for a moment. The experience here is a commonplace one for anyone who has ever had an installment loan. The idea that long-term loans involve payment of a larger amount of interest is also not novel for most people. Yet the implications of these simple facts have been systematically ignored in economic theory as it applies to capital investment. If capital is tied up in long-term projects, more of the yield goes to pay interest, and less is left over for the cost of producing the capital good (the car, the house, the equipment), particularly for the labor that goes into making it. This has tremendous implications for the ability of capital to promote employment or to stifle it.

The example above shows how the cost of a mortgaged house, or a debt-financed highway, or a debt-financed war can be mainly interest. But even if these are not debt-financed, they cost interest—the interest foregone on the equity capital.[2] Thus, if you live in a house, even if you own it free of a mortgage, you are giving up the income you could make by investing the equity in an alternative investment. Let us suppose that over a 50-year period, you could receive an average annual return of 8 percent on a $200,000 investment, compounded monthly. At the end of 50 years, you would have almost $816,000, or a "profit" of $616,000. Owning the $200,000 house instead, and not investing that money in the alternative investment, thus costs you that much in foregone revenue. So, whether you buy the house up front with cash or take out a mortgage, the result is equivalent. In one case, you have an out-of-pocket expense of $616,000 on interest (about 75 percent of the total cost); in the other case, you give up $616,000 in lost revenue.[3] (Since you would have to pay tax on the invested returns on stock, but you do not pay on the imputed return to owning the house, you can see that the tax code gives a huge benefit in avoided taxes to those who buy property and hold it.) Accordingly, it is understandable that housing starts are more sensitive to interest rates than to any other cost.

But note now how little of the salable service flow is produced by labor. If 75 percent of the cost of building a house is interest payments, only 25 percent is available for everything else: materials and labor. Since onsite labor is only about one-fifth of the construction cost, labor is only 5 percent (one-fifth of 25 percent) of the total cost. If you watch a house being built, it might seem that labor is a large part of the cost of building it. Based on that visual impression, it might seem that boosting housing construction is a good way to increase employment. But these are illusions—the kinds of illusions that cause us to invest in the wrong kinds of activities if we want to achieve full employment.

If 15–20 percent of the cost of building a house is in the materials, perhaps we can find some labor added to capital at the stage of producing those building materials. As it turns out, the labor involved in producing the lumber used in houses is insignificant. Lumber comes from trees that take decades to grow, and as we have just been reminded, long-lived capital represents mostly a return to capital investment and very little labor input.

On the face of it, growing trees may not seem like a form of capital investment, if we are accustomed to think of capital in terms of machinery, warehouses, computers, or inventories. But, in fact, growing timber is capital formation in its purest form.[4] When a company plants a tree farm, it does so with the expectation of making a return equal to an investment of an equal amount in some other venture. Let us imagine that investment of a dollar in an alternative would yield 8 percent, so that a given amount of investment in a tree farm will yield that much. On that basis, we will assume a known financial yield in advance, ignoring the change in lumber prices likely to occur during the life of the standing timber. At the end of nine years, an investment of $100 yielding 8 percent compounded annually will double to $200. It will continue doubling every nine years, so that it will be $400 after 18 years, $800 after 27 years, and so on. Let us suppose that the harvest time for a given stand of second-growth trees is 63 years, which means seven doubling times. Since 2^7 is 128, the initial $100 investment will have a value of 128 × $100, or $12,800. Of that amount, $100 is the initial cost of planting and $12,700 is the value added by capital formation or compound interest. Thus, 12,700/ 12,800, or slightly over 99 percent of value added, comes from capital, and slightly less than 1 percent comes from labor.[5] (If tree planting is a capital-intensive operation, far less than 1 percent comes from labor.) Of course, harvesting, hauling, milling, and selling apply more labor to add value, so lumber value embodies a higher share of labor value than timber alone. Still, timber is a splendid second example of capital-intensity in which it is largely capital, and not labor, that produces capital.

Timber growth is a good example of "passive investment." It is internally financed in the most literal way. Each year's growth is a product, an income to the owner, that is automatically invested in growing stock, adding to capital. But this investment employs no labor. It only employs capital and land, that is, growing stock and site.

Mature timber, finally, has not been produced by labor so much as by capital—the young growing stock—and land. Preferential tax treatment for timber, then, is a good way to make work for capital but a bad way for labor. Capital-gains treatment of timber sales, expensing of interest and property taxes, and preferential low property tax rates and assessments for timber tie up capital in the slowest of cycles and fence off land from labor, except once a century or so when the crop is cut. The job-creating efficiency of capital frozen this way is very low.

3. Half-Truth #3: A Fixed Amount of Capital Is Required for Each Job to Be Created

A third ancient error is that it takes a fixed quota of capital to "create" a job, visualized as a kind of niche made of capital in which we place one worker. The Obama plan to increase employment by investing in "green" infrastructure is based on this premise, as if each job required the investment of a specific amount of capital.[6] The idea that "capital creates employment" is also the basis on which economists attack capital gains taxes. They argue, with only limited validity, that the tax reduces capital investment and thus stunts employment growth.

If the premise were true, of course, then the way to make jobs is to create capital, case closed. But in fact, factor mix varies over a wide range. A little bit of land, labor, and energy can mix with a lot of capital, or any other combination. The timber-growing example above amounts to a lot of capital and few other inputs. A sidewalk hot dog vendor with a pushcart exemplifies a lot of labor relative to land, capital, and energy. There are many combinations between those two extremes. That means policies, such as the Obama infrastructure program, that are nominally intended to create jobs by adding capital may actually have the opposite effect by absorbing capital in uses that generate very few jobs.

Capital is capable of complementing labor, but the extent to which it actually does so depends entirely on how it is invested and used. It is a serious mistake to assume that adding capital will add jobs. The value of capital to labor depends on how active the capital is. In this case, "active" means the extent to which capital combines with labor, either in use or in the process of renewal or maintenance. Looking ahead, we will see that each time capital is recovered and reinvested, it can recombine with and reactivate labor. But torpid capital, like that in trees, many public works, premature exploration for minerals, suburban sprawl, and so on, is withdrawn from abetting labor.

Capital may preempt land as well, as the landlords' sheep did in 16th-century England by removing land from more labor-intensive forms of cultivation.[7]

C. Basic Principle of a New Macroeconomics: Increasing the "Valence" of Capital

These niceties have almost entirely escaped modern capital theory because they require paying attention to the reality behind the symbols that tend to hypnotize economists. In the growth models of and following Harrod (1948) and Domar (1957), macroeconomists have been quite comfortable with assumed constant ratios of capital to output, as if all capital were uniform in its relationship to labor. Growth was linked closely with capital formation. This harmonized nicely with the assumptions on which the Obama infrastructure plan is based. It has served to reconcile the Marxist streak in demand-side economics with the puritanism of capitalists. Alongside the Marxists, who have repeatedly (and incorrectly) foretold the declining marginal productivity of capital for over a century, the Keynesians and their allies viewed growth as an escape from the doom of oversaving. The capitalists, meanwhile, saw capital investment as their social duty, which rationalized the social value of entrepreneurs and investors and helped aggrandize their functions, prerogatives, incomes, wealth, and status. It has been a curious but powerful partnership, hardly ever challenged by economists.

It has had to exclude, however, from its intellectual substance and theoretical apparatus the good news buried in a few obscure pages of Wicksell (1934: 194–196), that capital can increase its "valence" (to borrow a chemical term) for labor easily, and combine with more or less, in response to relative prices. (This does not mean that a given piece of capital equipment, such as a factory building or a tool-and-die machine, can be used to employ more or less labor as a complement.

It is possible, however, to choose different types of capital equipment or buildings, some with long life, others with a shorter life. That is what Wicksell had in mind by saying the valence for labor could be changed easily.) We may not need to find a new theory, but to resurrect one. Like any entrenched system, macroeconomic orthodoxy was unassailable when things went tolerably well, regardless of its merits. Now that we face a global crisis of unemployment and the proposed solution is to pour on capital without regard to its "valence," it is time to review and reconstruct. The "New Economics" has grown old, and has become a terminal case. It had to break down because it was superficially based. The suffering is not welcome, but the opportunity for review is.

What is needed now is an entirely different approach to macro-economic problems, an approach that takes account of different types of capital, and the effects of those differences on bottlenecks in the real economy. The Keynesian solution to a stalled economy is based on symptomatic relief using a "one-size-fits-all" monetary approach that ignores the underlying cause of economic problems. In effect, Keynes said, when there is not enough liquidity, increase the flow of money. When people are not buying goods being produced, increase effective demand by spending more money on government projects.

This is not my caricature of Keynesian economics. It comes directly from one of its proponents, Nobel Prize winner Paul Krugman. In his "Introduction to Keynes's General Theory," Krugman (2007) writes:

> Although Keynes speculated about the causes of the business cycle in Chapter 22 of *The General Theory*, those speculations were peripheral to his argument. . . . Rather than getting bogged down in an attempt to explain the dynamics of the business cycle, . . . Keynes focused on a question that could be answered: . . . given that overall demand is depressed—*never mind why*—how can we create more employment? (Emphasis added.)

If Krugman is correct, then Keynes offered us a technical fix to a problem without any "attempt to explain the dynamics of the business cycle." If *The General Theory* does not even attempt to explain causes, how it can it possibly be "general"?

D. Environmental Benefits of a New Macroeconomics

Faced with a surplus of labor (high unemployment) and a shortage of land and capital (i.e., difficulty obtaining credit to buy either), an obvious way to adapt is to substitute labor for land and capital, at the margins of course, making all processes more labor-using. Thus we would increase the use of labor without pushing on the limits of the Earth, without invading others' land, and without needing more capital. It would be too crude and harsh to say that the wars in Iraq were a direct outgrowth of macroeconomics. Nevertheless, by ignoring the impacts of capital investment on the environment and resource consumption, post–World War II macroeconomics has been a contributing factor in the logic of imperialism.

It is not a question of stopping growth. There is no need to divide into factions for and against growth. We can grow by combining more labor with the same land and capital. It is simply a matter of modifying processes and products and consumption. Each time capital recycles it can embody new techniques as well. Growth of capital is not needed for progress; turnover is. Since one way to substitute labor for capital is to turn over capital faster, this also accelerates embodiment of new knowledge in real capital.

The principle that more rapid capital turnover would be socially beneficial may not be intuitively obvious. We perceive waste in physical terms—the amount of material we throw away because it has outlived its usefulness. We favor products that last a long time, and have contempt for shoddy goods and planned obsolescence. We admire houses that have lasted more than a century, and look down on cheaply built houses that will collapse in a generation or two.

Higher turnover of capital might seem on its face to support waste by encouraging investment in capital with shorter economic lives. That does not have to mean shoddy construction, however. In the case of buildings, which represent over 70 percent of the fixed capital stock in the United States, the physical meaning of higher turnover would mean more money spent on frequent maintenance and restoration. The replacement of capital does not have to take place by demolition and reconstruction from the ground up. It can also take place by repair and reuse. Even more important, from the perspective of the environment, each turnover allows the introduction of energy-saving technology. The introduction of "green" technologies of the sort promoted by Amory Lovins (Lovins et al. 2005) is hindered by the slow turnover of the stock of buildings and other capital equipment. A higher rate of capital turnover would enable reconstructed buildings to embody more environment-friendly building materials and insulation.

This study develops a thesis that we can employ ourselves as fully as we wish without any of the unpleasantness we now suffer in the name of jobs: without inflating, without borrowing, without fighting, without polluting, without any compulsion to grow, develop, and expand, without wasting, without price and wage controls, without invading more wilderness, without impoverishing posterity, without socializing labor or capital, without dirigisme, without giving up freedom, and without overspilling our national boundaries. Economic policy can offer better than dismal choices.

The problem is too much displacement of labor. It is "too much" because it results from biased institutions, a large set of them, operating over many years, that artificially induce substituting land and capital for labor. The way to solve the problem is to identify and remove the biases. This will increase demand for labor without requiring any more resources or capital.

No special rate of growth is required. We simply need to grow (or even not grow) in such a way as to combine each worker with less land and capital than now, to run with a leaner mixture of wealth, richer in labor. Until now, our policies have been strongly biased against the full employment of labor. Correcting this failure should not entail making the opposite mistake by arbitrarily restricting capital investment or creating make-work jobs to absorb labor. The sort of directive policies favored by socialists and proponents of "industrial policy" are not needed. We will invariably go wrong if we imagine that the plans of a few experts will be superior to the millions of decisions made daily by economic actors in the course of normal transactions.

The operation of a free market with flexible prices to serve as equilibrators can restore the right balance between labor, land, and capital, if we will simply let the market do its job. The idea is to make jobs not by waste but in the process of mixing inputs more efficiently.

This is the very sort of thing that a flexible economy can do. A wide variety of policies create an institutional bias against labor. Regulatory standards often require particular forms of capital equipment, even though a different mix of labor, capital, and land might be more efficient. In this essay, I will confine myself to taxes and subsidies that distort relative prices of inputs and promote wasteful use of capital, land, and resources.

Policies that create incentives to substitute labor for capital will achieve "structural" changes throughout the economy. I am proposing a new approach to macroeconomics because it addresses all of the conventional issues: unemployment, price stability, fiscal policy, and monetary policy. But this new approach refuses to stay in the pigeonhole of "macroeconomics" because it simultaneously achieves goals of resource conservation, environmental protection, and social equity. It achieves those latter goals indirectly through faster recovery of capital and faster ripening of capital into final goods. The first increases the rate of reinvestment; the second increases the flow of consumer goods. Thus the "structural" substitution is a macroeconomic effect of the most central kind.

E. Austrian-Georgist Roots of New Macroeconomics

The new approach to macroeconomics that I am following derives from two strands of economic tradition: (1) Henry George's theory of how macroeconomic instability, including unemployment, is associated with an artificial scarcity of land; and (2) the insights of Austrian economic theory that emphasize the substitutability of capital for labor and the instability caused by lending on capital with slow recovery periods.

Although the followers of Henry George in the 20th century primarily focused on the incentive effects of shifting the property tax from buildings to land, his theory has macroeconomic implications of global significance. He showed that land ownership tends to absorb investment and cause an economy to freeze periodically, which constricts the employment of labor and impoverishes workers. By taxing land, the passive factor, and removing taxes from active factors, such as labor and capital, it is possible to thaw the economy. George said there was no limit in a truly free economy on jobs, other than human desire for the fruits of work. This theme commanded attention because that was the problem that needed solving, even as today. He wrote his most famous work, *Progress and Poverty*, in the depths of the depression of the 1870s, which was as severe a contraction as the 1930s—or as the present crisis seems likely to be. With some modifications, his advice remains as relevant today as it was during that depression.

Again, like the Keynesians, George was weak on capital theory. He treated capital as an extension of labor rather than an independent factor of production. He saw their interests as united and set off against the interests of landowners. He overlooked the substitutability of capital for labor, which looms so large in Austrian School economics. Keynes and George alike treated the Austrians as their natural enemies, an unfortunate and needless impoverishment of their respective philosophies. The oversight in George was not so serious because he wanted to remove taxes on labor, not just on capital. The oversight by George's followers is serious because their emphasis has been on removing property taxes on buildings. But if we shift property taxes away from capital and continue to tax payrolls, we stack the cards against labor and bias the system to substitute capital for labor. It is important, as George said, to use more workers per unit of land and primary products. It is also important, as he did not say, to use more workers per unit of capital.

III

Combining Land, Labor, and Capital for Macroeconomic Health

IT IS NOW TIME to show how the economy could be reconfigured to avoid the dramatic oscillations that create false hopes and shattered dreams. My approach is not dramatic. My premise is simple: the economy would effectively regulate itself if distortions caused by faulty tax policy and public investments could be removed. To support that thesis, I have four points in what follows:

1. Factor mixes vary over a wide range and are by inference sensitive to relative costs and other stimuli like tax bias. The key

to intelligent macroeconomic policy is nothing more profound than enabling the factor proportions in production of both private and public goods to respond to the right signals. This is an idea that has been well developed in microeconomics, but it has been surprisingly neglected in macroeconomics.

2. Tax bias force-feeds land and capital into the production mix but militates against labor. Those tax biases are not obvious because the harm they cause is associated with a variable that has been largely overlooked—the rate of turnover of the nation's capital stock.

3. Demand for capital is not a sufficient or even necessary condition to make jobs. It often helps, but there is a tradeoff in the factor mix between labor and capital. We must distinguish among investment outlets and find policies to guide investment into more labor-using ones.

4. Using labor for capital means recovering and replacing capital more often, which increases aggregate demand for labor, as well as the flow of consumable goods and services as long as there is surplus labor to employ. It increases the flow of gross investment associated with any given kind of capital.

Based on that analysis, we can then see how to invest so as to put capital where the jobs are, to invest so that the "job-creating efficiency," if you will, of capital and land is higher—not a maximum, but an optimum, where idleness is only voluntary and the amount of capital suffices that people save voluntarily. We can also discuss which tax policies would serve to remove the present bias.

A. Factor Mix and Factor Prices

We can make more jobs by using more workers (W) per unit of land (L) and capital (K). Some employers already mix enough workers with their land and capital to employ everyone if only most other employers were moved to act a little more like them. What needs doing is already being done, it just needs to be done more. Of course, we do not propose to proselytize employers with this information or to use regulations to force them to hire more workers. We will identify the kinds of operations that use more labor in the mix, that is, a high

W/(L + K). Then we can see how to stop penalizing them, and how to get more like them, by changing the incentives created by different taxes and other institutions.

The goal is not to make work for its own sake. Combining labor with land and capital more efficiently not only creates more jobs; it also creates more goods and services. One can produce much more value from the same land by applying more labor, and without wasting labor.

1. Historical Observations About Land "Engrossment"

A good starting point is the observation by Adam Smith that the value of land and other resources depends on how actively the owners use it. In the following passage, Smith ([1776] 1937: 538–540) notes that land is the source of prosperity but that it fails to fulfill that purpose if the law permits concentrated ownership—what he calls "engrossment":

> In plenty of good land the English colonies of North America . . . are . . . inferior to those of the Spaniards and Portuguese. . . . But the political institutions of the English colonies have been more favorable to the improvement and cultivation of this land. . . . First, the engrossing of uncultivated land . . . has been more restrained in the English colonies. . . . The plenty and cheapness of good land . . . are the principal causes of the rapid prosperity of new colonies. The engrossing of land, in effect, destroys this plenty and cheapness. The engrossing of uncultivated land, besides, is the greatest obstruction to its improvement.

Henry George gave this theme center stage in his philosophy, attributing unemployment to speculative withholding of some land from use. Labor needed access to land. It had access to some lands, but these were oases in the speculative desert. Later commentators have mistakenly imagined that George was talking about farmland, when in fact his explicit emphasis was on urban land. The land today that employs most people is in cities, and a major source of underemployment lies in holding a surprisingly large portion of urban sites idle or in suboptimal uses. Anywhere from 10 percent to 40 percent of buildable lots in cities are unused or occupied by derelict buildings or low-value uses, such as parking lots. Urban sprawl, "scatteration," or "leapfrog development" leads to extremely different intensities of use on neighboring lands. Smith and George wrote in black and white contrasts. More generally, land is fallow, "engrossed," or "held in speculation" by degrees, and in this sense sprawl and scatter are the universal condition.

2. Tax Biases Affecting Land and Capital Combinations

Economists seem well aware that factors blend and mix in a range of ratios. They make use of the principle of variable proportions. They note the contrast among nations and regions resulting from different relative prices: more labor per log in European than Canadian saw-mills; more labor per acre on Japanese than Argentine farms; more capital per acre-foot of water in the citrus groves of arid Tulare County, California, than the rice fields of the Sacramento Valley. They have noted that larger companies and governments tend to favor more capital-using techniques.

They have been less good about attributing some of these contrasts to institutional bias, specifically to biases introduced by the tax system. There is a strong positive relationship between belief in tradeoffs and devotion to the price system. Too often contrasts of factor mix are adduced to rationalize the price system, when in fact they display the bias of institutions like taxation. Perhaps that is the result of specialization that leads economists to ignore important concepts and nuances in other subdisciplines. Industrial economists examine factor combinations, but they have little interest in the way they are influenced by tax policy. Public finance economists pay attention to different types of taxes, but they tend to treat capital as homogeneous and ignore different factor combinations. Those who work within the subdiscipline of macroeconomics ignore most variations in both factor combinations and taxes because their aggregate models abstract from those differences. The result is that specialists have completely ignored the possibility of a causal nexus between tax policies, factor combinations, and the periodic malfunctioning of the macroeconomy. At present those categories are examined separately, and it is our task to bring them together to show their connections.

In macroeconomic models, labor is treated almost as the only cost, so wage cuts might only lead to "vicious downward spirals," and wage boosts can only be shifted forward in "vicious inflationary spirals."[8] Since factor price flexibility up or down is vicious, the models (such as the Harrod-Domar model or the Solow model) assume either constant or growing capital intensity (a fixed or rising amount of capital per worker ratio).[9] Under those circumstances, the only way to make jobs is by "growth"—by adding to the stock of capital—and in the more pessimistic models, even that may not be adequate to prevent permanent stagnation. There is no thought of making jobs simply by enriching the mix with more labor. That would be retrogressive, lowering "productivity," or reactionary and unmentionable. There is, if anything, a sense of predestination that forces us to use ever more capital per worker.

3. Counterproductive Expansionism

We are left with a theory of compulsive growth. Worse, when it comes to intensifying the use of land, it often turns out to be land occupied by other people. We justified the conquest of North America on the grounds that Europeans used the land more productively than the native inhabitants. Alvin Hansen (1939) integrated Keynesian fatalism with traditional Americana by attributing stagnation in part to the closing of the frontier. Since recessions followed the sudden oil price hikes of the 1970s, many economists seize on our loss of cheap foreign oil and other primary products as the killer of jobs.

In fact, expansionism in pursuit of employment is counterproductive, whether it appears as the pursuit of new land, new energy sources, or new military spending (based on the idea that World War II saved us from the 1930s depression). In the past, the frontier was a great sink of capital. Overinvestment in canals and railroads on the frontier was a major source of the depressions that afflicted the nation repeatedly in the 19th century. Frontier expansionism neglects the inner frontier, the intensive use of labor on the land we already have.

The energy industry has also absorbed massive amounts of subsidized capital, in terms of production, consumption, and militarism. Energy-driven jingoism has at times been justified as a means of maintaining full employment (particularly after the Volcker recession of 1982), but more energy does not create new jobs. In fact, energy serves as a substitute for labor more often than as a complement. Consider the fact that cheap energy powers the farm machinery that drove labor off the farms in the past. In that case, energy combined with capital and land, not labor. More generally, capital, labor, and energy are substitutes for each other.[10] A significant rise in energy prices in the future (which is likely, after recovering from the current downturn) will help achieve full employment, if the market is allowed to work. However, if we tax labor to subsidize energy production (such as the current subsidy to corn farmers for biofuel), then we shall have cheap fuel and unemployed workers. Berndt and Wood (1979), in a comprehensive study of American industry, found that energy use is highly related to capital use, not labor.[11] Note that the "inner frontier" of energy does not refer mainly to producing more primary energy domestically, but to economizing on energy by substituting labor for energy at the margin.

By comparison with the many studies of energy efficiency, capital intensity, and the substitution of labor and capital for energy, comparatively little research has been conducted on how the inefficient use of land affects the economy. On the face of it, we have intensified the use of land through urbanization. Yet instead of urbanizing people, we have suburbanized cities. As housing has shifted from row houses to lots of one-sixth of an acre, to one-quarter acre, to one-half acre, and even larger, and as commerce has shifted from urban centers to suburban strip malls, we have been reducing the density of cities by about 50 percent every 40 years. Instead of intensifying land use, we have made it more extensive, sinking enormous capital into new roads, pipes, streetlights, and light-rail systems. We have extended police and fire services over an ever-expanding area. Providing urban water unleashes municipal hydro-imperialism, as cities range far away to capture remote waters rather than clean and develop nearby sources.

Thus American urbanization replicates the continental frontier and global expansion. As we expand urban boundaries, we use up our capital prodigally. It would be a mistake, then, to think that making jobs by applying more labor to land, the policy advanced here, would entail more conversion of farm to city land, more new towns, shopping centers, industrial parks, and the like. Territorial expansion generally raises the required complement of land per worker. It spreads people out over a larger geographic area. That might have worked well when people lived in self-sufficient feudal domains, but in an integrated modern economy of specialization and exchange, it raises the cost of water supply, road building, and of every other economic transaction without any corresponding benefit. The net effect of shifting activity onto marginal sites is to lower wages and reduce returns to capital. Investment in the extension of capital and energy over larger expanses of land is the clearest form of anti-investment and a major cause of economic downturns.

4. Varying Intensities of Land Use: Tax Biases and Employment Effects
Here follow some data to illustrate the varying intensity of the economic use of land. The data refer to neighboring lands, generally, of comparable quality and in the same markets.

The first data are from California farming. In the San Joaquin Valley, east side, land is versatile among many competing uses. Table 2 is a crop report gathered by the U.S. Bureau of Reclamation from its Friant-Kern Canal Service Area. Not all the land is versatile among all the options, but a close study of the area has shown that the margins between the uses are ragged (Gaffney 1961; Althouse 1942).

These data are five decades old, so the absolute dollar values of the various crops have changed, but the ratios are what we are interested in, and they have not changed. The reader is also advised that we have chosen an agricultural example merely for convenience because the relationship between land and production is more obvious. But land is also needed to make bicycles or jet engines or to provide hairdressing services. Farming is not in a separate category from industrial or service jobs. The same principles regarding the application of factors of production apply to all types of enterprise.

What we are looking for here is evidence of how the intensity of land use is affected not only by market conditions but also by tax policies that affect employment, not by design, but by accident. To the extent that the market determines land use, each unit of land will maximize rents (a more exact term than "profits") for its owner if inputs are added, as long as they add more value than cost. Taxes that distort land use intensities create the conditions that can culminate in macroeconomic problems. Faulty tax incentives filter through every decision in an economy. They lead to land use decisions by every operation from the humblest farmer or small business owner to the

Table 2

Crop Production, Friant-Kern Canal Service Area

Crop	Acres	Value per Acre ($)
Berries (all kinds)	80	1,215.6
Beans (fresh market)	75	975.3
Oranges and tangerines	24,952	915.5
Beans (processing)	27	900.0
Tomatoes (fresh market)	1,343	881.2
Prunes and plums	3,288	674.0
Peaches	6,371	644.4
Cantaloupes, etc.	507	547.0
Grapes, table	43,795	545.2
Onions, dry	86	495.7
Asparagus	1,383	418.7
Potatoes, early	12,711	366.0
Cotton, lint (upland)	108,928	352.8
Walnuts	1,374	338.1
Lettuce	423	336.5
Olives	7,172	327.5
Corn, sweet (fresh market)	254	205.9
Rice	907	167.7
Alfalfa	1,279	151.8
Alfalfa hay	63,460	144.1
Beans, dry and edible	4,293	107.1
Corn	10,490	96.7
Wheat	3,176	87.9
Irrigated pasture	17,388	77.7
Sorghums	17,279	74.8
Barley	15,696	51.1

Source: U.S. Bureau of Reclamation, Sacramento Office (1958). Minor crops omitted.

largest corporation, and those micro-level decisions add up to bank failures and macro-level instability and unemployment.

What do the data about the yields of different types of crop tell us? Land yields a little or a lot of value, depending on what you mix with it. According to the table, 80 acres of berries will yield roughly the same gross revenue as 300 acres of lettuce or 1,000 acres of wheat or corn. If gross revenue were all that mattered, everyone would plant berries. But costs are also higher for berries because planting, tending, and harvesting them requires much more labor than the other options.

Almost every parcel of land has several options, and many of them are choices between the highest and the lowest gross. Let us assume that a farmer can gross $15 by grazing animals or $1,500 by growing tomatoes. Labor's share of gross rises with intensity, defined here simply as nonland inputs divided by output. (To simplify the discussion here, we are combining labor and capital inputs into a single sum.)[12] For grazing, this is on the order of $6/$15 = 40 percent. For tomatoes, it is more like $1,400/$1,500 = 93.3 percent.[13] The remaining amount ($9 for the land used for grazing, and $100 for the land used for tomatoes) is the return to land, or rent.

Because the land growing tomatoes has a small (6.7 percent) ratio of rent to gross revenue (or "profit margin"), this production process is highly leveraged. That is true of any high-input, high-yield operation. Being leveraged means it is highly sensitive to small changes in input costs, such as wage rates. If those costs rise by seven percentage points, the economic rent is wiped out; a drop of seven percentage points more than doubles the rent. By contrast, the land used for grazing is not highly leveraged, which means it is also not sensitive to wage or tax changes. The same wage change that would bankrupt the tomato farmer would only imperceptibly change the returns to land from grazing.

Because of leveraging, the elasticity of demand for labor on land growing high-yield crops is quite high. A small change in the price of labor leads to a large change in the demand for labor. On the one hand, a slight drop of labor costs will encourage many farmers to shift land from low-yield crops, such as wheat or pasture, to high-yield crops, such as fruits and vegetables. On the other hand, the prospect of an increase in the payroll tax will have the opposite effect. It will economically sterilize land that has the potential to yield a lot of value per acre and turn it into land used only for growing relatively low-value crops.

The high-grossing crops use more labor per acre not just in the fields but also in the packing houses, the railroads, the stores, and the kitchens. A $900 tomato crop will use more labor at every step to the consumer than a $15 weight gain on a calf, and will use it sooner, and much more often. Thus a higher use of labor in the field increases demand for labor beyond the field. Going in the other direction—from store to farm—any policy that reduces labor costs in food wholesaling, retailing, and processing (either technical change or a cut in wage taxes) will lower the price to the consumer and increase the quantity demanded from the farmer. If that chain of events were to raise field prices by, say, 7 percent, that would (in our example) double land returns from tomatoes and increase demand for labor on the farm.

The scope for this kind of change is manifest in the fact that most of California's farm output comes from a small fraction of its good farmland, that which is used intensively. Of the 9.2 million acres of irrigable land in California, approximately 24 percent grows high-intensity crops.[14] The remaining 76 percent grows mostly low-intensity crops, using less labor to yield fewer dollars' worth of barley, alfalfa, forage pasture, hay, sorghum, safflower, rice, or cotton.

In irrigated farming, water is an indirect land input, since a water right is the right to the water yield of a vast watershed. One might then think the tomatoes really use a lot of land in the form of irrigation water. But in fact, the high-grossing crops such as tomatoes, citrus, peaches, and berries are modest users of water. Pasture, alfalfa, and rice are thirsty crops, and they yield only $50–$200 per acre, not one-tenth of the high yielders. Marc Reisner (1993) and other critics of the massive water transfers in the American West correctly point out the absurdity of growing water-intensive crops in the middle of a desert. What those critics have failed to grasp is that the misallocation of water (and land) is a direct result of their tax treatment.

Let us summarize what we have discovered thus far. High marginal tax rates on labor—from 15 percent to 50 percent of wages—discourage highly leveraged uses of farmland that rely heavily on labor (e.g., growing strawberries or broccoli). (The same principle applies to urban land, but we are concentrating for the moment on farming.) Wage taxes therefore cause land to be shifted toward capital-intensive uses, such as cattle grazing or mechanized farming, or toward water-intensive uses, such as rice or alfalfa. The highest-value uses of land cannot compete, at the margin, with uses that involve a high capital/labor ratio, particularly uses that add capital with a slow payout period. Low-turnover capital requires little labor. Low tax rates on land, and no taxes on water rights, exacerbate these biases. Because land is underutilized (used for purposes with low value-added), farmers and businesses bid up the value of marginal land and expand into territory that would remain untouched except for the biases created by the tax system. A society will keep expanding its use of resources and capital in order to achieve a given level of value-added. Economic overexpansion and imperialism are symptoms of the failure to get the value needed from the use of a more limited range of resources.

Farmland use in general varies so much from farm to farm that "farm sprawl" and "horticultural sprawl" are as common as urban sprawl. But this reminds us that all our cities are dominated by sprawl, which is essentially a condition of extremely different intensities on adjacent lands.

Different mixes of land with nonland inputs are not the exception but the rule.

5. Concentrated Land Ownership and Diminishing Labor Intensity

It does not surprise tax economists, of course, to learn about differences of factor proportions, for that is at the heart of the problem of tax enclaves. As everyone knows, localities compete to attract capital-using plants and to repel labor-using ones, and they find large differences among them. Factor mix also tends to change with size of business and wealth of individuals. As a broad statistical truth, the application of labor to property tends to be regressive. Larger farms and industrial plants use less labor per unit of property value than smaller operations. The U.S. Census of Agriculture ranks farms by value of gross sales. In 1950, "Class I" farms, those grossing $25,000 or more, had 22 percent of the land in farms but 7 percent of the farm labor (U.S. Census Bureau 1953: 51). The ratios of capital to worker and land to worker both increased with the size of the farm. The small producers, of course, made the figures balance by applying more labor per acre.

A large number of studies in many countries have demonstrated statistically that labor inputs diminish with the size of farms. Berry and Cline (1979: Ch. 4) document the decrease in labor per acre in developing countries and the lower output per acre on large farms than on smaller ones. As farm size increases, land, water, and capital displace labor. In addition, the economic intensity of land use diminishes. That is to say, value added per acre declines as farm size increases. To the extent that capital has substituted for labor because of increases in technical efficiency, that has been a social benefit. However, to the extent that taxes have distorted decisions about the proper mix of land, labor, and capital, the displacement of labor has been social folly that results in unemployment and financial instability.

Turning to "industrial" corporations, the regressive use of labor on property may be inferred from data in *Fortune* magazine's yearly report on the largest 500 corporations.[15] The larger the corporation, the higher the proportion of its income comes from land and capital rather than from labor. I tested the thesis by ranking corporations by "net worth" or invested capital, and calculating profits (after taxes) per employee. Table 3 shows the broad results. Profits per employee are 11 times greater (3,291/297) for the largest firms than for the smallest firms.

The choice of profits per employee to test the case is based on the premise that profits are the best index of the real assets of a firm. In fact, if the larger firms use their property less intensively (as this and other evidence suggests), then their realized profits as an index understate the assets of larger firms compared to smaller ones. Larger

Table 3

Profits per Employee, Large and Small Industrial Firms, Ranked by Net Worth

Group	Net Worth ($000,000)	Profit After Taxes ($000,000)	Employees (000)	Profits per Employee ($)
Top 10	40,090	5,470.0	1,662.0	3,291
All 500	133,660	14,839.0	9,966.0	1,489
Lowest 10	116	8.8	29.7	297

Source: Calculated from data in the *Fortune Directory* (1964).

firms also tend to be more highly leveraged with debt than smaller ones, since the large ones have better access to credit. For that reason, profits will underestimate the total assets of large firms more than small ones. Thus, the biases reinforce the conclusion that small firms combine more labor with their assets than large firms.

6. Expansionism: Civilian and Military

If there is something about size of business that discourages labor use, it would follow that mergers tend to result in reduced jobs on given assets. Jon Udell (1969) found just that in his study of mergers in Wisconsin. A wealth of fragmentary evidence suggests that this finding would be duplicated elsewhere.

The largest organization is government. The public sector is the most property-using of all. It has a reputation for wasting labor, and in some cases conspicuously does. But it pays the market for labor, while the interest rate on money it borrows is well below the market rate. As to land, it still holds much more than anyone, tax-free and unmortgaged, with little internal pressure or shadow price to reflect the foregone gains.

The military, for example, holds 20 percent of San Francisco and Washington, D.C. virtually idle. The annual value of this kind of lavish land input does not appear in the budget. The national forests use much more capital (as timber) per man employed than do private ones, especially small private ones, a fact that Forest Service doctrine makes a virtue. Richard Muth (1973) has concluded that the outstanding distinguishing trait of public housing is its higher capital intensity. Civil engineers, generally working for governments, have become notorious for producing white elephants by treating capital—not labor—as a free good, and for overstating future benefits next to present costs by using low interest rates (U.S. Congress Joint Economic Committee, Subcommittee on Economy in Government 1969). One can justify any project using a low enough interest rate and ignoring land costs. In the limiting case, using a zero rate of interest, the present value of future rents in perpetuity equals infinity.

Private utilities are capital-using, of course. But governments supply the most capital-using utilities, like water and sewer, which are increasingly costly because of urban sprawl. Governments are always called on to put up social front money, to push back and invade frontiers, territorial and otherwise, where the payoff is too slow for private capital.

Since the 1950s, a number of studies have analyzed the costs and benefits of peripheral expansion of public services, particularly water and sewer lines (Isard and Coughlin 1957; Mace 1961; Downing 1969; Real Estate Research Corporation 1974). Most such studies were motivated by growth controversies. They framed the question of growth in terms of whether new developments generate enough tax revenue to pay for themselves, regardless of location and timing. Our concerns here are location and timing. Even if developers now pay for the infrastructure costs within new developments, the taxpayers of older areas characteristically finance the expansion of treatment facilities, trunk lines, and other capital costs of development of new areas for years, sometimes decades, before the newly serviced lands return enough taxes to pull their weight (Gaffney 1977). It is another long span of years before they return the advance of capital by generating fiscal surpluses above their share of public costs. Such is the lag of private building behind public works that the public capital is sunk for years before payout.

A perfectly analogous case that has received detailed study is the lag of private behind public capital in irrigation projects. The classic is Weeks and West (1927). Public capital flowed into irrigation 10 to 30 years ahead of complementary private capital, leaving the public to finance dead capital in the meantime. But that was before the great explosion of state and federal financing, and later problems have grown larger. Factor mix also changes over time. We often read of declining capital/output ratios, but these do not show declining capital intensiveness because labor/output ratios are declining faster. (As noted earlier, capital intensity has more than quadrupled since 1950, not including the public sector, where the ratio has undoubtedly grown more quickly.)

7. Longevity of Capital and the Displacement of Labor

Marxists and other technological determinists have averred that changing techniques are inevitably more capital-using, but most economists today would recognize that the course of inventions and their application depend on relative costs. Technology evolves in response to costs, rather than being an autonomous mover of history. We are left with institutional bias as the likely cause of the failure of the economy to soak up surplus labor.

The source of this bias is not far to seek. To enrich the mix with labor, we would need to encourage the things that humble folk do, and take the fun out of many things that the rich and mighty do. It is not impossible, but it does call for a more effective philosophy than the poor and needy have embraced in modern macroeconomics.

Let us underscore what the facts just cited imply about the elasticity of demand for labor. On some lands and in some firms, labor is 90 percent of costs. Property gets 10 percent. The return to property is here highly leveraged by changes in the price of workers. An 11 percent drop to labor doubles the rate of return to land and capital; an 11 percent rise in wage costs wipes out those uses of land. At the other extreme, where labor is 10 percent of costs, halving or doubling the wage rate raises or lowers property income by only 5.5 percent.

All of the above may seem only marginally relevant to some readers because of their beliefs that (1) land is a minor input relative to capital and (2) labor produces capital anyway. As to the first belief, I have marshaled evidence against it elsewhere (Gaffney 1969, 2009). According to the second belief, industry employs labor to produce the capital, and such investment is the motor of the economic machine.[16] What then is the labor content of capital?

Let us say farm machines displace farm labor. Looking upstream, we see labor helping produce the machines. Is capital displacing labor, or is it merely labor stored in machines displacing onsite labor? We know the machine needs fuel, and fuel is capital-intensive to produce, but that does not tell us much until we know what "capital-intensive" means, for refineries, too, are produced by labor. So let us just focus on the farm machine. Keeping it simple, we ignore marketing costs between factory and farm.

Let us say a new super-harvester displaces farm labor. Looking upstream, we see labor helping produce the harvester in Peoria. Is capital displacing labor, or is labor stored in harvesters displacing onsite labor, or some of each?

To answer, let us follow one harvester through its life. It costs $100,000. The buyer lacks that kind of cash, so he finances it at 7 percent over 10 years, its expected life. To avoid any early cash drain he agrees to make a "balloon" payment after 10 years. The lender, to get her 7 percent, must require $197,000 at that time, about double what she advanced ($1.07^{10} = 1.97$). The harvester's service flow over life must be roughly double the initial cost. Even if the labor content of the new harvester were 100 percent, which of course it is not, and even if the fuel used were entirely a labor product, which of course it is not, wages as a fraction of the harvester's service flow are just 50 percent.

More commonly, of course, borrowers pay on the installment plan. They repay the lender bit by bit, year by year, together with interest on the unpaid balance. This holds down interest charges, because the lender recovers most of her capital sooner. Interest does not fall, however, to anywhere near zero. The level annual payment that will return lenders' capital with interest over 10 years is the capital recovery factor.[17] At 7 percent and 10 years, the factor is 0.142, or $14,238 annually for the loan of $100,000. Over 10 years, that comes to $142,380, or 42 percent more than the original cost. The harvester, in equilibrium, must yield its owner that much more than its labor cost. Wages as a fraction of total service flow are $100,000/$142,000, or 70 percent.

The 70 percent figure is based on a 10-year total life (or "carcass life") of the harvester. In the tenth year the harvester is not much more than a hollow shell, economically speaking. The capital is actually committed only a little more than half that time, on the average, because the lender recovers part of it each year and reinvests the income in new projects. So the payback time is really only about six years, to lower wages to 70 percent of the product, and raise interest to 30 percent of it.

Either way, capital contributes a big share of the service flow, and claims an equally big share of the harvest. This is basically because the capital is tied up a long time before payback. With shorter payback times, capital's share is less. For example, if the investor recovers capital at the end of one year, interest adds only 7 percent to the total cost, and the ratio of wages to total product is $1/1.07$, or 93.46 percent.

On the other hand, if the carcass life is five years, the wage share is 82 percent; if 10 years, then 70 percent (as we have seen). If the carcass life is 20 years, then the wage share is 53 percent; if 40 years, like a cheap house, 33 percent; if 80 years, like a mid-rise office building, 18 percent.[18] Throughout the economy, the share of labor in the flow of service from capital falls as the life of capital lengthens.

Table 4 shows the same calculation for buildings or equipment with a life of 5 to 80 years, with an interest rate of 8 percent. The comparison with 7 percent (in the preceding paragraph) indicates that the wage share goes down slightly as the interest rate rises.

We have slurred over the land input so far, but it is easy to deal with now. Labor is applied less frequently to land where labor is embodied in capital of long life, so the share of land rises relative to labor with life of capital.[19]

Figure 1 shows the relationship among land, labor, and capital graphically. The graph presupposes that an even flow of investment is

Table 4

Relative Shares of Construction Wages and Interest in
Cumulative Cash Flows from Capital Goods of Varying Lives,
Using Interest Rate of 8 Percent

Life of Capital	Investment Cost Divided by Annual Cash Flow	Wage Share of Cumulative Cash Flow (B/A)	Interest Share of Cumulative Cash Flow Interest (1 − C)
A	B	C	D
5	3.99	80%	20%
10	6.71	67%	33%
20	9.82	49%	51%
40	11.92	30%	70%
80	12.47	16%	84%

In Column B, investment cost means the initial cost of the capital equipment or building. The annual cash flow is the annual payment required if even payments are made over the life of the loan. So, if a building costs $5 million and lasts for 40 years, the annual payment would be about $419,000. If there were no interest, the loan would be paid in 11.92 years, but with 8 percent interest, the borrower repays $5 million every 11.92 years.

Figure 1

Components of Service Flows of Capital Investment

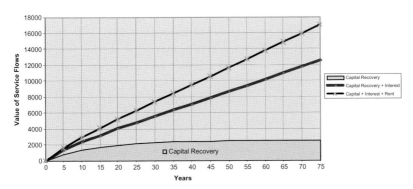

made each year in an equivalent unit of capital equipment (such as one harvester per year in the above example). Thus, the graph represents service flows from all units in service over the entire life cycle of the equipment. Each curve represents respectively the shares of cumulative service attributable to *capital* goods (buildings and equipment), *interest* as the value of time, and *rent* as the value of location. In the figure, the horizontal (X) axis represents the life (in years) of a unit of capital equipment. The distance between the X-axis and the lowest curve is the maximum amount of service flow that can be attributed to labor, on the exaggerated assumption that 100 percent of the cost of producing a piece of capital equipment comes from labor. The distance between the lowest curve and the heavy line is the amount of service flow dedicated to interest payments. The distance between the heavy line and the highest line represents the amount of service flow that covers ground rent.

Ignoring ground rent for the moment, the graph shows that most of the service flow of capital can be attributed to labor if the carcass life is less than 20 years. For capital with a short life, the shaded area is larger than the triangular area above the shaded area and below the dark line. For capital that endures longer than 20 years, the longer its life, the more of service flow pays interest rather than labor.

The triangular region above the heavy line but below the thinner line represents the service flow for rent. The service flow for one year is the site rent (the value of the location of the building or where the capital equipment is used). Better locations add greater value, and the best use of each site is the one that maximizes the rent or economic surplus. Thus, if sites are being used optimally, the service flow from rent will be greater for investments of longer duration. The area of the topmost triangle in the diagram, representing the service flow added by rent, is annual rent times the number of years a site is occupied. Even though the wedge represented by rent rises with the durability of the capital on the site, it does not increase as rapidly as the service flow from interest. This leaves us with two important conclusions: (1) the share of service flow created by land rises relative to labor with the increasing life of capital; and (2) the share of service flow created by land falls relative to interest with the increasing life of capital.

8. Growing and Flowing Capital

There are two kinds of capital: growing capital, which is storing up value, and flowing capital, which is releasing it in the form of service. The one is growing in value, the other shrinking as its value flows out into goods and services.

The above all refers to the latter, flowing kind of capital, which shrinks (depreciates) with time. The same relationship between long life and labor's share also obtains with growing capital, only more so. We follow $1 through the life of a tree it is invested in to plant. The tree is cut after 60 years and sold on the stump for $58 per dollar of initial labor, for a rate of return of 7 percent per year (because $1.07^{60} = 58$). So labor's share is 1/58, or 1.7 percent. I omit any table or graph because growth at compound interest is so familiar. Labor's share falls steeply as time passes.

For a fuller picture we would add the cost of logging, which is mostly labor, and that may equal the stumpage in value. This would raise the wage share, but it remains true that the longer the rotation age, the less often these wages are paid.

The share of labor in growing capital is less than for flowing capital of the same carcass life. The labor in flowing capital starts to flow out early on, but that in growing capital is locked in until the product is ripe, and joined by yet more capital that is not produced by labor at all but by land and other capital, the invisible inputs.

With growing as with flowing capital, the basic principle is unaffected by having a going concern. If we have a normalized forest of 60 cells (loggers call them "chances"), and cut and regenerate one chance each year, then we must keep 59 chances in inventory drawing interest for every one that we pay workers on. As before, the function relating labor's share to life is the same, whether we look at one chance of trees over life or at one normalized forest over one year of its life—which is not surprising, considering that the normalized forest is a cross-section of the whole life of one chance of trees, there being one chance of every age. Knut Wicksell (1934: 176 ff.) demonstrated this long ago in his *Lectures*. His example was wine, so wags call it "the grape juice model," but the ideas are the same. As before, there is less labor per acre when labor is used less often.

The crucial point is that there is less labor content in the machine that lasts longer. In general, the share of labor in the flow of service from capital decreases as the life of capital lengthens. Once again, we return to the central point of this essay: capital with a long life displaces labor, because it turns over and is replaced slowly. Capital with a short life enhances the demand for labor. In the extreme, direct services like haircuts are almost all labor, except for a small element of rent on the premises.

An important corollary is that an investment in enduring capital also increases the share of land in the value of production. Labor is applied less frequently to land where labor is embodied in capital of long life, so the share of land rises relative to labor.

Here are some familiar, recognizable traits of capital-using objects and enterprises, a sort of Field Guide to Capital Intensity (i.e., to capital that endures and does not turn over quickly):

1. The payout is deferred. The benefits are strung out, so that the object has to yield a large surplus over investment to cover interest. This surplus is the value added by capital, the Austrian "agio."
2. The cash flow, when it comes, is largely interest income. Recovery and depreciation are a minor share of cash flow. By the same token, if the object is financed, most of the periodic payments are interest for several years. The installment needed to retire the

   debt with interest is not much higher than simple interest on the
   original principal.

3. Demand is very sensitive to changes in interest rates, as with
   housing and all durable capital. Demand is also sensitive to the
   property tax, since it functions much like interest in raising the
   cost of investments in durable capital. Because a large portion of
   each installment is interest, a 10 percent increase in the interest
   rate (say, from 5 percent to 5.5 percent), imposes an 8 percent
   cost increase in a 40-year investment and a 10 percent increase
   in an 80-year investment.

4. Only a small share of the objects are normally replaced each
   year. The slow turnover of the buildings or equipment means
   less demand for labor.

5. A large share of the objects suffer obsolescence at any given
   time. For example, a significant part of the housing stock in
   many cities has outlived its useful life. High interest rates and a
   high property tax on buildings prolongs the life of housing by
   discouraging new construction, which bears the major brunt of
   the tax on buildings.

6. If the objects are attached to a site, as the most durable ones are,
   labor is applied onsite in a bulge, a one-shot payroll. There is
   no fund quickly recovered to reinvest to sustain the payroll.

7. The services stored up do not flow through to consumers for
   a long time, so production creates incomes without yielding
   up the goods to match them. This is true of both growing capital (like trees or cattle), and flowing capital (like buildings or
   trucks).

8. The fund-to-flow ratio is high: a large stock per unit volume of
   sales.

9. Finally, it is fair to say that the owners and other beneficiaries of
   these objects often demand relief from the test of competitive
   interest rates, a test they cannot pass. They also demand, and
   often get, special relief from property taxes.

For any purpose for which land and capital are used, there is a full
range of technical options. The choice depends on relative input costs,
that is, the cost of labor versus the rate of interest. High labor costs

(including labor taxes) screen out labor-using investments, and high interest rates screen out capital-using investments. Capital that matures or turns over in a short period is highly labor-elastic (responsive to changes in the price of labor). Long-lived capital is highly interest-elastic. High annual payments for land (either in the form of interest or taxes) have the same effect as high interest rates on capital; they discourage durable capital and promote forms of capital that turn over rapidly.

If wages are high, firms invest more in capital, specifically in durable capital. Where labor is 90 percent of costs, a 1 percent increase in labor cost reduces property income by 9 percent.[20] Rising labor costs, either from a wage increase or an increase in a tax on labor, induce investors to conserve on wages and spend more on interest. High wages and other labor costs screen out short-term, labor-using capital; high labor costs promote long-term investments in durable capital.

If interest rates are high and wages low, the reverse is true. The shorter maturity gains an advantage or premium over the longer one. Long-term capital investments (such as buying a house or building a dam) are screened out by high interest rates because most of the cost of long maturities is interest. They are prodigal of capital, so naturally a high price of capital screens them out. These are the adjustments made routinely as a result of market signals.

9. Activating Capital by Encouraging Faster Turnover

The ready answer to our current crisis of capital shortage (and to the more general problem of avoiding liquidity crises) is to invest in shorter maturities, deliver the final goods more quickly to consumers, recover and reinvest the capital more quickly in payrolls to use the whole labor force. That is my thesis in a nutshell.

Problems arise when the government adopts demand-management solutions to a credit shortage. That is particularly true if those solutions include investment in "infrastructure," which necessarily means capital with long maturities (roads, transit systems, dams, etc.). Such projects lock capital up in projects that will pay back slowly, employ few people per dollar of investment in construction, and even fewer in capital turnover.

The key to full employment, then, is raising the labor-combining valence of capital by turning it over faster. Active capital moves labor, while torpid capital merely occupies land and often displaces more labor than it employs.

The key to activating capital in this way is to let labor costs fall and the cost of capital rise. Conservative economists have long advocated something like that, by putting a lid on wages. Those of more analytical bent have stressed the "Ricardo effect," the substitution of cheaper labor for capital. Labor, of course, has resisted that message. They have all, however, failed to observe that we can lower wage *costs* without lowering wage *rates*, or take-home pay. This can be done by abating institutional biases like payroll taxes, withholding taxes, and sticking employers per se with social overhead costs like pensions, workers' compensation, medical insurance, etc. Likewise, we can raise capital costs without raising interest rates by removing income tax loopholes for capital and taxing property more heavily. Thus one can advocate lowering wage costs and raising capital costs without lining up with the demons in the House of Labor. But neither does this preclude one from faulting excessive wage demands, even as the conservatives do. In short, this is not a gut issue pitting "liberals" against "conservatives" in tired routine combat rituals, but a new issue calling for some cerebration and promising a way out of old dead ends.

The capital stock of an economy is a great revolving fund. Each time a unit of it recycles, it combines with workers. To combine the whole great fund with surplus labor, we need only turn the whole faster. This will deliver ripe goods to consumers at a faster rate: Growing capital will spend less time growing before harvest, and flowing capital will spend less time frozen in cold storage before thawing and flowing. Reinvestment of the recovered capital will increase incomes with which to buy the augmented flow of goods and services.

Here we collide with one of the firmest biases in our cultural impedimenta, the bias against rapid replacement. To many people that connotes waste, shoddiness, flimsiness, speculation, demolition of treasured antiquities, planned obsolescence, and ticky-tacky. That those are indeed only connotations and perversions of the principle, not the essence, does not placate some people. Long life to them connotes reliability, stability, soundness, trustworthiness, and old-fashioned goodness. These values lie deep in the cultural subconscious and will not yield easily. They are indeed part of what sustains the institutional bias that causes unemployment and inflation.

An economist cannot plead against them so well as point to the high price of indulging them: inflation and unemployment, as well as neglecting the positive values of flexibility, adaptability, early embodiment of technological advance, reduced capital requirements and easier entry, replacement of obsolete equipment, stimulus to creativity, mobility, and evolution.

It may help some to note that the "life" of flowing capital, as the term applies here, is not carcass life but service life. The idea is not to shorten carcass life, but to speed the delivery of value to consumers, and with it the recovery of capital invested. If the carcass survives, well and good; it is a bonus.

The purpose in demolishing an old carcass of, say, a house, is to recycle the site it preempts. This offends the preservationist in many people, but two observations are in order.

First, demolishing old buildings and replacing them with new is a way of preserving more old capital than is demolished, just like replacing a car's dead battery, or pulling a sick tooth. Surgical demolition is preservation, in the larger sense. Replace the sick house and preserve the neighborhood; preserve the neighborhood and preserve the city, with all its capital infrastructure and all its valuable land. In the past year, foreclosures of houses with subprime mortgages have depressed the value of nearby property, causing a spate of further foreclosures. This "neighborhood effect" reveals why there is a high social cost in preserving capital beyond its economic life.

Second, the best way to renew many sites is not to demolish but to rehabilitate. In that way, the policies advanced herein are in tune with Jane Jacobs's (1961) image of the good city life. Rehabilitation is labor-using, compared to new construction. So is operating the older buildings: maintenance and operation of buildings eats up an ever-larger share of rent as they age. Shelter from old buildings is a product of labor more than of capital.

Thus, we are led to a second paradox. The first paradox, which we have discussed above, is that reducing wage costs (by cutting taxes on wages) will increase wage rates by increasing the turnover of capital that combines with labor. The second paradox is that more rapid capital turnover will prolong the life of buildings. Our present taxes are biased in favor of durable capital over labor. One might assume that a capital-intensive bias would cause buildings to last longer, but that is not the case. Ironically, it promotes premature abandonment of old buildings, which is why entire sections of some cities are slums. Reducing wage costs and investing in capital of shorter service life favors extending the carcass life of old capital by patching it up with investments of shorter life than a wholly new structure would have, and by using more labor to operate it. Effective neighborhood reconstruction is achieved not by mass demolition and new construction but by continuous upkeep.

We have shown now that labor benefits when both land and capital are frequently recycled, rehabilitated, upgraded, and reused. That depends on how actively the owner combines those factors with labor. We have shown that the elasticity of demand for labor is high for combining with both land and capital, when the factor mixture is rich on labor. This is owing to the leverage that labor costs exert over returns to land and capital, if policies are not biased against labor. We have shown that there is a great reserve of land and capital on the "internal frontier" (torpid land and capital that are underutilized and turning over slowly) ready to combine with more labor, in response to small additional incentives. We have hinted at what such incentives might be. Next we look closer at tax bias against labor.

B. How Taxes Induce Land and Capital to Displace Labor

The tax system affords few shelters for the wage or salary earner. Income and payroll taxes are withheld, beginning fifteen and a half months before the tax is otherwise due. All wage income is "ordinary" and taxed at the full rate. If you have any question that the income tax is largely a payroll tax, ask yourself when you last heard of an oil man taking salaried work as a tax shelter. Harry Kahn (1968) found that labor income rose from 66 percent to 81 percent of the base of the personal income tax from 1939–1963.

There was a time when wage tax enthusiasts argued that such taxes posed no disincentive to work because the tax rate was a percentage, and your best choice before tax was the same as that after tax. (If this logic is valid, it applies equally to income and to payroll taxes. The latter rose from 2 percent in 1949 to 15.3 percent in 1990. They are imposed on the first dollar of earnings, and provide no exemptions or deductions.) If the marginal tax on your wages is 30 percent, combining the payroll and income tax, that argument amounted to a claim that $14 an hour was as attractive as $20 an hour, at the margin.[21] This presupposes that leisure activities, such as going fishing, watching television, spending time with friends or family, or sleeping do not compete with earning an extra dollar. It is reasonable to assume that wage taxes have *some* effect on behavior at the margin, so that some withholding taxes are shifted forward to employers. They, in turn, naturally look for substitutes for labor.

In addition, public policy has influenced the cost of employing an additional worker in recent decades for reasons other than taxes. Any health and safety regulations that vary with the number of employees will affect hiring behavior. The costs of providing fringe benefits, particularly health insurance, have risen dramatically.[22] Although pension plans are declining in importance, relative to 401(k) plans, they have had a significant impact in the past.[23] Since those costs have risen precisely because fringe benefits are not taxed, they are indirectly a result of tax avoidance. These hidden costs strongly discourage hiring workers at the margin and thus encourage substituting capital for labor.

The net result is that wage costs (wages, taxes, benefits) are strongly influenced by public policy. The tax system says to employers: "Hire labor, and government will charge you in many ways so that your labor cost is much higher than the worker's real wage." Businesses respond to this upward pressure on labor costs by using more land and by investing in longer-maturing capital than the market would otherwise impel them to do.

The bias against labor and in favor of capital of long duration takes other forms than policies that raise wage costs directly. In order to recognize these biases, we should compare the treatment of taxes on land and capital with taxes that fall on labor.

Consider taxes on the sale of most consumer goods. These taxes raise labor costs either directly (if they are borne by sellers, since about 70 percent of value added comes from labor) or indirectly (if buyers bear the main brunt of these taxes from their wages). By contrast, sales and excise taxes bear lightly on land. Implicit property income, such as the service flow of one's house, avoids sales taxes. This creates a bias toward property income and encourages over-investment in land and durable capital.

1. Property Tax Treatment of Land

There are taxes on the transfer of land, but these discourage selling as much as buying. They have a net impact on the motive to hold land, by gumming up the market, which adds to the incentive to buy in advance of need (by destroying the confidence that one can buy at time of need). When it comes to holding land, the tax system is geared to make the burdens light and the rewards great. The incentive to hold land rather than transfer it also encourages longer-term capital invest-ment, which reinforces the anti-labor bias.

The only tax that adds to holding costs is the property tax, and then only the part that is levied on land value discourages holding and encourages the use of high-turnover capital. Even then, the pressure by the land portion of the property tax to promote a higher labor/land ratio in production is relieved by assessment practice. Most assessors give a good deal of weight, in valuing land, to its current use, based on the existing improvements and the gross business conducted there,[24] rather than on highest and best use. That is, the "land" tax becomes a tax on using land, not holding it. Preferential assessment laws now require this in many states. (The effects of the property taxes on buildings will be treated below.)

A good deal of land is exempt (although hardly any wage or salary is exempt from income tax). Government land is the largest exempt class. Much of it is let to private people for inadequate fees. Their possessory interests are seldom assessed adequately or at all, and the low fee structure tells them to waste government land to substitute for highly taxed labor. Low grazing fees, for example, let stockmen hold cattle on grass too long, just as low parking rates in cities let parkers hold scarce street space too long.

Turning to the income tax, it bears very lightly on land. The basic abatements for land may be classified and summarized as follows:

1. Covert write-off of appreciated land value, by allocating part of it to an old improvement on the land. Of course, the tax laws do not formally allow land to be depreciated. But since depreciation rules allow property to be depreciated and traded multiple times, the net effect is to allow land to be depreciated in the guise of continuing depreciation of improvements that have been fully depreciated.

2. Many categories of exemptions: (a) imputed income (homes, resorts, hobby farms) coupled with deduction of interest and property taxes; (b) unrealized appreciation (as of advance purchases held until needed); (c) capital gains at death; (d) bequests; and (e) capital gains of exempt "nonprofit" owners.

3. Several ways in which property income is deferred or reduced while costs are treated as current and fully allowed. On the income side: (a) deferred tax on appreciation until realized by sale; (b) deferral of tax beyond date of sale, by several devices; (c) deferral of land use income where there is intertemporal interdependence of income (as by planting orchards); and (d) application of a low "capital gains" rate to realized appreciation. On the cost side: carrying costs and (some) losses are allowed to offset ordinary income.

I have treated some details of these devices elsewhere (Gaffney 1967b, 1970a, 1970b/1971). Some of these abatements are so gross as to amount to 100 percent exemption from tax, and some of these, like covert write-off, are repeatable, resulting in actual subsidies in lieu of taxes for holding land. This is double-, triple-, and quadruple-"dipping" much more serious than what currently goes by that name.

While keeping taxes on land holding low, government arranges high rewards for landowners by building public works, as well as by the whole complex of allied policies to support and sustain land values. Local works may be charged in part to local property taxpayers, but there are large federal tax favors here, too. Local bonds are exempt from federal income tax,[25] and are repaid from local taxes that are expensible (debt amortization in advance of economic depreciation should really be capitalized). Incomes peculiar to land like ground rents are not taxed as sales. Capital gains and imputed income also escape.

The result of all of these tax biases is a highly inflated incentive to buy more land than needed, sooner than needed, and to hang onto it longer than needed. Ernest Fisher (1933) describes this process as "the advance of urban uses into the penumbra" of a city, which involves premature platting and subdividing of land far from current residences and worksites. This in turn results in spreading people and capital thinly out over much more land than needed, and the next chapter will reveal how this creates instability in the banking system. This process of spreading out necessitates pumping billions of dollars of capital into stretched-out roads, pipes, lines, wires, and other linkages that tie the fragile web of society and economy together. Localities attract large capital resources to sink into extensions of low productivity, high risk, and deferred or imagined benefits by mortgaging the tax power to general obligation bonds. State and federal governments pour in additional capital, as by the Highway Trust Fund. None of this public capital is subject to any property tax, and only an eccentric public accountant would add a shadow tax to the capital to show its real social cost.

Yet it is just such an eccentric public accountant who is most needed now. The federal government is poised to engage in an orgy of capital investment in high-speed rail lines and other infrastructure with either negative returns on the investment or, at best, very slow and delayed payoffs. The possible elimination of the capital gains tax will exacerbate the problem of capital lock-in. All of this is being done in the name of creating macroeconomic leverage, to get the economy moving again.

Investing in infrastructure will create fewer sustainable jobs per million sunk than it would if invested in almost any other way—as it would have been if not taken for this use. There is a one-shot payroll only. After that, the value added by the facilities is added mainly by the unrecovered capital and land, and the factor input is mainly capital measured by interest, the hire of unrecovered capital. The capital per job is uncommonly, inordinately high above the mean.

As to investing in land, this creates no jobs at all, it is a zero-sum transaction for the whole nation or economy. A buys, B sells, they create nothing, destroy nothing. It is the same with most old buildings and other capital, and with most common stocks. The stock exchanges are mostly just casinos where people bet on the futures of existing assets. Only a few stock sales, the initial public offerings (IPOs), raise capital for new net investing, the "I" of standard macro models. Earlier Keynesians such as Walter Heller understood this full well. Over the years since then, owners of land and old buildings have slowly induced Congress and various economic advisors to gloss over the difference between creating new assets and buying old ones, so tax favors to the latter are now granted with the rhetoric of fostering the former. This has become a major source of confusion in the public dialogue, and of counterproductive tax policy.

Returning to the money spent on durable infrastructure, it recycles, but that will simply create inflationary pressures, since the economic activity generated will be slow to yield benefits. The fund of real capital stops revolving; active capital is converted to a torpid form. Ripe goods are not delivered to consumers, and the investor does not recover his capital to reinvest. The real capital advanced to workers now lies buried in the ground, unavailable to meet money demand in the next round of consumption. The policy only makes sense on the premises built into modern macroeconomics: (1) that there is a bottomless cornucopia of latent capital formation waiting for demand; and (2) that inflation is a remote danger. That premise has proven contrary to fact in the past. We will return to these macroeconomic questions below.

In addition to tax-induced waste of "land" in the narrow sense, there is the same for minerals. The set of tax subsidies to hype up minerals exploration and production are by now well known, and I merely remind you of the depletion allowance based on a value whose accrual was never taxed as income, use of wellhead value rather than *in situ* value as the base of the allowance, expensing of dry holes and intangibles, and capital gains treatment.

When it comes to extracting foreign resources, there are the foreign tax credit, tax exemption of ocean shipping, transfer of profit to lowest tax jurisdiction, tax deferral on unrepatriated profits, and the like. As to the property tax, assessment is at its lowest when it comes to minerals. There is negligible property tax pressure to utilize domestic minerals, nothing at all comparable to the income tax incentives to go after foreign minerals.

The results of the complex of tax measures are of course complex, and as Alfred Kahn (1964) has shown, they must be interpreted in terms of the cartelized industries, and to this we should add other institutional biases, like the establishment of tenure through exploration and military pressure (Gaffney 1967a, 1972). But the broad results are analogous to those for other land. We spread ourselves too thin by overstimulating foreign production relative to domestic, and overstimulating exploration and capture relative to production and conservation. We thus involve enormous extra outlays for pipelines and infrastructure, and the foreign investments involve even greater outlays for military support. Military outlays may be regarded much like the extension of a municipal service such as police protection to new suburbs.

The mercantilist metropolis makes the world its suburb. Like other outlays, these tie down capital until the flow of benefits returns the costs. It is symptomatic of the capital intensity of military outlays, if not definitive, that the $343 billion in interest on the national debt in FY2008 (U.S. Council of Economic Advisers 2009: Table B81) about equals the U.S. military budget prior to the wars in Afghanistan and Iraq (Sharp 2008). As the debt is rolled over, its cost can only go up.

In their efforts to promote full employment with indiscriminative investment incentives, dominant modern macroeconomists tend to think of all production as good. But extracting more primary products with a high natural resource content, like oil or aluminum, is the substitution of land for labor, just as much as is spreading labor thin over farmland. In addition, lavish use of materials and energy for labor is the prime source of pollution and generation of residuals, both of which in turn require space and drive away people. Thus, in respect to minerals and hydrocarbons and most exhaustible resources, as with other land, the tax system induces the use of too much, and requires large capital outlays to do so (Rose 1974; Gaffney 1967a, 1976b, 1982).

2. Property Tax Treatment of Capital

Next we look at the tax treatment of capital. The property tax hits some kinds of capital, and rather hard. But public capital, as noted already, is exempt, and affords a wide avenue of escape. Much other capital is also exempt, or given preferential low assessment. Timber makes a good example. Timber is almost everywhere underassessed by custom or law. The argument is that the investment would not pay if taxed, because of its long life—that is, its heavy use of capital. Yet when is the payroll tax or income tax abated because a labor-using business cannot survive it? Preferential treatment of timber is granted in almost as many ways as there are states. Ellis Williams (1968) has summarized these as exemption or rebate, modified assessment, modified rate, deferred payment, yield tax, and severance tax.

A good deal of other capital is exempt as well. Anything on legs or wheels or water is hard to catch on assessment day, as are consumer durables, and most jurisdictions have stopped trying. But business inventories, which are short-lived, are hit hard.

Buildings, which are durable and capital-using, are hit hard, too. This would seem to constitute a bias against use of capital, and it certainly is a bias against improving land. But the effect on the individual building is reversed because the property tax is levied locally, and local governments use zoning and other controls to protect and fortify their tax bases. The thrust of local zoning, building codes, subdivision controls, occupancy limits, condemnation power, and "sewer power" is to raise the capital requirements of residing in a town. The net result is doubly bad. We get more sprawl, raising infrastructure capital needs, and more capital per dwelling unit on the land that is used.

3. Income Tax Treatment of Capital

Turning to the income tax, it contains many loopholes and abatements for capital, and these generally are geared to favor capital of longer life. I will itemize five basic classes of preferences for flowing and growing capital, beginning with flowing.

1. Fast write-off and expensing. Whenever one writes off an asset faster than it actually depreciates, the effective tax rate is lowered below the nominal rate (for mathematical proofs, see Gaffney 1967b, 1970b/1971, 2006). Expensing is best of all, of course, being the fastest, and it lowers the effective rate to zero. It means the treasury in year one puts up a share of the capital investment equal to the tax rate, and thereafter gets only a return on its own investment.

Some important capital outlays that Congress lets be expensed are costs of minerals exploration, intangible drilling costs, research and development, advertising, rearing breeding livestock, starting orchards, soil and water conservation, many costs of land development[26] (Hoover 1970: 42), interest and property taxes incurred to carry growing capital, losses incurred to create goodwill or appropriate resources allocated by user rights (like air routes or water rights), any investment of unrepatriated profits abroad, price-war losses incurred to capture markets, movie making,[27] and so on. One can see from the list that expensing is granted more freely to growing than flowing capital. Growing capital is the kind that ties up capital longer before any is recovered.

It is a constant theme of interest groups, both private and public, that profits are not profits but costs if reinvested in the same business in which earned. Strange as it seems to an economist, there is a ready audience for this fallacy.

Almost all income-yielding capital is fully tax-depreciable well before its service life is over. About the only kind depreciated slowly is that of regulated utilities, to maintain the rate base and pass through the higher taxes to consumers.

2. Recapture of excess write-off. There is double-dipping allowed when capital is sold and redepreciated. The excess of sale price over book value is taxed as a capital gain, to "recapture" the excess depreciation, but recapture is several years after write-off and at the lower capital gain rate. The longer capital lasts, the more dips are possible. Buildings are the main beneficiaries. Besides their long life, they have the advantage of being confusable with land, and a good deal of land value is written off normally with each dip, even though the land value is rising.

"Recapture" of excess write-off is based on a sliding scale, the lower rates applying the longer the capital is held. This helps limit the number of dips, but adds to the favoritism shown to longer-lived capital.

3. Tax-free imputed income from housing. Consumer capital in houses and hobbies yields a tax-free imputed income, just as land does, coupled with deduction of interest and property taxes and indefinite deferral of capital gains taxes. If I am solvent and never move to a cheaper house, I can defer the gains until fiscal extreme unction, forgiveness at death. The capital gain may derive mainly from the land, but to claim the land as residential I must have a house.

If I hire workers to build or improve my house, that is not deductible. If I pay out for repairs and upkeep, that is not deductible. The exemption is to the return on capital, the service flow in excess of cost. The more durable and capital-using the house, the greater share of the service flow that is. A cheap house or trailer, a shelter of low capital requirements, benefits little from this exemption. The benefit is to capital.

Here we meet an exception to the rule of no loopholes for labor. Labor on one's own house is tax-free. There is even some inverse relationship between the capital in shelter and the labor input required to keep it going. On the other hand, the opportunity for tax-free labor requires that one own a house, and the more land around a house, the more the opportunity. The greatest outlet for home labor is when combined with land and capital.[28] A material share of the value of country estates and farms doubtless derives from their outlet for tax-free labor. The farther one gets from the exchange economy of cities and the nearer to self-sufficiency, the more labor is tax-free. In addition, it is relatively wealthy men who can afford to keep wives at home who do not work for cash. The tax-free labor of housewives is a bonus for the leisure class, of much less value to the waitresses, seamstresses, scrubwomen, and maids who labor in the houses of others.

The income tax is a tax on sale and exchange of labor rather than on home labor—a critic might say on social behavior rather than narcissism. But on larger landholdings there is room to reap the benefits of specialization, cooperation, exchange, and society and still avoid taxes, by internal barter. In the later days of the Roman Empire *patrocinium* became common, evolving into the early feudal system. The overtaxed citizen commended himself to be a "client" of the large landowner "patron" to escape the heavy hand of the publican (Thompson and Johnson 1937: 293–295). Today on large paternalistic ranches we see the same forces in a less aggravated stage, and in tax-free religious brotherhoods of Hutterites and Mennonites the modern counterparts of old ecclesiastical benefices. There are many reasons why Houthakker (1967) found the farms of Texas to report no net taxable income whatever, but one reason is the outlet they offer for tax-free exchange of labor.

Thus the tax loophole for labor is open mainly to those owning land and capital. This narrows the loophole so that it hardly compares in scope with the exemption of imputed income of owned land and capital. The landless proletarian seeking tax relief has to resort to welfare and crime. For sentimental reasons, tax benefits to homeowners are popular, along with many other subsidies, like cheap credit pumped in via the Federal Home Loan Bank Board and the host of predecessor and ancillary agencies. In result, capital is diverted from commerce and industry (the taxpaying branches, at least) to homes. Yet capital in homes complements labor less than capital in offices, stores, factories, inventories, and so on. It makes no workplaces, it needs no processing, and it lasts much longer.

4. Deduction of interest and property tax. These costs of carrying capital are fully deductible from ordinary income, even though the income from capital is wholly or partly exempt from tax.

5. Investment tax credit. This on-again off-again device lets investors in many kinds of capital reduce their taxes by 7 percent of the investment. After that, one may depreciate the whole amount as well. This device has the potential of favoring shorter over longer investments. In form, it is a premium on replacement, and thus labor-intensiveness. It could be a powerful device for quickly causing capital to combine with more labor. But Congress has forestalled this by permitting the credit only on a sliding scale, favoring longer investments. The credit is not fully allowable for investments whose estimated economic life falls short of eight years. The net result is a lower overall tax rate on capital than on labor.

Those five abatements move investors to prefer capital-using over labor-using techniques, and combine more capital per worker in all processes. In addition, the abatements are biased among forms of capital, consistently favoring those lasting longer. Capital cycling in less than a year is treated very harshly. It hardly achieves the status of "capital" in the eyes of the law. Economists have strung along, letting "investment" refer to buying capital to last longer than a year and appearing quite unconcerned over the logical, definitional, and modeling problem in drawing so arbitrary a line between "investment" and consumption spending.

The investor who recovers capital inside the year reports his costs and revenues on the same tax return, even though they may be nearly a year apart. He might gain by straddling the year-ends, but the IRS, so careless with intertemporal advantages gained by owners of durables, is vigilant to this and forbids him to deduct the cost of goods not sold.[29] The effect is the same as requiring that increased inventories be reported as income. The Treasury will not help anyone finance working capital as it does durable capital. *Eisner v. Macomber*, the 1920 case that protects land, timber, mineral reserves, stocks, and so forth from taxes on unrealized gains, does not apply to accumulation of inventory. The rules are bent against goods of higher labor content.

There is a concession to phantom inflationary inventory profits in LIFO accounting, but "very complex rules are involved and . . . LIFO is not ordinarily used by small business" (U.S. Department of the Treasury, Internal Revenue Service 1965: 26). It is tailored for larger business—the ones that need more capital per worker.

As noted before, recapture of excess depreciation is taxed on a sliding scale, the rate declining with years held—another favor to long life.

Improvements to land that add to sale value receive capital gains treatment, with all the many favors that implies. Unlike the cost of inventories, which is not deductible until sale of goods, these costs are often expensible and nearly always depreciable long before sale. Land improvements are of course more durable than inventories.

Depreciable lives are generally based on arbitrary classes of assets, regardless of actual service life. The more the service life exceeds the write-off life, the lower is the effective tax rate, a clear tax incentive to build in more durability. Depreciation paths are also important. Straight-line tax depreciation is most common, but shorter-lived assets like, say, a delivery truck, depreciate like the *Blue Book* value of cars, faster than straight line. They get the tougher break. Buildings, on the other hand, depreciate slowly at first, along a path like the declining balance of an installment debt. But the IRS allows them accelerated depreciation (double-declining balance and sum-of-the-years'-digits.)

Thus there is a consistent and pervasive tax bias in favor of capital, and among capital assets in favor of the longer-lived. That this is so consistent, and often explicit,[30] points to some sort of conscious intent, or systematic bias.

The above referred to flowing capital. Growing capital, which on the whole ties up capital longer, and admixes more interest input with the original labor input than does flowing capital, is treated even better. The basic tax subsidy to growing capital is deferral of tax to date of sale. Income, in the meaningful definition of Haig (1921) and Simons (1938), occurs when value accrues, that is, each year as the value grows. Thus growing capital is taxed after the income accrues, and the longer the wait, the greater the benefit. In effect, by deferring taxes, the Treasury helps finance growing capital (except ordinary inventories of short life).

Associated with that is a greater propensity of Congress to allow expensing of the capital cost of growing than flowing capital. Agriculture makes a good example (Dangerfield 1973; National Planning Association 1972). Under the cash-accounting privilege allowed to farm business, a "farmer" can deduct expenses of materials and services that "actually go into or are a part of a final salable product—such as feed, seed, stud fees, and management services" (Dangerfield 1973: 15989) Machinery and building improvements have to be capitalized— they are flowing capital. Capital that falls in a twilight zone between the classes includes costs of raising livestock held for draft, breeding, or dairy purposes, and costs of starting up orchards and vineyards. These, too, are expensible, even though some orchards may bear for 80 years. Breeding stock may be depreciated as well—another case of double-dipping—and their sale not be taxed until the "herd" is liquidated, an incredible package of special privilege for the kind of livestock that requires the most land and capital per dollar of value added, to say nothing of per unit of nutritive value (Houthakker 1967).

Some large classes of growing capital are timber, livestock, minerals (the portion of their value added by discovery and development), some kinds of knowledge, orchards and vineyards (for part of their lives), and liquors. Most inventories are growing capital, but the bulk of them turn over within a year and enjoy no tax subsidy. Most of those listed are greatly favored, however.[31] As a result, investors seek to maximize tax-sheltered assets and minimize assets that are not sheltered. They substitute growing capital, like cattle, for flowing capital, like machinery or buildings.

Again we take timber as an example. Although the tax is deferred until sale, the carrying costs of timber, interest and property taxes, are expensible as you go. On the other hand, the cost of labor used to reforest bare land is not an expense; it must be capitalized and not deducted until sale. In addition, timber sales get capital gains treatment, although the interest and property taxes are expensed from ordinary income. The labor cost that had to be carried forward to sale is now deducted only from the capital gain.

The main labor cost is logging. We omit that here because we are illustrating just the stage of timber growth, terminating in stumpage. Logging begins a new cycle, one of processing the stumpage to make wood products. This in turn terminates in delivery of finished lumber to a building site, where a new cycle begins with onsite labor converting lumber into housing.

Ordinary profit from vertically integrated downstream sawmills may be shifted to timber and get capital gains rates by the firm's nudging up shadow transfer prices. The IRS watches these prices with some diligence, and it is not certain that fictional internal prices get by. But there is every incentive to raise nonfictional transfer prices by letting timber add more value on the stump at capital gains rates before becoming a log, processed by labor at ordinary rates. In the mills, value added by labor is taxed at ordinary rates, and so is the value added by profit.

4. Inflation as a Tax

Some of the gains subject to tax are illusory results of inflation, and on this basis one might think tax preferences are needed merely to prevent higher effective rates on growth of capital. The undeducted cost basis of ripe timber is however negligible, in any case, next to its merchantable value, so this does not amount to much. Carrying costs have been expensed right along.

In general, inflation adds to motives to hold real assets, for these reasons:

1. Inflation of property values has outpaced wage rates. The illusion would be to overlook that wealth holders as a class have gained on tenants, young people, pensioners, and depositors.

2. Inflation is an annual tax on holding money. Taxing the rise of equity values merely redresses the balance, and fails in that by a wide margin, because the inflationary loss is immediate, while the gains tax is deferred. Inflation hurts the most those whose need for liquidity is high relative to their real assets. These are those whose volume is high relative to their capital because liquidity needs vary with volume. That is, these are those whose capital turns over fast. Lampman's study (1962) of the concentration of wealth found that money and near-money as a share of wealth declines with total wealth, so that inflation as a tax has a regressive quality compared to taxes on real wealth.

3. Inflation lowers the real cost of borrowing. Owners of real wealth are the major borrowers, and leverage is the name of the game. Inflation has advanced them capital at very low real rates of interest, another subsidy to holding capital.

4. In terms of bias between long- and short-lived capital, gains on short-lived capital are equally the product of money illusion but are taxed sooner, and at ordinary rates.

Some economists have argued that "phantom profits" should not be taxed. By that they mean that capital gains should be indexed for inflation.[32] That would result in larger depreciation write-offs over time. This strikes me as a one-sided and unbalanced view, which overlooks points 1 through 4 made here. Inflation on balance favors the longer-lived assets. Indexing would only worsen this bias (Gaffney 1991).

5. Corporate Income Tax

Turning to the corporate income tax, it is biased against income from corporate property by double-taxing it, or so it would seem. Yet the corporate form is so useful a device for sheltering property income, regardless, that some wealthy people set up personal corporations for tax avoidance. This calls for a second look.

Corporations are able to avoid the double tax by not taking cash out for a long time, thereby converting the shareholders' ordinary income into capital gains, forgivable at death. Public corporations, too, are moved to plow back profits. This puts more capital each year back in the control of corporate managers to reinvest, whether or not they have any good ideas. The capital does not have to meet the test of the market; it is free of all cost but the range of opportunities of the particular management. Thus the net impact of the tax system is to make internal capital artificially cheap to corporations, and push them into ventures of deferred payoffs.

In addition, of course, corporations avoid double taxation by financing with debt, and their collateral security rises in step with their retention of earnings. They also finance internally from pension funds, totaling $2.7 trillion in 2007 and $1.9 trillion in 2008, the income free of income tax (Board of Governors of the Federal Reserve Board 2009: L.118b). Borrowing requires collateral, and law and custom favor solid, durable capital as the thing to pledge. As to excise taxes, which raise about twice as much revenue from business as corporate income taxes, their impact is like that of income taxes, only more so, because costs are not deductible. Excise taxes, in effect, tax capital each time it turns over. The busy merchant who turns his capital several times a year is taxed on it as many times. But the same capital in a tree is taxed only once at the end of 80 years or so.

If tax bias were the only institution to favor wealth over labor, we could say it may offset other biases, but in fact there are reinforcing biases, which I will merely list:

- regulatory bias and the Averch-Johnson effect, or the tendency of rate-regulated firms, such as utilities, to expand their capital base beyond an efficient level to maximize returns (Averch and Johnson 1962);
- licensing laws that dispose of resources, franchises, and monopolies subject to heavy capital requirements; for example, a taxi medallion in New York City in 2007 cost $600,000, and the price

has appreciated 14 percent per year over the past 50 years (Business Wire 2007);

- subsidized low-interest loans and use of low interest rates in planning public works, both of which encourage investment in projects with excessively long maturities and slow payout;
- ignoring opportunity costs of public land, which encourages government to substitute land for labor at the margin;
- logrolling, overcommitment, and resulting stretchout of public works, all of which is justified politically by the claim that public works provide employment;
- the Highway Trust Fund, which promoted overbuilding of the federal highway system in the past, and that now imposes a large maintenance burden on present and future generations;
- the price-umbrella effect that builds excess capacity into cartels and allows cartel members to overinvest in capital.

There are more, and I know of no comparable set of biases favoring inputs of labor.

C. Capital Investment and Capital Turnover

We have already laid the basis of the present argument and recapitulate briefly before moving into the macroeconomics.

If there were no capital, the way to make jobs would be clear and simple. We would tax land value as the property tax does, as a regular fixed payment based on value, not varying with use. This would put pressure on owners to intensify. We would not tax them for hiring labor and selling products. They would use more labor on less land and solve our problem. And this is still a big part of any solution, regardless of capital. We must use more workers per acre.

Since there is capital, the problem has a third dimension. We need to use more workers per acre, and also do it more often. The form of capital we create affects both relations—that is, how many and how often.

When capital is short and land is dear, we not only need to use less land per worker, we also need to use less capital per worker. It is not that more capital would not be good if we had it. Voluntary saving is splendid, and taxing land will doubtless encourage it by lowering the value of that asset and prompting people to fill the void with real capital formation. But at any time, we want to make do with what there is, and just now we need to make a short supply go around much further. The market will do it for us if we let it.

Investments differ widely in "valence" for labor, how much labor they mix with capital. So investments that take capital from job-creating uses of high-labor valence to sink it into other uses of low-labor valence are not helping make jobs. Unrepatriated capital overseas is not making jobs in the United States, except as Americans emigrate with it. Some capital, like cattle, has a high valence for land and deprives labor of land, as well as of capital in other forms. Some capital, like that in a giant strip-mine excavator, combines one operator with millions in capital and land, and hardly compares with one sewing machine, which also requires one operator and a few square feet of floor space. But our well-intended effort to increase output per worker and thereby increase wages tells us we should subsidize investment to employ labor, reduce taxes on capital, and finance tax-exempt public works, and so on.

They tell us that labor produces capital anyway, so how can capital displace labor? In effect, they tell us that if capital does not always combine well with labor in parallel, it still combines in series. In other words, even though we know a machine may replace several workers, we take comfort in the fact that labor was required at an earlier time to make the machine. It seems in that vague way that creating labor-saving capital and creating jobs balance out. So, as politicians and economists rationalize, the key to jobs is investment. And here they lead us into folly.

We see investment in, let us say, a large storage dam as using workers, but not as freezing up scarce capital. We can *see* the labor that goes into producing the dam, but we *cannot see* the service flow from the dam produced by the capital input. That invisible flow of services is comprised of the interest on the unrecovered principal over the life of the dam, which accounts for and soaks up most of the imputed cash flow. We see the demand for construction labor and think it is a net increase, but forget that the financing takes funds and thus real capital from alternative uses. Since those other uses of capital are likely to combine with labor more frequently than the capital tied up for decades in the dam, this is an example of how heavy construction slows down the aggregate economy and destroys labor opportunities. Each dollar frozen in concrete contributes to shortage of capital reinvestment and reemployment. We pay bread today for stones tomorrow.

It might be thought that I am overemphasizing the life of capital and should consider that capital combines not just with labor that produces it, but also with labor that works with it. Thus a factory "makes jobs." However, the factory produces goods, too, which are capital of some life. If we think of an economic matrix in which we match all capital with the labor that produces it, then we have a comprehensive tableau. Further matching would be redundant and might double-count. That is, we can measure factor proportions by vertical integration, as I am doing; or alternatively by horizontal integration, as in a normalized model; but not by both at once.

We think that "intensive land use" must be good for labor, but forget that trees and livestock and farm machines and fully automated plants and the blank sterile walls of many modern city buildings drive labor off the land and last too long to hire reconstruction labor very often.

Long life of capital can mean high intensity of land use without much labor. The problem is that to encourage investment we lower the cost of capital, and move investors to use it lavishly in place of taxable labor. We forget that the job-creating efficiency of capital varies from one use to another, and our measures to promote investing lead capital into the least job-creating uses, where capital substitutes for labor, because we make capital look cheap and labor look dear.

D. *The Microeconomic Basis for a Correct Macroeconomics*

The great, the overriding fault of modern macroeconomics is its homogenized treatment of investments. One investment is as good as another; only the aggregate matters. We must distinguish among investments. Adam Smith, as so often, gave us a morning star of light on the subject. Smith said:

> The quantity of that labor, which equal capitals are capable of putting in motion, varies extremely according to . . . their employment . . . A

capital . . . employed in the home trade will sometimes make 12 operations, or be sent out and returned 12 times, before a capital employed in the foreign trade of consumption has made one . . . the one will give four and twenty times more encouragement and support to the industry of the country than the other. ([1776] 1937: 338, 341, 349)

1. Historic Recognition of Capital Turnover: Smith, Mill, Wicksell

Mill was like-minded. He and Smith saw "circulating" capital as "setting labor in motion," and "fixed" capital as not. Mill said:

[C]apital may be temporarily unemployed, as in the case of unsold goods . . . [D]uring this interval, it does not set in motion any industry (§2, p. 41) . . . [C]apital may be so employed as not to support laborers, being fixed in machinery, buildings, improvement of the land and the like (§3, p. 41). . . . Capital is kept in existence from age to age not by preservation, but by perpetual reproduction (§6, p. 47). . . . To set free a capital which would otherwise be locked up in a form useless for the support of labor, is, no doubt, the same thing to the interests of laborers as the creation of a new capital (§9, p. 52) (Mill 1872: BK. I, Ch. V) . . .

[A]ll increase of fixed capital, then taking place at the expense of circulating, must be, at least temporarily, prejudicial to the interests of laborers. . . . Suppose . . . a capital of 2,000, . . . half . . . effects a permanent improvement. . . . He [the capitalist] will employ, in the next and each following year, only half the number of laborers. (Mill 1872: BK. VI, §2, p. 59)

Unfortunately, Smith and Mill never got the bugs out of their wages fund theory, which never became fully coherent and operative. In spite of the above quotations, it seemed to some that the "fund" could not increase except by slow increments of capital formation. Knut Wicksell (1934: 194–196) corrected this with:

a true view of the famous wage-fund theory . . . Capital in its free form is employed to advance both wages and rent. . . . If . . . a given capital . . . is employed year after year, . . . then each year about an equal part of that capital will be set free. That part . . . constitutes the whole production of finished commodities and services [of capital] of the year. When the capitalist class has taken the surplus . . . it must, in order to maintain its capital, reinvest the remainder—which it does by hiring labor and land for new production. This part, therefore, is . . . the annual wage-fund. . . . The wage-fund may undergo considerable changes, in so far as the average period of turnover of capital is lengthened or shortened . . . it is only the part [of capital] annually set free which can purchase labor (or land).

"*It is only the part of capital annually set free which can purchase labor (or land).*" Here I think we have the basis for a correct macroeconomics, one that can exorcise the fallacy that investment of any kind adds to real demand for labor merely by recycling money. The only kind of investing that purchases labor truly, without the fraud of inflation, is investing that corresponds to delivery of real goods to consumers at the end of the pipeline. These real goods are the "capital set free which can purchase labor." This is what turns paper money into real money.

This device suddenly ties together micro- and macroeconomics nicely. The way to use more workers with capital is to turn and recover the capital more quickly. This is also the way to increase aggregate demand for labor. By far the bulk of the gross investment that generates payrolls has its source in the recovery of capital by sale of ripe goods and the services of flowing capital to consumers. Recovery and reinvestment of capital are the prime movers of the economic machine.

Wicksell saw capital soaking up any surplus labor:

> If . . . more labor is available than can be employed . . . a shorter period of production . . . is adopted, and the capital which was before insufficient is now able to give employment to all workers. (1954: 127)

He saw social capital as a wage fund, but a fund that can sustain any rate of flow because it revolves. This Great Revolving Fund does not limit wages. By recycling faster it employs more workers up to any needed number, and it speeds up when stimulated by lower wage rates and higher interest. In the idiom of modern macroeconomics, this increases replacement demand. Aggregate demand can fall short of full employment if capital turns slowly, but faster replacement corrects things and fills the gap. Thus, "the existing capital must just suffice to employ the existing number of workers" (Wicksell 1954: 160). The greater replacement demand is financed by greater capital recovery, and matched by a greater flow of finished goods, so it is not diluted by inflation.

Let us look at Wicksell's device[33] as a way of meeting the national payroll with a small capital. He was telling us, in effect, that the economy can do what the small businessman has to do all the time. He has to recover his capital quickly each time he sinks it, if he is to meet the next payroll without dropping workers.

2. A Homely Example of Business Turnover

Consider a baker on a busy corner open 365 days a year, with working capital of $200. To keep it simple, assume payments are made daily, and he spends the first day setting up, making no sales, but sinking the $200. Half goes to pay the payroll for the first day, half for feedstock, and we will ignore overhead for simplicity. Thereafter, the baker sells out each night. The $100 that turns over each day will finance a daily payroll of $100 or annual payroll of $36,500, plus an additional $100 flow of net production above cost. To this amount, he need add only $10 for 10 percent interest on $100 of his working capital.

As a rough rule, the flow (F) one can handle equals the capital (K) times turnover (T). So, $F = K \times T$. The average payout period (P) is the reciprocal of turnover ($P = 1/T$). So, $K/F = P$. Using the above example:

K = $200 of working capital

F = $200 per day of output ($100 for payroll, plus $100 of net production)

T = 1 (capital turns over every day); $P = 1/T$ also equals 1

$F = K \times T$, so $200 = 200 \times 1$

$K/F = P$, so $200/200 = 1$

In annual terms:

$F = \$73,000 = K \times T = 200 \times 365$

T = 365 (stock turns over 365 times per year), so $P = 1/365$

If it took two days instead of one to sell out, then T would be 0.5 (meaning half the stock turns over each day) and therefore P (or $1/T$) is 2. (In annual terms, T is $365/2$ and $P = 2/365$.) In order to balance the equation, so that $K/F = 2$, the baker would have to find another $200 of working capital, or drop half the staff. From this simple example, we can see that turnover is both a substitute for capital and a generator of employment. The slower the turnover, the more capital the owners must provide for each person hired.

The baker must hold down that payout period by scheduling sales so that cash flow balances outgo before running out of capital. If it takes six days to turn over the $100 of stock, then $K/F = 6$, so $K = 6F$.

The baker must sell the first cohort of goods out in six days, or fail to meet payroll on the seventh day.

As a business gets into financing slower inventories, such as a camera store might have, compound interest adds to the capital required and K > FP. If the average payout period (P) is seven years,[34] then compound interest at 10 percent doubles the value of each item by the time it is sold. (That means, roughly speaking, that half the price of a typical camera that has sat on the shelf for seven years, waiting for a customer, is the cost of interest for holding it in inventory that long.) The capital required to sustain a payout period of seven years will be 10 times the flow (or K/F = 10), rather than seven times, because the cumulative value of an annuity of one over seven years equals 10. Ten percent interest on 10 equals one, meaning the interest cost is the same as the cost of the capital (the stock of cameras in the shop, in this case). The memorable thing about this period is that the annual interest bill now equals all other costs, and takes half the cash flow.[35] Meantime, the capital has virtually stopped sustaining any payroll. Instead of being 1/365 of volume (in the bakery, with extremely fast turnover), capital is now 10 times volume, or 3,650 times as much per job.

The demand for labor does not depend primarily on the amount of capital, then, but on how fast it turns over—how active it is. Each time capital cycles, it combines with and activates labor: every investment in payroll creates labor income equal to capital on the first round. But for sustained impact it must keep recycling. Paybacks deferred are payrolls denied.

If you recover capital slowly, you constantly need more money, until you reach an equilibrium with cash flow balancing outflow—which by this time includes very large interest payments on all the unrecovered capital.

Some firms and agencies have gone on for decades without reaching that balance. The Bell Telephone Company is notable. In 1971 it went to the market for $4.5 billion in outside capital, about 20 percent of all the new capital raised from stocks and bonds by American industry. "But it will take another 30 years, according to Bell's plans, for electronics switching systems to displace the older (electro-mechanical) equipment in the telephone network" (Business Week 1972: 57–58).

3. The Great Revolving Fund

The U.S. Bureau of Reclamation makes another case. In 1902, Congress endowed the new bureau with the Revolving Fund, to be recouped and reused every 10 years. By now it was to have completed 11 cycles ($11 of dams for each $1 of capital), and might have, except for one problem: it has yet to complete the first. Each new project has drained capital from elsewhere—and frozen much of it tight. Instead of activating much labor, the bureau has deactivated much capital. In the process it has also frozen scarce waters in farm uses in areas where that use is seriously obsolete, so the capital is a public nuisance.

Normally, a company can be viable only if the cash flow from its operations allows it to recoup its capital periodically. To do that, its payback period must be short enough that its income is not entirely consumed by interest expense (or imputed interest in the case of government projects). Many companies invest in excess of depreciation, which means their revenues are insufficient to recover their capital after paying interest. A company can do that—but only by tapping others. An economy cannot, except by new saving. It is a closed system with a zero sum of capital transfers. To meet the national payroll, the economy must deliver the goods, or cut the payroll. The national capital is indeed a Great Revolving Fund. The fund receives inputs from labor and delivers to consumers. Labor and consumption set limits on the throughput, as we know. But so does turnover of the fund—and that has been neglected.

Meeting the national payroll has two sides: spending money for work, and delivering real goods to back up the money. Turnover generally balances the two sides nicely. Replacement anticipates liquidation. The keepers of the fund—capitalists—anticipate the maturity and sale of their goods, and pay workers to replace them. This gives workers the income to buy the ripe goods. (Along with turnover there are net saving and investment, but these are small next to turnover— too small a tail to wag so big a dog, as mainstream macroeconomics would have it.)

Most macroeconomists take care only of the spending side, the money payroll. Their fault is to assume that delivering the goods takes care of itself. Turnover is assumed mutable, totally accommodating in response to the touch of spending.

The fact is that turnover itself determines spending, since replacement anticipates liquidation. In other words, the production for which workers receive wages is primarily the replacement of capital that is worn out, moved out of inventory (by final sale), or otherwise depleted. Consumer goods are technically capital (inventory) until the moment they are sold to a household, so the basic reason for sluggishness of an economy is the buildup of capital so that it does not need to be replaced. In that way, turnover becomes a bottleneck. The flow of income cannot exceed $K \times T$, capital times turnover (plus direct services).

Mainstream macroeconomics cannot address this problem any better than the guns of Singapore, facing out to sea, could turn around to meet the Japanese attacking by land. "Think spending" and "Discourage deliveries" are its motifs. That Keynesian adage presupposes that the fundamental macroeconomic problems are underconsumption, oversaving, underinvesting, and liquidity preference. If the problem is perceived as how to remove surplus goods from the market, the doctrines and policies that result will welcome investments with only deferred benefits. These create money incomes and no consumer goods. The result has to be inflation.

The "New Economics" mocked Say's Law and taught two generations that supply does not create its own demand. Today's problem seems to be that demand does not create the answering supply. Merely spending money is cheap, and easy to arrange when you have your hands on the levers that control money supply and government debt. Delivering real goods is harder.

Smith and Mill sound quaint today when they say that the office of capital is to advance subsistence to labor. We should have more such quaintness, rather than doctrines that would advance money to labor without subsistence to back it up, so that it shrinks in your hand. We have traded on the symbol and denied the substance until the symbol has lost its power to command.

4. Capital Replacement as the True Source of National Income

Mainstream macroeconomics does not omit turnover from its equations. Rather, it buries and obscures it by keeping it implicit. This occurs when one treats "consumption" as an income-creating expenditure. Consumer spending as such does not create much income; it takes off the shelf goods already produced. Replacement of liquidated capital is the spending that creates income. There is disinvestment and reinvestment. In macroeconomic logic these two transactions are netted out, so consumption creates income, and only the uncleared balance shows up as net investment—which is what "investment" means in modern macroeconomic logic.[36] The great mass of gross investment is called consumption. The turnover of capital required is assumed to occur passively, automatically, accommodatingly. Only it doesn't. Turnover has its own set of determinants, including the tax biases we have surveyed. Furthermore, since replacement anticipates liquidation, and the time for liquidation depends largely on the physical character of the capital in question, turnover plays a strong role in determining income and consumer spending, rather than the other way around. It is the pacer, not the paced. Consumer spending is the result, not just the cause, of the ripeness and sale of goods. It is this that keeps balance between aggregate demand and supply.

This is the missing link in typical macroeconomic thinking, enmeshed in its doctrine of consumer determinism. It is replacement, mainly, that determines gross investment, which generates most income. Replacement in turn is determined by the schedule of maturity of capital in being.

This analysis would seem to explain better than orthodox macroeconomics our current predicament. Contrary to that orthodoxy, replacement spending falls short because of a shortage of ripe goods, not a surplus. If too much capital is invested in capital of long maturity, which loses its value when interest rates rise in a downturn (e.g., buildings on marginal land), it ties up capital that might have been invested in short-term working capital (e.g., the feedstock used in a bakery). Excess production of the former prevents sufficient production of the latter. If there are not enough jobs to go around, it results from too few goods flowing out the pipeline, not too many. In the aftermath of a period of explosive investment in long-term projects, there will be a shortage of ripe goods, which requires that they be rationed. Unemployment is the rationing agent. If there is not enough consumption to employ all workers, it is because there is too little to consume. It sounds very much like stagflation.

What's happening is that turnover is too slow. A lot of good capital is simply wasted and lost forever, too, which is worse in the long run but not very different in the short from freezing it up for 20 years. This means slow delivery of final goods, and slow recovery of capital to reinvest. Reinvestment demand is not inflationary because it anticipates or accompanies delivery of real goods. Lacking adequate reinvestment, modern macroeconomic policy seeks to simulate real demand by creating and recycling money faster. But the policymakers have omitted the second half of meeting the national payroll. They are feeding out paper but not delivering the goods. How can capital be short when there is so much, and when you can buy it so cheap on Wall Street now? Easy. There is plenty of capital stuck in the ground. The shortness is of readily recoverable capital for reinvestment. The shortness raises discount rates and devalues common stock, but cannot transmute concrete into peaches or recycle telephone poles into sugar. The moving finger has written. We have gone astray by thinking that what is good for capital is good for labor. It is a half-truth, and we now have to face up to the other half.

The microeconomic solution to unemployment also contains a macroeconomic solution. An important aspect of substituting labor for capital and land is to apply labor to land more often and recover and reinvest capital more often. This increases replacement demand, which is almost all of aggregate demand, and does it without any inflation. The key to good macroeconomic policy is not net new investment and growth of capital, but turnover, recovery and reinvestment of capital. Favors to capital are not favors to labor unless they come in such form as to accelerate the cycling of capital, as the investment tax credit could.

IV

Conclusion

WHAT CAN WE NOW SAY about how to allocate capital so that its job-creating efficiency will be greater? A number of general rules follow from our analysis.

A. Directing Capital to Enhance Employment

We need to stop regarding high output per worker as an adequate index to efficiency, when this index mainly reflects overapplication of land, primary products, and capital. Labor's interest is in having high marginal productivity, not necessarily average.

We need to foster things that humble folk do, directing capital where its valence for labor is high, and for land low. This does not call for subsidies, but for neutrality in taxation. There is some truth in the old slogan that the rich can best help the poor by getting off their backs. This calls for a considerable shift in values and attitudes, even on the part of the poor, who often think as their own worst enemies (and so remain poor). We need to extract less from the Earth, and to process, recycle, maintain, and service more that we do extract. There is no rigid fixed multiplier, as spokesmen for primary industries allege, by which downstream jobs depend on upstream mining or logging. Cheap logs are butchered; dear ones are cherished laboriously. Cheap wood chips and natural gas are burned off as waste; dear chips and gas are handled with labor and love as feedstock and fuel.

We need to use and improve land more, especially land already within the perimeter of existing streets and roads and utilities. We need to expand less into, and even contract away from, submarginal peripheral hinterlands that soak up so much capital, and return so little, so slowly.

We need to invest capital nearer the consumer, on the whole, and farther from the bowels of the Earth, for the labor content of value-added and service flows generally rises downstream, in processing, manufacturing ("making with hands"), services, trade, and so on. Even housing, much of which is lavish of land and capital, complements labor by sheltering it.

Yet I would not legislate on any of the above generalizations, for they are too vague, too exceptionable. That is why we have a price system, to pinpoint more exactly our goals, and help achieve them. Thus there are sharp differences among extractive industries. Oil is capital-intensive, to be sure, and cartelized as well, which makes it more so. But market gardening is labor-intensive, as shown in Table 1. Strip-mining is land-using and capital-using, but pit-mining uses labor.

We need something more subtle and accurate than a spasm of outrage against primary products. We need pressures that will encourage those primary producers that use more labor, and discourage those that waste capital and land, and will apply the same pressures in the same measure right down the line to the consumer. Again, that is what the market and the price system are for. We can achieve our goals best by working with them, not by throwing them out. The abstract generalizations of price theory often seem sterile and irrelevant because not clothed in material examples, yet they are more relevant to our actual policy needs than anything else because they deal with universal qualities of specific examples.

B. Faster Recovery of Capital

A general rule is that we should invest so as to recover capital more quickly. This means that more of cash flow will be recovery of principal, and less will be net income to the investor (i.e., interest payments). This will cause a faster flow of reinvestment to employ labor, and a faster flow of goods to feed us all. As an example, most investment in drilling oil and gas wells is financed from the cash flow of extant wells on stream; that is, it is internally financed by recycling capital already in the industry. Each time capital goes into the ground, it makes jobs. Then we must wait until it comes out again to make another round. The longer the wait, the fewer jobs created per decade by each million of capital. Oil and gas owners happen to carry an inventory of proven reserves whose minimum estimated life index is 12 years (and probably ranges much higher), making the job valence of capital here very low. As a corollary, most of the cash flow is property income, not capital recovery.

As another example, we could lower the capital cost of buildings a good deal by shortening their service lives. This might seem like a bad trade, since to reduce the cost by one-third we would reduce the life about two-thirds. But we could then build 50 percent more houses each year with the same capital, increasing the annual service flow by 50 percent. We would increase jobs three times, since each building would be replaced in one-third of the time. This example is highly oversimplified, ignoring maintenance and rehabilitation as alternatives, but gives an idea of how many jobs we destroy by sequestering a nation's capital in forms that pay out slowly.

Long advance inventories and durable flowing capital are not bad in themselves. Deferral of recovery is the bad, and durability is the good that usually accompanies it. The point here is that this good is forced on us beyond our voluntary willingness to pay for it, and part of the cost is involuntary unemployment.

The life span of particular capital items is not to be judged in isolation. Durable capital like that in a barn, a sewing machine, or restaurant furnishings may complement and have a high valence for labor "in parallel," that is, labor applied in using and operating the equipment and short-term investments in maintaining it. And the aggregate capital needs of the overall operation, in a consolidated accounting, may be a modest share, if the material moving through the process is finished and sold quickly.

The point about capital turnover is not that all durability is bad for labor, but that capital that appears to drive labor off the land really does so, even though labor helps produce the capital. And opening new lands, seemingly so favorable to labor, may actually damage labor by pulling capital into forms where it turns more slowly than before and so has a low valence for labor.

Or it may be that an operation uses little labor in parallel with capital but a great deal downstream. Thus pulp mills use more capital per man than sawmills, yet paper requires little downstream capital per man, while lumber needs a lot. Newsprint turns over daily, while lumber in buildings ties up capital for decades. Looking upstream, too, pulp mills use smaller logs, and chips, and so require much less capital in timber than sawmills do. It is the price system that weighs these compensating factors in the same balance and lets us achieve an optimal total deployment and mixture of labor, capital, and resources.

Again, some durable capital may help labor by obviating even more durable capital. Thus utility cores and elevators in high-rise buildings may yield back capital slowly, but they use much less (for the functions performed) than one alternative, that of expanding the city laterally by extending streets and utility lines (they return it faster, too, and with taxes to boot). Also, high-rises help labor by substituting capital for land, releasing a good deal of the latter for other uses.

Of course, there may be still better alternatives in rehabilitating older houses, in low-rise garden apartments, and so on, depending on particulars. The price system is what supplies us with these particulars.

The point is not to regard capital as a threat. Labor needs capital, and labor suffers now from the shortage of capital available to invest where its job-creating efficiency is high. The point is rather to mobilize capital and redeploy it so that its valence for labor is higher. This means making it available to small businesses, especially, and others that combine a little capital with a lot of labor. And this means keeping capital out of sinks and traps.

C. Monuments and Frontiers as Capital Sinks

Among sinks and traps of capital, the worst are monuments, frontiers, and wars. Let us survey these three sinks of capital. By "monuments" I mean things built with one eye on eternity, like the pyramids, and things that resemble them, like many works of governments and of other large organizations, the family seats of the very wealthy, and overmature timber. Many monuments are built to make jobs. The intent is lost in the execution, for monuments soak up a maximum of capital per job created, and yield a minimum of subsistence to advance to labor for the next job.

Public works to make jobs are one of history's great self-defeating, self-deluding, tragic ironies. There is only a one-shot payroll, after which the capital stops recycling for a long time, often forever. One of the great stupidities of all time, surely, was the English effort to relieve the Irish potato famine of 1845–1849 by hiring Irishmen to build roads. A large fraction of the working population, 570,000 men, toiled for the Board of Works, while food prices took off like a bird and half the people died of starvation (Woodham-Smith 1964: 137–160). The people needed subsistence for tomorrow morning, while public policy directed their effort to the next century. An unrecognized self-defeating policy is the most dangerous concept imaginable, for its failure will be taken as a sign that more is needed. Could this be why some civilizations left such amazing tombstones as the pyramids of Egypt, the temples of Angkor Wat and Greece and the Aztecs, the Incan canals, and the famous Roman roads, aqueducts, and public buildings? It is grand to amaze future archeologists, but not at the cost of destroying a civilization.

The monument-building syndrome has many aspects. Generally, a monument is anything too far ahead of demand. A great deal of heavy construction and civil engineering is monumental because tax-financed and tax-free. Advance extensions of transport-utility networks, sized for anticipated higher future needs, show monumental proclivities. They are often financed by cross-subsidy from the central system, and calculated to maintain the rate base, and/or internalize the profits. Excess capacity is often monumental, unless geared to reasonable forecasts of early need.

Monumental excess capacity results from the use of capital as the ante in some of life's poker games, where it is used to claim quotas: a share in a cartel, a water right, a bank charter, an air route, an oil lease, or what have you. "Buying business" is the current phrase for it. Inventories of extractive resources are commonly excessive for a complex of reasons (Gaffney 1967a).

"Master plans" and "fully integrated development" are usually monumental, unless carefully staged; splendid examples are the California Water Plan, the California highway system, the U.S. Interstate Highway System, and the sterile city of Brasilia. "Internalizing externalities," "economies of scale," "planning for future expansion," and "foresight" are excellent catchwords for monument builders. Meanwhile, life is what happens while we are making other plans, and obsolescence is what happens to big plans under construction or soon after. Governments, world banks, and Wall Street all tend to favor monuments for their publicity and promotional value. Hothouse "regional development," often promoted by local unions and contractors seeking jobs, has all the monumental traits. The headquarters and towers of large public and private organizations of every description tend toward the monumental, as do many of their other works. Every large organization seeks to internalize profits and keep the capital under control of the management.

Turning to "frontiers," gaining access to land via conquest and expansion is the imperialistic variation of Henry George's observation that labor applied to marginal land creates poverty. There is some truth in the old idea of the frontier as a safety valve for labor, but a generation of revisionist economic historians now has established that the frontier attracted more than its quota of capital per man, much of it prematurely. This led to recurrent crises of capital shortage in the 19th century. We tap frontiers by building monuments like the canals of the 1830s, the premature western railroads, and the dams of the Army Corps of Engineers. The payout from much developmental infrastructure capital comes in the form of increased land values. But to private owners this increment is income, most of which is normally consumed. Thus the capital is dissipated.

Frontiers of science and research and invention are another Lorelei for capital. As Boulding has rhymed,[37] they yield "benefits hereafter." These are tax exempt because the capital cost is expensible. Yoram Barzel (1968) has shown that the patent system, too, hyperactivates research in the same way that an open range overstimulates grazing. Research in subsidized agriculture experiment stations has gotten decades out ahead of dissemination and application. We need to embody more quickly in real capital what we already know, and adapt it more frequently to changing needs and scarcities, prices and costs, by replacing capital faster.

The energy frontier—including investments in alternative energy sources—is the current vogue. Incredible figures like $1 trillion are tossed off as capital "requirements" of pipelines, drilling, solar energy farms, tankers, ports, and so on, requirements that will obviously never be met because the capital does not exist or cannot be spared and will not be saved. As a broad generalization, where we use capital to substitute for land, or open frontiers, the capital is very durable. It lies in close with land and resembles it and takes on some of its durability. Wicksell (1954: 105) called such objects "rent-goods" because they so resemble land. Examples are surveying and exploring, cuts and fills, drainage, leveling, clearance, foundations, pipes, tiles, wells, pits, shafts, canals, tunnels, bridges, dams, and roadbeds. The permanence of land warrants building long life into capital that develops it. The rise of land values converts flowing into growing capital.

The upper levels of skyscrapers are also land substitutes of long life and high capital input. While intensive improvement of the best sites is generally desirable on balance all around, we suffer today from uneven improvement of sites, that is, high-rise sprawl or scattered hyperintensification. This pattern is more capital-using, as a total system, than more uniform improvements at moderate densities.

Frontier governments often go overboard competing for seed capital. They put a high value on immediate payrolls from construction—an aspect of their high time-preference. They give away too much to get it: tax holidays, de facto pollution easements, resource leases on giveaway terms, land grants, charters, franchises, special services, and so on. These nonmarket fillips pull capital into premature and marginal development on frontiers. The form of the lure for capital, like borrowing a city's credit, often prompts excessively capital-intensive forms of investment. Granting pollution easements lowers the capacity of surrounding land to house labor and attract people generally. During a boom, frontiers drain capital from older centers without doing much obvious immediate damage, but when it is time, as now, to renew the older centers, the frontiers do not return the capital. They demand more and more, having fallen into the seed-capital fallacy initially.

Subsidies to tap frontiers make land artificially abundant. This is supposed to help make outlets for labor, and in some ways does. But frontiering taps new land at the cost of sequestering capital. Frontiers soak up scarce capital and hold it so that it stops cycling and creating payrolls. Abundant land can still be badly used, and centuries of Caucasian expansion in the New World in a futile flight from unemployment have shown that frontiers are not enough. Labor does not need great reservoirs of underused land so much as pressure to use the land we already have, and working capital to help labor use it.

The third great sink of capital is war, and the policies of mercantilism and imperialism that attend it. War combines the frontier fallacy and the public works syndrome and the waste-makes-jobs doctrine into a claim on the national treasure that can become greatly inflated above the simple cost of police protection. It costs money to win land—and one does not always win. Someone, indeed, always loses. Policing marginal outposts after they are supposedly "won" can be a continuing drain, as in Japan, Korea, Berlin, Israel, or Iraq. If and when land is won and secured, finally, the net benefits of the whole military outlay often accrue to a very few large owners of the land in question, as in California and Hawaii, or to foreign potentates like

Mohammed Reza Pahlevi (the former Shah of Iran) or King Faisal who turn around and exploit us and drain us of more capital, or to multinationals that reinvest mainly abroad and bed down with the foreign potentates. Imperialism has generally been an economic catastrophe for most of the players for the benefit of a few.

To keep capital from wasting into those sinks calls for massive institutional and attitudinal changes. Attitudes are surprisingly adaptable, and we see evidence on every hand of eagerness to adapt life styles to scarcity, even in advance of need. Institutions are something else. They are the stubborn rear guard, shutting out the signals of the times and resisting our efforts to budge them. But this, too, will pass in the coming time of troubles, as the lag of institutions behind current needs creates overpowering tensions.

D. The Role of Taxes

Here, we focus on tax policy. The question is, are we prepared, once the rear guards yield, to budge tax policy in the right directions? Rule One is to retain and strengthen the price system as much as possible, and be wary of rules couched in other terms. The price mechanism is the only way we have of treating the economy as a total system and applying rules consistently in the same measure throughout.

The best tax on all counts is the part of the property tax that falls on land values. The part that falls on capital is far from the worst tax. It is the surest way to tax capital without favoring longer lives over shorter. So we should make greater use of the property tax at the same time as we increase the share of it that falls on land. The property tax on holding land presses landholders to use the land. This employs labor and produces goods and services. It also abates the pressure to waste precious capital developing new lands. The land tax pressure should be applied with greatest force to land already serviced by extant underutilized capital.

There is a hard choice to make when we know that some extant public works, roads, and lines are badly placed in terms of long-run good planning. The choice has to hinge on particulars. Today one overriding particular is the crisis of capital shortage, and the choice should often go to pressing into use land presently serviced. As there is a surplus, however, we have some choices and can begin immediately an orderly retreat from the most remote submarginal extensions and outposts. But infilling of some good land bypassed by public works may now wait a while until capital is cheaper.

Optimal infill calls for land assessments more influenced by near than far future income. But then, high interest rates that signal capital shortage will push market values that way anyway. There is a lot to be said for having assessors simply follow that most useful of pilots, the market. Added revenues from land taxes should be used to lower other taxes. But the property tax on buildings should not be the first to go. It is the only tax based on capital standing still instead of moving. It serves much like an increase in the rate of interest, to steer capital into forms cycling more quickly, with higher valence for labor. Realization or liquidation of capital, the base for income and excise taxes, is what feeds us as consumers and employs us as workers. Passive investment, the base for the property tax, employs no one.

We must prepare to accept the decline in investments of high capital intensity that a less-biased tax system would cause. For that is the whole point, to spare scarce capital and release it for higher uses. Even overmature trees, a form of extravagant monument revered by many otherwise thrifty and ascetic outdoorspersons, must yield, although it consoles some to note that capital shortage also dictates using more labor on each log after cutting, and fewer logs in each house.

The first taxes to cut are payroll taxes. The major payroll tax is the personal income tax on earned income (wages and salaries). How far to carry this gets into value judgments beyond our present scope, but some first steps are clear enough. We should forget about revenue sharing, which substitutes federal payroll and other activity-based taxes for local property taxes. This taxes labor to relieve property. Federal grants to local people should go to persons, not governments, and what better way to do this than lower the personal income tax on earned income?

Among other benefits, the shift from area-based grants to person-based transfers would help make localities more hospitable toward workers as residents. Currently, central government taxes individuals to subsidize local governments, which turn around and zone out poor individuals because their disposable after-tax income is so low they might dilute local property tax bases. Ideally, central governments would relate to individuals as their net benefactors instead, and localities would compete to attract persons. Lowering payroll taxes increases the incentive both to work and to hire, and a secure employed worker would be as good a neighbor as one usually finds.

We should decline current proposals to widen income tax loopholes for property. This can only shove more of a burden onto payrolls and make our income tax resemble more that of England, the sick man of Europe.[38]

Labor is supposed to benefit from *greater investment,* but our analysis has shown that labor needs *faster reinvestment.* Ignoring this central truth is one of the truly great and damaging economic fallacies, leading us to think we must spoil capital to employ labor. It is, rather, payroll taxes that slow down reinvestment, by making labor look artificially dear to employers and motivating them to substitute capital and land for it. Special tax favors for capital almost all favor deepening capital and slowing reinvestment. The only exception would be the investment tax credit, if stripped of the present sliding scale.

Instead, we should plug the loopholes for land and capital so that we can lower the tax rate, relieving payrolls. It would be a good idea to reinstate a generous lower rate on earned income as well, for we will be a long time plugging a hundred clever loopholes, some subtle and others complex beyond easy reform.

We should remove biases that favor long over short investments. It is too much to expect that we could tax accruals and imputed income annually, as the Haig-Simons logic would have it, and the more workable alternative is to strengthen the property tax, which reaches the same end by a different route. But we could remove all explicit biases granting lower rates to longer investments. Capital gains treatment is the greatest of these, with all it implies, and we could also do away with all the sliding scales that apply higher rates against shorter investments. Although we cannot easily tax appreciation other than by the property tax, we can and do deduct depreciation, and a neutral tax policy here will key tax depreciation to real asset value depreciation, removing biases against shorter-lived capital. Having turned the personal income tax back into a tax that includes property income, we could abate the corporate income tax, with its powerful bias for internalizing new capital. A progressive corporate rate would break up the largest corporations, which, as we have seen, employ the fewest workers per unit of capital, and become "too big to fail." Undistributed profits should be taxable to stockholders on the same basis as dividends.

Public works are major sinks of capital. They need to pay property and income taxes, and the agencies in charge should show these in the budget, if only as shadow costs, along with interest at full market rates. Here we need tread carefully, remembering the logic of marginal cost pricing, and remembering that the right works in the right place, like subways in New York, can save much more capital than they consume. Let us look last to the subway for revenue, and first to the capital and land in highways, cars, trucks, terminals, gas stations, parking lots, garages, refineries, and car lots.

A decreasing-cost distribution system should be priced to yield a deficit because a price based on marginal cost cannot cover fixed costs. The value of service at the low price is imputed to the land served, and that is the proper tax base. The deficit-yielding subsystem has no value and should pay no property tax, but receive a subsidy. This is the principle of "marginal-cost pricing." That is a good principle in its place, but it is hard to keep it there. Cross-subsidies and submarginal extensions become the rule, wasting capital. Here the solution is user charges, especially peak pricing and area rates, which force users to economize on the capital and serve as substitutes for excess capacity. Fortunately, there is a wide literature on this subject to supplement these spare and summary words.

Another needed change is the tax treatment of income from offshore. We cannot suddenly create much new capital, but we can summon back a great mass of it now lost to us offshore by removing the egregious special loopholes for U.S. capital invested abroad.

These are some steps toward a tax system less biased for monuments and frontiers, more geared to help make jobs by mobilizing and activating wealth. If we do this, and like the results, we can go further. Meantime, these steps represent substantial progress. They will help us find full employment on our present land base, permanently, freed from the compulsion to grow and expand that we inherited from generations of ancestors who had not yet learned the finite limits of the Earth. We can continue to create capital, and we can apply new ideas more quickly than now as faster replacement lets us embody new techniques in capital in a shorter time. Thus we can grow in every good sense by substituting real progress for the random lateral expansion of the past. We can find full employment in peaceful labor on our share of this small planet and, doing so, drop the burden of imperialism that may otherwise destroy us.

Notes

1. Since land is not depreciable, these tax preferences theoretically do not apply to land income. In practice, however, land income is as sheltered as capital income. See Gaffney (1970a: 405–415). Mainstream macroeconomists have not been at all alert to this problem.

2. They are simply financed with owned instead of borrowed capital. The relevant "term" is how long the capital sunk is tied up before being fully recovered. "Recovery" is the residual after deducting interest from cash or service flow, and may be very slow and even negative when interest rates are high and cash flow low.

3. If the interest rate on the mortgage is only 4 percent, the proportion of the total cost paid in interest falls from 75 percent to 57 percent. If the interest rate rises to 10 percent, it rises to 80 percent.

4. A full accounting of the capital value of a tree would have to consider the stream of ecological benefits it provides while it is growing, particularly in the form of the offsite benefits of preventing downstream flooding. As important as those spillover benefits are, they take us away from the central point of this discussion—the effects on labor of capital investment.

5. A more correct analysis would take into account the return to the land on which the trees are growing. Since timber grows on relatively marginal land with few alternative uses, the rent is low. For the initial capital investment of $100, the land under those trees might be $5 per year, and the future value of those payments in 63 years (at 8 percent) would be $7,900. Thus, the return to land could be as great or greater than the return to capital. For now, however, the point is simply that labor receives little.

6. As Scherer (2008: 1) reports: "For every $1 billion in government infrastructure spending, 28,000 new jobs are created, according to a federal study quoted by Kenneth Simonson, chief economist at the Associated General Contractors of America. But only about 25 percent of those jobs are for construction workers. Another 25 percent are supplying industries, such as for concrete or lumber. The rest are jobs like retail and others created indirectly because workers are spending money."

7. The sheep were capital in exactly the same sense that trees are: they are assets that ripen in value over time, depreciate, and require maintenance. In contrast to trees, sheep provide an economic service annually after an initial period.

8. An assault within the economics profession on the assumption that capital is homogeneous was launched decades ago by Pierro Sraffa and Joan Robinson, leading to very technical and abstract debates, without clear practical implications. Nevertheless, Paul Samuelson and other neo-classical economists conceded that their models of capital were faulty and that measures of capital intensity are necessarily ambiguous (and involve some amount of circular reasoning). These debates did not, however, influence mainstream economic thinking in the United States. As one recent summary explains: "In the United States, . . . mainstream economics goes on as if the controversy had never occurred. Macroeconomics textbooks discuss 'capital' as if it were a well-defined concept—which it is not, except in a very special one-capital-good world (or under other unrealistically restrictive conditions). The problems of heterogeneous capital goods have also been ignored in the 'rational expectations revolution' and in virtually all econometric work" (Burmeister 2000: 310). For our purposes, the relevance of the controversy is that American macroeconomic theory has simply assumed away all of the differences in capital intensity associated with alternative factor mixes, so that the issues being raised here have been entirely ignored.

9. The growth model developed by Robert Solow posits technological change as the factor needed to overcome the diminishing returns associated with additions to the capital stock per worker. In effect, this means more capital per worker is needed just to stay in place, which reinforced the bias in favor of capital intensity that was already present in the Harrod-Domar model.

10. There was a lengthy debate in the 1980s as to whether rising energy prices would cause demand for capital to rise (if they are substitutes) or fall (if they are complements). Inconsistent statistical results fueled the debate until improved statistical techniques resolved the question on the side of substitutability. For a discussion of three different statistical measures of elasticity of substitution, see Chambers (1988) and Thompson and Taylor (1995).

11. An older, perceptive treatment is Rose (1974).

12. Gaffney (1976b: Appendix 3) explains mathematically the separate effects of labor and capital inputs. The result can be described intuitively as follows. If the capital invested on land depreciates quickly and must be renewed every two or three years, labor-demanding production processes will be chosen over low-intensity uses. But if the tax system encourages capital investment, labor will be displaced. This is particularly true of capital with a

long payout period, where the durable investment locks land into a single use for a long period, and labor will be largely displaced from that land over the life of the investment.

13. Of course, the return to land from tomatoes is highly leveraged and volatile as a short-run gamble, but that is not our concern here. We are averaging out the good years and the bad.

14. The irrigable acreage is from California Department of Water Resources, Division of Planning and Local Assistance (2001). Crop acreage is from U.S. Department of Agriculture, National Agricultural Statistics Service, California Field Office (2005: 1). There were, in 2004–2005, around 800,000 acres in grapes, 550,000 acres in almonds, 300,000 in other nuts, 240,000 in citrus fruit, and about 300,000 in various other fruits and nuts.

15. We have drawn data from 1964 because the data in more recent years did not include the number of employees in each firm. There is no reason to assume that the relationships we are investigating here between capital and labor have changed over time.

16. An example of such thinking, unrelieved by any apparent doubt of its adequacy, is Hickman (1965). Nor could I name any Brookings economist who takes a different view. Close to power and the application of economic ideas to policy, Brookings plays a central role in defining the orthodoxy that has dominated policy to date.

17. In general the CRF is $i / [1 - e^{-ni}]$, where i is the interest rate, n is the number of years, and e is the base of the natural exponential function. If i = 0.07 and n = 10, then CRF = 0.139. That calculation is slightly different from the one actually used in accounting, however, because it assumes continuous, instantaneous interest calculations. If interest is computed on the remaining principal once a year, the CRF is 0.142.

18. The same wage shares apply if investments are "normalized" by staggering purchases and retirements over time. If new harvesters are produced and old ones retired at a constant rate, say, one a year, there must be 10 units out bearing interest for every work crew making a new one. The share of labor in the income falls as the capital pays off more slowly, with the wage share the same as for an individual harvester.

19. A mathematical treatment of the way land rent and the life cycle of capital influences the ratio of labor to capital can be found in Gaffney (1976b: 153–158).

20. Conversely, a *decrease* in unit labor cost to employers leverages an increase in property income with a nine to one multiplier. So, 1 percent off labor cost adds 9 percent to property income, drawing new investment into labor-using enterprise in the most compelling way.

21. The arguments about who bears the tax burden have nothing to do with who directly pays the government. The issue is whether the tax on work affects hours of work. If it does, then employers have to raise wages to attract

workers, meaning that part of the final burden falls on business. If taxes on work do not influence work behavior, then the tax falls entirely on workers, including the half of the payroll tax currently contributed by employers. If taxes do not affect willingness to work, then employers can reduce wages by enough to compensate for the payroll tax they pay. The marginal tax rate of 30 percent that I have posited in the text is based on the assumption that workers end up paying 100 percent of the payroll and income tax. That would occur only if wage earners work as many hours per week regardless of the size of their take-home paychecks, so employers do not have to pay higher wages to compensate for the taxes they take out. However, if wage taxes discourage work at the margin (overtime, second jobs), then part of the cost of those taxes is borne by employers. Most business owners already take this for granted.

22. The U.S. Chamber of Commerce reports that benefits are 39 percent of payroll costs, of which 11 percent are from health insurance, 10 percent are compensation for time off, and retirement and savings plans are 8 percent (Taub 2003). Median health insurance costs per worker covered rose 62 percent between 1999 and 2005, according to a study by the Henry J. Kaiser Family Foundation (2008), which is based on U.S. Bureau of Labor Statistics data from the National Compensation Survey, 1999–2005.

23. Interest earned by pension funds is tax-deferrable, but that helps the pensioner as a capitalist, not as a worker. Some pension plan deductions (like those of the state of Wisconsin) are not tax-deferrable—the worker pays tax on unrealized income, even though property does not.

24. There is a wide literature on this, including Holland (1969).

25. Before World War II, salaries paid by state and local governments were free of federal income tax. Then salaries became taxable, while the cost of hiring capital remained exempt.

26. See Forbes (1965: 27), showing how housing builders can expense water supply systems. William Condrell, writing in the *Timber Tax Journal*, October 1970, also discusses how Section 175 of the Internal Revenue Code lets "farmers" expense soil and water conservation, and Section 182 lets them expense land clearing.

27. Via defaulting on nonrecourse loans. See Forbes (1974: 40–41).

28. "Combining with capital" refers to producing durable improvements. These might be for personal use or for later resale with capital gains treatment. Both are common.

29. An exception may be poultry. That is, however, very unusual. It is part of a general bias for agriculture inherent in cash basis accounting allowed for livestock.

30. There are several points in tax law, besides those already noted, in which excess depreciation is recaptured using a sliding scale where the amount recaptured declines with the number of years before sale.

31. Liquor, of course, is highly taxed outside the income tax, by excises, but the excise tax levied upon sale has a bias for longevity, and greatly favors Scotch, maturing in 10 years, over vodka, which can age in the bottle in as little as 10 days.

32. Bartlett (2009) describes the way the indexing debate has fared in recent decades: "For many years, economists have advocated indexing capital gains for inflation so that taxes would apply only to real gains. . . . Rather than adopt inflation indexing for capital gains, Congress has generally allowed a lower rate on capital gains than that on ordinary income. . . . During the George H. W. Bush administration . . . the Treasury Department [tried] to bypass Congress and institute indexing of capital gains for inflation using its regulatory power, [but] . . . the Justice Department issued a legal opinion saying that this was not possible. Since then, the issue of indexing mostly died, with Republicans concentrating their efforts on cutting the tax rate on capital gains to its present level of 15 percent."

33. He credited it to Böhm-Bawerk, who, however, expounded it very roundaboutly, if not obscurely.

34. 7.273 years, to be more exact.

35. Instead of K = FP, the proper formula is now $K = (F (e^{Pi-1})) / i$, which is greater than FP.

36. In practice, "investment" is used very loosely by macroeconomists for spending on durables, without careful distinctions of net and gross, as the logic would require. No careful effort at all is made to estimate real depreciation, the problem being buried by using GNP instead of national income.

37.   In modern industry, Research
       Has become a kind of church
       Where rubber-aproned acolytes
       Perform the ceremonial rites
       And firms spend funds they do not hafter
       In hope of benefits hereafter.

—K. Boulding

38. Ironically, the data come from Joel Barlow (1973: 432–433) of Covington and Burling that British taxes bear more lightly on capital than do those of other major capitalist nations.

References

Althouse, Irvin H. (1942). *Water Requirements of Tulare County: Report to Tulare County Board of Supervisors.* Mimeo.

Averch, Harvey, and Leland L. Johnson. (1962). "Behavior of the Firm Under Regulatory Constraint." *American Economic Review* 52(December): 1052–1069.

Barlow, Joel. (1973). "The Tax Law Bias Against Investment in Production Facilities." *National Tax Journal* 26(3): 415–431.

Bartlett, Bruce. (2009, March 13). "A Strategy for Capital Gains." *Forbes.* Available online at: http://www.forbes.com/2009/03/12/obama-capital-gains-treasury-opinions-columnists-federal-reserve.html

Barzel, Yoram. (1968). "Optimal Timing of Innovations." *Review of Economics and Statistics* 50(3): 348–355.

Berndt, Ernst R., and David O. Wood. (1979). "Engineering and Econometric Interpretations of Energy-Capital Complementarity." *American Economic Review* 69(3): 342–354.

Berry, R. Albert, and William R. Cline. (1979). *Agrarian Structure and Productivity in Developing Countries.* Baltimore, MD: Johns Hopkins University Press.

Board of Governors of the Federal Reserve Board. (2009, March 12). "L.118.b Private Pension Funds Defined Benefit Plans." *Flow of Funds Accounts of the United States (Z.1).* Federal Reserve Statistical Release. Available online at: http://www.federalreserve.gov/releases/Z1/Current/accessible/l118b.htm

Burmeister, Edwin. (2000). "The Capital Theory Controversy." In *Critical Essays on Piero Sraffa's Legacy in Economics.* Ed. Heinz D. Kurz. Cambridge: Cambridge University Press.

Business Week. (1972, March 25). "Why Ma Bell Constantly Needs More Money." 57–58.

Business Wire. (2007, May 29). "Taxi Medallion Sale for Record $600,000 Reported by Medallion Financial Corporation." Available online at: http://www.businesswire.com/portal/site/google/?ndmViewId=news_view&newsId=20070529005784&newsLang=en

California Department of Water Resources, Division of Planning and Local Assistance. (2001). "California Land & Water Use: Irrigated Crop Area." Available online at: http://www.landwateruse.water.ca.gov/annualdata/landuse/2001/landuselevels.cfm

Chambers, Robert G. (1988). *Applied Production Analysis: A Dual Approach.* Cambridge: Cambridge University Press.

Dangerfield, Jeanne. (1973). *Sowing the Till: A Background Paper on Tax Loss Farming.* San Francisco: Agribusiness Accountability Project. Reprinted in *Congressional Record*, May 16, 1973, Vol. 119, Part 13, 93rd Cong. 1st Session: 15988–15996. Page number cited is from *Congressional Record.*

Domar, Evsey D. (1957). *Essays in the Theory of Economic Growth.* New York: Oxford University Press.

Downing, Paul B. (1969). *The Economics of Urban Sewage Disposal.* New York: Praeger.

Eckstein, Otto. (1974, January 5). "Resharpening the Tools." *Business Week* 56.

Fisher, Ernest M. (1933). "Speculation in Suburban Lands." *American Economic Review* 23(1): 152–162.

Forbes. (1965, August 15). "One Man's Poison." 27.

———. (1974, August 15). "A Loophole for Pigs." 40–41.

Fortune Directory. (1964). New York: Time, Inc.

Friedman, Milton. (1968). "The Role of Monetary Policy." *American Economic Review* 58(1): 1–17.

Gaffney, Mason. (1961). "Diseconomies Inherent in Western Water Laws: A California Case Study." In *Economic Analysis of Multiple Use: The Arizona Watershed Program; A Case Study of Multiple Use.* Denver, CO: Western Agricultural Economics Research Council. Available online at: www.masongaffney.org/publications/H3-DiseconomiesInherentinWestern WaterLaws21.CV.CV.pdf

———. (1967a). "Editor's Conclusion." In *Extractive Resources and Taxation.* Ed. Mason Gaffney. Madison: University of Wisconsin Press. Available online at: www.masongaffney.org/publications/B1Extractive_Resources_ Conclusion.CV.pdf

———. (1967b). "Tax-Induced Slow Turnover of Capital." *Western Economic Journal* 5(4): 308–323.

———. (1969). "Adequacy of Land as a Tax Base." In *The Assessment of Land Value.* Ed. Daniel Holland. Madison: University of Wisconsin Press. Available online at: www.masongaffney.org/publications/G1Adequacy_ of_Land.CV.pdf

———. (1970a). "The Treatment of Land Income." In *Economic Analysis and the Efficiency of Government.* 91st Congress, 1st Session, Part 2. Washington, DC: U.S. Government Printing Office.

———. (1970b/1971). "Tax-Induced Slow Turnover of Capital." *American Journal of Economics and Sociology* 29(1): 25–32; 29(2): 179–197; 29(3): 277–287; 29(4): 409–424; 30(1): 105–111. Available online at: http://www. masongaffney.org/publications/I11-TaxInducedSlowTurnoverofCapital. CV.CV.pdf

———. (1972). *Benefits of Military Spending: An Inquiry into the Doctrine That National Defense Is a Public Good.* Unpublished ms. Available online at: www.masongaffney.org/workpapers/1972_Benefits_of_Military_ Spending.pdf

———. (1976a). "Objectives of Government Policy in Leasing Mineral Lands." In *Mineral Leasing as an Instrument of Public Policy.* Eds. Michael Crommelin and Andrew Thomson. Vancouver: University of British Columbia Press. Available online at: http://www.masongaffney.org/publications/ B4-ObjectivesofGovernmentPolicyinLeasingMineralLands.CV.pdf

———. (1976b). "Toward Full Employment with Limited Land and Capital." In *Property Taxation, Land Use and Public Policy.* Ed. Arthur Lynn, Jr. Madison: University of Wisconsin Press.

———. (1977). "When to Build What." In *Local Service Pricing Policies and their Effect on Urban Spatial Structure.* Ed. Paul Downing. Vancouver:

University of British Columbia Press. Available online at: http://www.masongaffney.org/publications/E5-WhenToBuildWhat-LocalServicePricingPolicies.CV.pdf

———. (1982). *Oil and Gas: The Unfinished Tax Reform.* Working paper, Department of Economics, University of California–Riverside. Available online at: http://www.masongaffney.org/publications/B13-Oil&GasUnfinishedTaxReform.CV.pdf

———. (1991). "The Partiality of Indexing Capital Gains." *Proceedings of the 83rd Annual Conference on Taxation of the NTA-TIA.* Columbus, OH: National Tax Association.

———. (2006). "A Simple General Test for Tax Bias." *American Journal of Economics and Sociology* 65(3): 733–749.

———. (2009). "The Hidden Taxable Capacity of Land: Enough and to Spare." *International Journal of Social Economics* 36(4): 328–411.

George, Henry. ([1879] 1979). *Progress and Poverty.* New York: Robert Schalkenbach Foundation.

Haig, Robert M. (1921). "The Concept of Income—Economic and Legal Aspects." Pp. 1–28 in *The Federal Income Tax.* Ed. Robert M. Haig. New York: Columbia University Press.

Hansen, Alvin. (1939). "Economic Progress and Declining Population Growth." *American Economic Review* 29(1): 1–7.

Harrod, Roy. (1948). *Towards a Dynamic Economics: Some Recent Developments of Economic Theory and Their Application to Policy.* London: Macmillan.

Henry J. Kaiser Family Foundation. (2008, March 14). "Employer Health Insurance Costs and Worker Compensation." Available online at: http://www.kff.org/insurance/snapshot/chcm030808oth.cfm

Hickman, Bert G. (1965). *Investment Demand and U.S. Economic Growth.* Washington, DC: Brookings Institution.

Holland, Daniel (ed.). (1969). *The Assessment of Land Value.* Madison: University of Wisconsin Press.

Hoover, Dale M. (1970). "An Economic Analysis of Farmland Development." *Agricultural Economics Research* 22(2): 37–44.

Houthakker, Hendrik. (1967). "The Great Farm Tax Mystery." *Challenge* (January–February): 12–13, 38–39.

Isard, Walter, and Robert E. Coughlin. (1957). *Municipal Costs and Revenues Resulting from Community Growth.* Wellesley, MA: Chandler-Davis.

Jacobs, Jane. (1961). *The Death and Life of Great American Cities.* New York: Random House.

Kahn, Alfred. (1964). "The Depletion Allowance in the Context of Cartelization." *American Economic Review* 54(4): 286–314.

Kahn, C. Harry. (1968). *Employee Compensation Under the Income Tax.* Princeton: Princeton University Press.

Kendrick, John. (1961). *Productivity Trends in the U.S.* Princeton: Princeton University Press.

Krugman, Paul. (2007). "Introduction." In John Maynard Keynes. *The General Theory of Employment, Interest, and Money.* New York: Palgrave Macmillan. Available online at: www.pkarchive.org/economy/GeneralTheory KeynesIntro.html

Lampman, Robert J. (1962). *The Share of Wealth-Holders in National Wealth, 1922–1956.* Princeton, NJ: Princeton University Press.

Lovins, Amory B., E. Kyle Datta, Odd-Even Bustnes, Jonathan G. Koomey, and Nathan J. Glasgow. (2005). *Winning the Oil Endgame: Innovation for Profit, Jobs and Security.* Snowmass, CO: Rocky Mountain Institute. Available online at: http://nc.rmi.org/Page.aspx?pid=269&srcid=269, after registration with Rocky Mountain Institute.

Mace, Ruth. (1961). *Municipal Cost-Revenue Research in the United States: A Critical Survey of Research to Measure Municipal Costs and Revenues in Relation to Land Uses and Areas: 1933–1960.* Chapel Hill: University of North Carolina.

Mill, John Stuart. (1872). *Principles of Political Economy.* Boston: Lee S. Shepard.

Murray, Charles. (1984). *Losing Ground: American Social Policy, 1950–1980.* New York: Basic Books.

Muth, Richard. (1973). "Capital and Current Expenditures in the Production of Housing." In *Government Spending and Land Values.* Ed. Lowell Harriss. Madison: University of Wisconsin Press.

National Planning Association. (1972). *The Effect of Federal Income Taxes on the Structure of Agriculture.* Washington, DC: National Planning Association.

Phelps, Edmund S. (1968). "Money-Wage Dynamics and Labor-Market Equilibrium." *Journal of Political Economy* 76(4): 678–711.

Real Estate Research Corporation. (1974). *The Costs of Sprawl.* Washington, DC: U.S. Government Printing Office.

Reisner, Marc. (1993). *Cadillac Desert: The American West and Its Disappearing Water.* New York: Penguin.

Rose, Sanford. (1974, March). "The Far-Reaching Consequences of High-Priced Oil." *Fortune* 106–112, 191–196.

Samuelson, Paul A. (1955). *Economics,* 3rd ed. New York: McGraw-Hill.

——. (1970). "Nixon Must Alter His Game Plan." *Washington Post* (August 23): G1.

Scherer, Ron. (2008). "US Task: Put Jobless Into Jobs; With Biggest Job Losses Since 1974, Obama Plans Massive Public Works." *Christian Science Monitor* (December 8): 1. Available online at: http://www.csmonitor.com/2008/1208/p01s04-usgn.html.

Sharp, Travis. (2008, February 20). "U.S. Defense Spending, 2001–2009." Center for Arms Control and Non-Proliferation. Available online at: http://www.armscontrolcenter.org/policy/securityspending/articles/defense_spending_since_2001/

Simons, Henry. (1938). *Personal Income Taxation: The Definition of Income as a Problem of Fiscal Policy.* Chicago: University of Chicago Press.

Smith, Adam. ([1776] 1937). *Wealth of Nations.* New York: Random House.

Stockfisch, Jack. (1957). "Investment Incentive, Taxation, and Accelerated Depreciation." *Southern Economic Journal* 24(1): 28–40.

Taub, Stephen. (2003, February 5). "Benefits Nearly 40 percent of Payroll, Survey Finds." Available online at: http://www.cfo.com/article.cfm/3008274

Thompson, James W., and Edgar N. Johnson. (1937). *An Introduction to Medieval Europe.* New York: W. W. Norton & Company.

Thompson, Peter, and Timothy G. Taylor. (1995). "The Capital-Energy Substitutability Debate: A New Look." *Review of Economics and Statistics* 77(3): 565–569.

Udell, Jon. (1969). *Economic and Social Consequences of the Merger Movement in Wisconsin.* Madison, WI: Bureau of Business Research.

U.S. Bureau of Economic Analysis. (2009). "All Fixed Asset Tables." Available online at: http://www.bea.gov/national/FA2004/SelectTable.asp

U.S. Bureau of Reclamation, Sacramento Office. (1958). *Report on Crop Production in the Friant-Kern Canal Service Area.* Mimeo.

U.S. Census Bureau. (1953). Census of Agriculture. Vol. V. Part 6. *A Special Report: Agriculture 1950—A Graphic Summary.* Washington, DC: Government Printing Office.

U.S. Congress Joint Economic Committee, Subcommittee on Economy in Government. (1969). *The Analysis and Evaluation of Public Expenditure: The PPB System.* Washington, DC: U.S. Government Printing Office.

U.S. Council of Economic Advisers. (2009). *Economic Report of the President, 2009.* Available online at: http://www.gpoaccess.gov/eop/tables09.html

U.S. Department of Agriculture, National Agricultural Statistics Service, California Field Office. (2005). *California Fruit and Nut Review* 25(8). Available online at: http://www.nass.usda.gov/Statistics_by_State/California/Publications/Fruits_and_Nuts/200508frtrv.pdf

U.S. Department of Energy, Energy Information Administration. (2006). "Table E-1p, World Energy Intensity: Total Primary Energy Consumption per Dollar of Gross Domestic Product Using Purchasing Power Parities, 1980–2006." *International Energy Annual 2006.* Available online at: http://www.eia.doe.gov/pub/international/iea2006/iea_2006.zip

——. (2009, March 10). "Short-Term Energy Outlook." Available online at: http://www.eia.doe.gov/pub/forecasting/steo/oldsteos/mar09.pdf

U.S. Department of the Treasury, Internal Revenue Service. (1965). *Tax Guide for Small Businesses.* Pub. No. 334.

Weeks, David, and Charles West. (1927). *The Problem of Securing Closer Relationship Between Agricultural Development and Irrigation Construction.* Agricultural Economic Service Bulletin 435. Berkeley: University of California Printing Office.

Wicksell, Knut. (1934). *Lectures on Political Economy,* Vol. I. Trans. E. Classen. New York: Macmillan.

——. (1954). *Value, Capital and Rent.* Trans. S. H. Frowein. London: G. Allen & Irwin.

Williams, Ellis T. (1968). *State Forest Tax Law Digest, 1967.* USDA Forest Service, Misc. Pub. No. 1077.

Wilson, John. (1974). Personal correspondence to Dwayne Chapman (January 16).

Woodham-Smith, Cecil. (1964). *The Great Hunger.* New York: Signet.

3
Money, Credit, and Crisis

By MASON GAFFNEY*

ABSTRACT. The financial crisis of 2008–2009 has antecedents in earlier crises, including the Great Depression. In order to understand how the current crisis arose, we must review the most fundamental principles of banking. Doing that, we find that the main service performed by banks is the creation of liquidity, a collective good that can be destroyed by the behavior of individual financial institutions. The key element in creating liquidity is the monetization of various types of collateral. When collateral takes the form of land or capital that turns over slowly, banks lose liquidity. That is why major banking crises have frequently been associated with real estate lending. The best way to restore health to the financial system is by restoring the principles of the "real bills" doctrine that requires loans to be self-liquidating.

I

Introduction

THE MOST OBVIOUS CULPRIT in the recent economic quagmire is the errors in judgment made by the managers of banks and other financial institutions.[1] As a result of these errors, a number of them have gone into receivership or been merged with better capitalized banks. According to the U.S. Federal Deposit Insurance Corporation (2008), an average of 3.4 banks failed per year from 2000 through 2007, followed by 25 bank failures in 2008, and another 25 failures by April 17, 2009. The failure of Washington Mutual Bank (WaMu) in 2008 was the largest bank failure in U.S. history. It held nearly $307 billion in assets when it was declared insolvent. IndyMac Federal Bank, with

*Mason Gaffney has been a Professor of Economics at the University of California, Riverside for 33 years; e-mail: m.gaffney@dslextreme.com. He is the author of *The Corruption of Economics*, an explanation of how land became excluded from neoclassical economic models. He has also written extensively on various aspects of resource economics, urban economics, tax policy, and capital theory.

American Journal of Economics and Sociology, Vol. 68, No. 4 (October, 2009).

$32 billion in assets when it went into receivership in July 2008, was the largest savings and loan in the Los Angeles area. Its failure was the fourth largest in U.S. history.

To provide a bit of perspective, the deposits of suspended banks in 1931 and 1933 amounted to around 0.6 percent and 2.9 percent of GNP in those two years, respectively (U.S. Bureau of the Census 1960: Series X-173, F-1). The combined failures of WaMu and IndyMac alone amounted to 2.4 percent of GDP in 2008. This does not include (a) the failure of many smaller banks; (b) the more than $500 billion of write-downs and credit losses as of September 2008 (before the bankruptcy of Lehman Brothers, valued at $639 billion in May 2008) (CNBC.com 2008); or (c) the billions in additional asset losses around the world after the Lehman bankruptcy led to liquidation of commercial real estate holdings at fire-sale prices. Surpassing all of the above liquidations, however, was the decline of asset values sustained by the Federal National Mortgage Association, Fannie Mae, and the Federal Home Loan Mortgage Corporation, Freddie Mac, which owned or guaranteed over $5 trillion of the $12 trillion mortgage market before they were placed under the conservatorship of the Federal Housing Finance Agency (FHFA) on September 7, 2008. By that time, their share prices were down about 90 percent from their high in 2007 (Goldfarb, Cho, and Appelbaum 2008: A1).

Crises involving large numbers of bank failures have occurred with some degree of regularity in the United States and other countries, although the current crisis would appear to be on a larger scale than previous contractions. In each case, the pundits have attributed the most sensational cases to personal fraud and malfeasance. Certainly, there are individuals who manipulate markets, gamble with invested funds instead of acting prudently, or extend loans to people or institutions with bad credit histories. There are also regulators who look the other way rather than enforcing the rules strictly. So it is easy to view the debacle entirely through the lens of personal morality.

The more important question, however, is who or what creates the *conditions* under which imprudent and fraudulent behavior by banks and regulators take place. To find out the answer to that question, we have to go behind the headlines to understand the fundamental nature of banking and what kinds of regulation are appropriate to prevent crises of the sort we currently find ourselves in. As we shall soon see, the fundamental problem lies in bank lending in which real estate serves as the collateral. By lending for housing and nonresidential land and buildings, banks risk losing their capacity to remain liquid, which thereby puts the entire financial system in jeopardy.

A. The Trap of Conventional Wisdom

In our effort to learn about the underlying causes of financial crises, we cannot simply turn to standard textbooks on money and banking. Of course, they are useful for explaining some of the basic mechanisms, such as fractional reserve banking. But a subtle bias enters into all conventional writing about the financial system, which creates the illusion that banks can be either healthy or insolvent independent of the real economy, as if finance operated in a different universe than the world of work and production.

The ordinary economist, even more than the ordinary person, is terrified of being thought different, or outside the loop, or "poorly trained," or "unaware" of what others are saying. Ordinary texts therefore keep in step with each other, in stupefying conformity. Conformity has some social value, especially, of course, to the extent that the conventional wisdom is true, and when the alternative is chaos. However, conformity breeds habits of suppressing observation, and shutting out facts that do not fit one's model. It also lets a few influential people manipulate and intimidate and exploit others by controlling their "training," and defining quality, and dehumanizing those outside what they call "the mainstream." This leads to error at all times, but more so in times of change and crisis, like the present.

B. Misleading Keynesian/Monetarist Orthodoxy

Keynesian/monetarist orthodoxy so dominates the minds of many leading economists that they ignore other perspectives almost entirely. Since orthodox macro has failed to prevent crises, or to cure them when they occur, one would imagine that some economists would look elsewhere for inspiration.

According to the Keynesian view, financial contractions can be explained in purely monetary terms, without any reference to real economic relationships. The chief symptom of a financial crisis is a "liquidity trap," in which people prefer to hold cash instead of investing in capital goods. This preference is often deemed to be a psychological phenomenon, which is to say that it is inexplicable.

I agree that the loss of liquidity is the fundamental symptom of a financial crisis. The basic difference between my approach and the neoconventional one is that I believe and can show that the loss of liquidity has a real basis. The previous chapter considered the ways in which tax policy influences the kinds of capital into which investments flow. Overinvestment in long-term capital goods has the effect of constraining liquidity. Now we will examine the same problem from the side of banking.

II

Liquidity and the Real Economy

IN ORDER TO PRESENT an alternative view of how we might think of the monetary side of economics, I will begin with the most basic elements in order to explain how current thinking leads to instability.

A. The Amount of Money

There was about $1.5 trillion of checking deposits and currency in circulation in 2007. Deposits and currency constitute *M1*. They are about one-eighth of the GNP.

The ratio of GNP/M1 is what the usual macroeconomics text today calls "velocity." More exactly it is "GNP velocity." "Velocity" alone, in proper banking parlance, means transactions velocity or deposit turnover. This is a much higher figure that covers the use of money in all intermediate transactions, not just those that enter into GNP. This may seem insignificant, and economists tend to overlook the difference, but it is of great importance.

The banking system is essential to the health of a modern economy, and its contribution lies largely in its ability to maintain liquidity. That refers to the ability to permit a smooth flow of transactions. The biggest factor reducing liquidity is the lumpiness of certain investments, which pay back investors over a period of many years. Tying up capital in long-term projects effectively depletes the liquidity of the banking system and the economy. Balancing those long-term projects are other forms of capital, such as retail inventories, that turn over in periods ranging from a few days to a few months. The high turnover of that capital is a major source of the liquidity of any economy. That sort of turnover is directly related to transactions velocity in a business or a bank, but it is not considered at all by economists who specialize in finance. They are concerned only with GNP velocity. As a result, the financial indicators that economists use to evaluate the health of the banking system are systematically biased because they cannot recognize liquidity problems that result from a slowdown of the turnover of capital in intermediate transactions. The previous chapter explained why the rate of capital turnover is important.

B. How Liquidity Is Created

The social problems that banking solves are (1) coordinating the savings and investments of diverse individuals and institutions; and (2) mediating between short-term lending and long-term borrowing. Because banks borrow short to lend long, there is a fundamental imbalance in any financial system. That structural vulnerability is entirely separate from irresponsible behavior of individuals. Financing long-term assets with numerous short-term liabilities creates a perennial risk of insufficient liquidity.

Thus, the systemic problem for the managers of any banking or financial system is how to maintain sufficient confidence to avoid liquidity crises. To understand how that is done, let us begin with the basics.

How can anyone or any bank create net liquidity? A's asset is always B's debt on its flip side, so some have argued that there is no net effect when debts are created. That would be a false inference from a true premise. Banks do create liquidity, in spite of the flip side. The flip side makes banking tricky and hazardous. Nonetheless, people have been doing it for centuries.

How do banks do it? Basically, it is a matter of exchanging IOUs. When a bank creates new deposits, it works like this. It finds a borrower who will pledge some asset (collateral) to secure payment of a loan. It takes the borrower's IOU and records it on the asset side of its balance sheet. In return, it gives the borrower the bank's IOU, now called a demand deposit (dd).[2] (Originally, it was a bank "note," a piece of paper reading "will pay to the bearer on demand . . . .") This "demand deposit" goes on the liability side of the bank's balance sheet.

In the American colonial period, the original banks did not even accept deposits. They started, rather, with a certain amount of equity, and then created bank notes as loans. (Like deposits, those bank notes were demand liabilities, meaning that anyone could come to the bank and instantly redeem them for cash.) There was little currency circulating for them to accept as deposits, so instead they *created* a currency by accepting collateral in return for issuing bank notes.[3]

These bank notes were pieces of paper that linked the exchange process to real assets. This is how assets are "monetized," transformed from something like solid to liquid form so they can circulate. In principle, those real assets can be seized to make whole those who rely on the pieces of paper, which is how those assets serve to "back" the value of money and other financial instruments. The effect of issuing notes backed by real assets is the same as though title to the collateral were now chopped into small units, circulating in bearer form. (As we shall see later, land has been a major form of collateral accepted by banks. The bank notes are thus the equivalent of a small interest in the land used as collateral by borrowers. But there is no reason land has to serve this role. Many other assets can serve as well.)

This begins to explain the great mystery whereby banks create money, seemingly out of nothing. This process is deeply disturbing to many people, who regard banking as fraudulent and the interest as a form of social theft. Since fears and prejudices associated with lending have led to conflict in the past (including attacks on Jews in Europe and Chinese in Southeast Asia), the mistaken view that banks have no positive social function can have serious social consequences.

Thus, it is best to think of bankers not as creators of money, but as facilitators of liquidity. Currency and credit are two very important instruments of liquidity. They facilitate transactions and contribute to prosperity in a real way. Banks thus perform a role in the production of real goods and services, as real as the person who makes computer chips or who serves meals in a restaurant. Without liquidity, economies would fail.

The "drying up" of liquidity is precisely what most concerns bankers and the managers of a national economy. This occurs when the money creation process (or liquidity creation process) works in reverse. Instead of assets being monetized, money is turned into assets. We might say the assets are then "demonetized." That happens when banks seize collateral when borrowers fail to perform (i.e., can no longer make payments on their loans). When the bank accepted a claim on the asset as its collateral, it created a counterbalancing liability that was liquid. When the bank seizes the asset that served as collateral, the same process retires the deposits, a liquid asset, that had monetized the collateral. The net effect is to reduce money supply by that amount. Since banks cannot meet demands for liquidity with those assets, this poses a problem unless banks can sell the assets quickly. In 2007, as banks foreclosed on the holders of nonperforming mortgages, the banks became less liquid, less monetized. Taking liquid assets out of circulation restricted the ability of banks to lend working capital, which has endangered the entire economy. (In addition, the value of the assets had shrunk, so the equity or capital of banks also declined, which will be addressed below.)

C. The Rationale for Interest

Why does the borrower pay interest to the bank? As I explained earlier, a loan from a bank is actually a quid pro quo, an exchange of IOUs. If the value of the two is equal, why should the borrower pay interest? The answer is not obvious unless one understands that what the bank is "selling" is liquidity.

The bank's IOU is worth more than the borrower's because it is liquid. The borrower can spend it immediately. Banks borrow short, but lend long. If the borrower instead received a note that merely gave partial title to a large and bulky asset (a particular mortgage, for example), other people would be reluctant to accept that note, because it would lack easy convertibility or fungibility. The borrower could not buy groceries with notes assigning ownership to particular assets. The bank creates liquidity by breaking the value of large assets into small pieces of uniform size that are universally recognized. That practice is what gives banks the ability to cover loans and enables borrowers to spend the borrowed money freely.

The bank's IOU is liquid because the bank spends money to make it so. That is how it uses the interest it receives from borrowers. Banks use their income to create liquidity by creating social trust, which is what enables the whole system of banking to work. Without trust, it would be impossible to transform fixed assets into liquid forms that permit complex transactions. Some degree of mystery is an inherent part of the banking function because trust can only be created indirectly by creating conditions that will quiet fears. That is why the earliest banks were temples and why many banks are still built to look like ancient temples.

A great social benefit can be achieved if people will trust the banking system. How exactly do the banks invest in building trust? They do it by:

- guarding your money;
- paying cash on demand, from an attractive building in a convenient location;
- clearing checks;
- attracting enough other depositors so their clearing balances are not negative for long;
- holding reserves;
- having some net worth as a cushion (and justifying it by paying dividends on their capital);
- maintaining a reputation for always meeting their obligations on demand.

For those benefits, depositors are willing to forego interest income. If they do not like what they are getting, they "disintermediate," meaning they can make their investments directly in other financial instruments or in direct loans. Then bank balance sheets have to contract. They have fewer assets and fewer liabilities.

Banks play the percentages, and are never literally in a position to perform on their contracts, that is, to redeem all their deposits on demand. Some have advocated "100 percent reserve" banking to avoid that. This cause is a remote dream and a diversion from reality.[4]

The workable alternative is to retain a fractional reserve system and to require banks to stay highly liquid by restricting their loans to commercial paper or "real bills" secured by highly liquid collateral like accounts receivable. Banks and their economist-spokesmen resist this policy, which they parody and flay mercilessly with all the considerable influence and authority at their command. Nevertheless, banking based on "real bills" would permit capitalism to function without repeated cycles of sudden expansion and contraction. We will return to the subject.

D. Cost of Creating Liquidity

It should now be clear that bankers provide a social benefit by serving as intermediaries between borrowers and lenders and by creating liquidity in the process. The fact that liquidity is a more abstract service than car repair or even health insurance does not make it any less a real service. Like other real services, it requires real resources to provide it.

The cost of creating liquidity varies with several factors, some of which have natural equilibrating effects. The basic principle is that each transaction is a cost. For example, teller services for ordinary deposits and withdrawals are expensive to maintain in retail banking, but banks maintain those services because they instill confidence in customers. Since liquidity depends on trust, teller service is an important element of producing that service.

The cost per dollar of deposits rises with:

- velocity (deposit turnover);
- renewal frequency of loans (loan turnover);
- cost of borrowing funds (i.e., the interest rate at which banks borrow funds from other banks);
- share of assets that must be held in dead reserves;
- cost of bank capital—required dividend rate times required volume of capital;
- cost of suitable location and improvements;

- taxes on banks (generally very light);
- operating expenses (such as teller services in retail banks).

Cost per dollar of deposits falls with:

- average size of checks;
- average size of loans;
- average period of loans (converse of renewal frequency, already cited, repeated here for emphasis to offset usual neglect).

I have emphasized loan turnover here as a cost of maintaining liquidity. There is a tendency for banks to seek out lending opportunities that allow them to cut those costs. From the perspective of the individual bank, it is better to have loans that turn over slowly than to have short-term loans that require a lot of processing time. However, from the perspective of the banking system as a whole (and for society as a whole), long-term loans decrease liquidity for reasons made clear in the previous chapter.

Each bank would like to shift the cost of maintaining social liquidity (in the form of high-turnover loans) onto other banks while keeping its own costs low by issuing only long-term debt. That poses a systemic problem that will continue to manifest itself in periodic liquidity crises. Rectifying this problem is an essential function of central banks. Unfortunately, Chicago School dogma rules this out as "selective credit control." This is a form of "intervention," a violation of basic principles to the followers of Milton Friedman.

E. Technical Limits on Destabilizing Effects

There are several normal equilibrating effects that tend to maintain stability and limit radical changes in deposit expansion. They may be overwhelmed by other destabilizing factors at times. Some stabilizing factors are:

1. Higher velocity translates into more bank transactions per each dollar of reserves. This raises the cost of maintaining accounts, and reduces incentives to create new demand deposits by lending money into existence. This is a natural limit on the expansion of M1.

2. High liquidity preference by the public increases cash balances. This reduces bank costs, which encourages expansion during downturns in the economy. Thus, even liquidity preference, the prime cause of "glitches" in Keynesian macro theories, is not all bad.

3. Low yields on investments reduce costs of holding capital and reserves, tending to offset the discouragement to expansion. Low yields for nonbank lenders and direct loans tend to drive funds into banks.

Those are not definitive observations. They are intended to show there are damping factors tending to limit instability. Some model builders get carried away showing major changes springing from positive feedback loops triggered by minor causes. They may do us a service to warn that instability is possible, but it is a disservice to misspecify the effective causes of instability. To destabilize, a cause must be powerful enough to overwhelm various natural equilibrating effects.

III

Sources of Equilibrium and Liquidity

THE ABILITY OF BANKS to create money at will has frightening inflationary possibilities. Yet banks do not routinely generate inflation or overextend credit in ways that make the banking system unstable. Although banks are ultimately a source of instability, it is helpful first to note the internal limits on banks that prevent more frequent catastrophes. It is apparent that any one bank is limited in its capacity to issue loans by the loss of its reserves to other banks. The question we consider in this section is what limits *all* banks from expanding together during extended periods of moderate growth (in contrast to periods of euphoric land booms and excessive lending on inflated land collateral).

A. Limit #1: Loss of Public Confidence

The most important factor limiting the growth of bank balances is the anxiety shared by depositors that banks might be unable to redeem deposits in cash on demand. The creation of the Federal Reserve system and deposit insurance allays those fears to some extent. Nevertheless, as recently as September 2008, there was a run on Washington Mutual Bank when it was rumored that it could not cover its liabilities. Customers withdrew $16.7 billion in deposits over a period of 10 days, leading the Office of Thrift Services to declare WaMu insolvent (U.S. Department of the Treasury, Office of Thrift Services 2008).

There are many episodes in history of cash withdrawals and runs on banks. It happened many times in the 19th century. The Federal Reserve Act of 1913 was supposed to end all that, but it failed in 1929. In 1933, there was a bank "holiday" to shortcircuit a dangerous positive feedback loop, "the fear of fear itself." However, bank panics have seldom been based solely on group psychology. In most cases, the fears of depositors were in fact well-founded, due to crashing collateral values.

The legislative remedies that were developed during the 1930s to instill public confidence in the banking system include deposit insurance; tighter bank examination and controls on quality of bank loans; "Glass-Steagall," or separating investment banking (floating new securities) from commercial banking (checking deposits);[5] and cartel protection for banks, that is:

- caps on allowable interest rates paid by banks to attract customers;
- limits on charters for new banks;
- tight limits on interterritorial competition, giving banks virtual franchises on their turfs;
- FHA insurance on mortgage bank loans;
- greater power for the Federal Reserve Bank to supply notes on demand;
- elevation of Federal Reserve notes to becoming the basic legal tender, as we went partially off gold (domestically), and gold clauses in contracts were illegalized.

Associated with the last two was a major expansion of federal debt, much of which the banks bought. With all its faults, federal debt supplied a more stable collateral security behind bank loans than the volatile common stocks and real estate on which they had been lending before, and that had collapsed. This may be the main real point behind the otherwise shaky Keynesian case for deficit spending.

B. Limit #2: Federal Reserve Board Controls

1. Reserve Requirements
One of the key instruments by which the Federal Reserve Board stabilizes the banking system is the requirement that banks hold cash in reserve, in order to avoid a situation in which banks cannot cover demands. Banks must hold a specified percentage of their deposit liabilities as a cash reserve deposited with the Federal Reserve Bank.

The Federal Reserve Bank also issues Federal Reserve notes (paper money) to facilitate exchange. Public demand for paper money (notes) determines the ratio between Federal Reserve notes and Federal Reserve deposits. The public demand for paper currency has increased dramatically in recent decades (U.S. Council of Economic Advisers 2009: Tables B-70, B-71). The ratio of paper currency to deposits by banks in the Federal Reserve Bank has grown almost sixfold—from around 3 to 1 in 1966 to 18 to 1 in 2007. Then in August 2008, to stave off a potential run on the banks, banks sharply increased their reserves. By November, reserve deposits were 14 times greater than in August, and the ratio of currency to deposits had fallen to its lowest level in over 40 years (1.3 to 1).

The Federal Reserve Bank can increase the amount of currency and deposits in circulation by making loans to the U.S. Treasury, which it does by buying Treasury securities (bonds, bills, and notes). It buys some from the Treasury direct, and others from the public, on the "open market." (To reduce the money supply, it sells the same securities and thereby reduces the currency and deposits in circulation.) These "open market operations" are the major operating variable in Federal Reserve Board policy. Federal Reserve Board intentions are traditionally treated like military secrets, lending an aura of mystery, intrigue, and class warfare to the whole business.

Treasury securities thus back Federal Reserve notes and deposits. The securities so used are said to be "monetized." Actually, any other asset used for collateral is also monetized, and I will so use the term. (Curiously, many economists are stuffy about the usage, and insist on reserving "monetizing" for what happens to U.S. securities.)

Federal Reserve Bank expansion is loosely limited by its own gold reserves. Under the international gold standard, it was tightly limited by gold. An import balance, if unrelieved by foreign loans, caused an outflow of gold and forced a tight money policy, correcting the imbalance.

Today, more or less the same effect is achieved, but without automaticity, by tightening money to correct an import imbalance. (If a country buys more than it sells, the value of its currency declines, requiring a decrease in its money supply and a corresponding increase in interest rates to restore balance.) This necessity greatly limits the power of central banks to pursue independent national policies.[6] They can reestablish their independent scope of action by devaluing their currencies. That, however, if done often, undermines confidence in the local currency and leads people to do business in a more stable foreign currency, totally undermining the power of central banks. Some think this only happens to lesser breeds and nations, but it could easily happen to us if our hubris continues blinding us to the hazard of deficit finance.

2. Federal Reserve Bank Lending to Member Banks

Another way the Federal Reserve system can provide liquidity to banks is by lending them money during difficult periods. This also creates deposits, usually on a small scale. The rate charged was formerly called the "rediscount rate," and now simply "the discount rate." It is symbolic of the Federal Reserve Board's mysterious intentions, and closely monitored for that reason.

During the crisis in the fall of 2008, when it seemed there might be a national run on banks (after Fannie Mae and Freddie Mac were nationalized), the Federal Reserve Bank lent member banks hundreds of billions of dollars to increase their reserves. This enabled banks to keep operating even though some of them were probably technically insolvent. The Federal Reserve lends money on the expectation that asset prices will recover, which will increase the capital of banks and also permit them to sell the assets and become liquid once again. It remains unclear when, if ever, that might happen.

3. Qualitative Controls on Bank Lending

Most discussions of the Federal Reserve Board and its power to maintain financial stability consider the question solely in quantitative terms. Through its reserve requirements, "open market operations," and the discount rate at which it lends to member banks, the Federal Reserve Bank can regulate (but not entirely control) the money supply and short-term interest rates. It has far less influence on long-term bonds (10- to 30-year maturities), which are determined by investor confidence in the future stability of the economy and interest rates.

Much less attention has been paid to the qualitative controls the Federal Reserve Board can exercise. It is my contention that these qualitative controls could prove more successful than purely quantitative controls have proven to be in avoiding crises.

The Federal Reserve Board has certain powers over the kind of collateral that is eligible to secure bank loans, in other words, to be monetized. The ones used today are primarily margin requirements applied to loans made for the purpose of buying and carrying common stock, and restrictions on loans for some kinds of consumption (but not consumption of housing, which on the contrary receives favored treatment). The first of these serves to limit the monetization of common shares of corporations. It does not, however, limit the monetization of the assets of corporations. These are monetized every time a corporation pledges them to a commercial bank as loan security.

The Federal Reserve Bank is one agency that examines banks as well. Here is an opportunity to apply qualitative controls more generally. Bank examination should see that banks remain liquid.

What does "liquidity" mean in this context? Required reserves provide an element of liquidity that is only specious. They are in dead storage and can never be used. So why are they required? Reserves are used largely as a matter of tradition. They are thought to help sustain confidence. But in practice, reserves provide stability only as a method of increasing liquidity quickly when a crisis emerges. Reserves are cure more than prevention, and not very effective at either.

What is called "secondary liquidity" is provided by keeping a substantial part of bank assets in short-term loans that are financing the working capital of businesses and that are therefore automatically self-liquidating in a few months. This "secondary" liquidity is actually primary, since the "primary" reserves are dead and cannot be used.

The idea that liquidity is important is known as the "commercial loan theory," also known as the "real bills doctrine." In England, it is called the "banking school" position. An early and eloquent advocate was Adam Smith in *The Wealth of Nations* (1776). "Real bills," like so many terms, conveys many meanings with different baggage to different people. Here we use it only to mean maintaining banks' liquidity by regulating them away from volatile real estate collateral and derivatives therefrom (of which there are now far too many).

Ordinary texts today wrongly dismiss the real bills doctrine, citing the studies of Lloyd Mints (1945), the predecessor of Milton Friedman at the University of Chicago. Adam Smith, the apostle of laissez faire, is too regulation-minded for the Chicago School of economics, the arbiter of modern market orthodoxy. Chicago orthodoxy, chiefly decreed by taste dictator Milton Friedman, brooks no twilight shadow of qualitative control on bank lending.

The valid idea in "real bills"—not to be confused with "real estate"—is that banks should avoid lending on real estate collateral and for long terms. The two previous chapters in this volume provide the reasons why real estate serves poorly as collateral. Land prices are too volatile and the payback period too long, which are the two characteristics of loan portfolios that create the conditions for financial crises to develop. Default on real estate loans was the major cause of bank failures from 1929–1933, the period in which half the nation's banks failed. Chicago orthodoxy has taken that disastrous cataclysm and stuffed it down the memory tubes. The resulting collective amnesia is one of the greatest, most brazen feats of thought control in history.

There are at least three reasons why Chicago School orthodoxy cannot tolerate the real bills doctrine. First, it questions absolute faith in markets. Second, it proposes the need for regulation of banks.

Third, it casts doubt on the social utility of private ownership of land, by revealing a weakness in the use of land as bank collateral. Let us consider those reasons in more detail.

1. "Real bills" rejects the dogma of market perfection. The real bills doctrine implies that there is some systemic weakness in the market, which lets collapses be generated endogenously. The ideology of the Chicago School demands that collapses be caused only by errors of short-term policy judgment by the Federal Reserve Board. That was one of the conclusions of Milton Friedman and Anna Schwartz (1963) in their study of the impacts of changes in money supply on the real economy. Although they recognize that economic expansions and contractions occur independently of monetary policy, they tend to view the business cycle as an unexplained phenomenon, leaving the regulation of the money supply as the only policy variable of any signficance. In particular, they attribute the banking crises of 1929–1933 to "panics" that made healthy banks illiquid, rather than to factors in the economy that reduced the value of assets and made banks insolvent.[7] On that basis, the Chicago School effectively ignores the reality of a land-value boom-and-bust cycle driven by its own internal dynamic—by factors outside the scope of monetary policy. Although the Keynesians differ in many respects from the Chicago School, they agree that the economic causation runs largely from financial factors to real events, rather than vice versa. As a result, the Keynesians make common cause with the "monetarists" in neglecting the obvious influence of land on the business cycle.[8]

2. The Chicago School rejects qualitative regulation. The premise that economic crises arise from problems in the real economy, not the financial world, implies that economic stability cannot be achieved solely through control of the money supply, interest rates, or other financial indicators. It further implies that financial institutions need to be monitored and regulated in terms of their operating practices. The Chicago School accepts general "quantitative" controls, and rather tight ones at that, in order to be rid of all specific "qualitative" controls. It is this ideology, in the name of Reaganomics and deregulation, that led directly to the savings and loan (S&L) fiasco of the 1980s and 1990s, in which over 1,000 S&Ls failed and taxpayers lost about $124 billion (Curry and Shibut 2000: 31, Table 4). In brief, the Tax Reform

Act of 1981 encouraged real estate speculation (primarily commercial real estate), which accelerated the growth of land prices. Home mortgages outstanding grew by 66 percent from 1981 to 1986; mortgages on commercial property grew by 102 percent (U.S. Council of Economic Advisers 2009: Table B-75). Deregulation of savings and loans, combined with deposit insurance, enabled those institutions to make imprudent loans without fear of loss. In addition, the equity held by S&Ls became tied to real estate when the Federal Home Loan Bank Board in 1982 allowed buyers to put up real estate as equity, instead of cash, permitting S&Ls to be far less liquid than banks (U.S. Federal Deposit Insurance Corporation 2002). When land prices began to fall in 1987, hastened by the Tax Reform Act of 1986, many savings and loans became insolvent for the same reasons banks would become insolvent 20 years later. As L. William Seidman, former chair of the FDIC, concluded in 1996: "The banking problems of the 1980s and 1990s came primarily, but not exclusively, from unsound real estate lending" (Seidman 1996: 57). But all of this history is ignored by both the Chicago School and the Keynesians, who focus exclusively on the financial cause of crises.

3. The unconventional idea that real estate matters. In the 1960s debate between the Keynesians and the monetarists (Chicago School), the Friedman and Schwartz (1963) book discussed earlier was instrumental in shifting attention away from real events as explanatory variables. I am not disputing the idea that the money supply influences economic outcomes and that many of the real variables previously emphasized in explaining inflation or unemployment involved ad hoc explanations. My issue with Friedman and Schwartz (1963) (and with the Chicago School more generally) is not so much with what they say as with what they leave unsaid. Their analysis simply ignores the easily observed fact that land speculation has preceded major economic crises and deprived banks of liquidity. They choose not to recognize that "real estate matters" because doing so would withdraw a major support from the value of real estate, an interest with which the Chicago School identifies. The real bills doctrine also tends to desanctify property as a good in itself, property for the sake of property. Rather, it points up the danger of using land as a "store of value" instead of using it simply as a factor of production.

Thus, the theoretical question about whether banks should be regulated by means of quantitative restrictions (on reserves or interest rates) or qualitative regulations (on the kinds of collateral that can be used to issue loans) turns out to have ideological consequences concerning the autonomy of the market and the types of government regulation that are deemed legitimate.

But the issue is not ideological. On purely pragmatic grounds, the historical evidence strongly indicates that past efforts to prevent economic crises with quantitative regulations of banks have failed. That is why banks are in such trouble today in 2009, as they were in the 1930s and the early 1990s. They followed the principles of the Chicago School and flouted the real bills doctrine. As a result, they became stuck with nonperforming (defaulted) long-term loans backed by real estate collateral. In a larger sense, most corporate debt is secured by pledging corporate real assets, in every industry.

Why is the real bills doctrine still important? Why should the government regulate the kinds of assets used as collateral? Adam Smith recognized that there are things that individuals can do one at a time that they cannot do collectively. One of those things is liquidating real estate investments: an individual can sell real property, but from a social perspective that is a transfer, not a liquidation. Real bills, as a policy, would make the banks stick with "self-liquidating" loans that turn into money through sale of the collateral to consumers. (An example is a printing company that buys paper and turns it quickly into a printed product and sells it, so the capital turns over quickly.) That is something that can be done collectively, because the process of liquidating the loan is done routinely, daily, in the normal course of production and exchange.

Land, in sharp contrast, is not self-liquidating because the corpus of land is not sold to consumers in the course of ordinary use and consumption. Land is never liquidated, it just changes hands. The cash flow from unappreciating land is just enough to pay interest on its purchase price. The cash flow from appreciating land is less than enough, and must be augmented each year by additional outside payments. In that sense, land does not "throw off" capital during periods of growing prosperity. Instead, it absorbs liquid capital and solidifies it. That is why it is the wrong sort of collateral for the banking system.

C. Limit #3: The Market

In addition to Federal Reserve regulations that limit the expansion of bank balance sheets, the market also constrains bank lending that would otherwise cause inflationary pressure. Each bank has an incentive to survive and to maintain its reputation for stability, because that is how it attracts the deposits that enable it to extend loans and make money. Even if the Federal Reserve Bank did not exist, banks would show some restraint in order to preserve their assets and their reputation.

As the banks expand their balance sheets, they need to squirrel away more capital and surplus to maintain a safe ratio of equity to liabilities payable on demand. For this they must either save, sell more stock, or borrow long-term. In addition, if existing loans are not self-liquidating, the slow return of loans outstanding chokes off the flow available for new loans. Those two factors increase demand for liquid assets and reduce the supply. Since the supply of and demand for liquidity determine loan rates, new loans must be financed at higher interest rates. The higher rate screens out projects for which the rate of return is too low or too slow. Thus, the market has an automatic feedback mechanism that slows down investment as banks become overextended. Since the decline in the demand for loans takes place at the same time that banks are increasing their capital and reserves, this explains why there have been periods when banks have had excess reserves, and still did not expand their loans. Some attribute this to lack of demand for loans, caused by lack of "investment opportunities." In fact, that is more effect than cause. The true problem is that banks lack liquidity.

1. "Creditworthiness" of Borrowers

We have seen that the share of eligible collateral that is monetized by banks depends on their costs relative to those of competing lenders. Next we ask what determines the sum of "bankable" collateral that may be pledged to secure loans. The amount of money is the product of the two factors.

The basis on which lenders ration or allocate credit among borrowers is not marginal productivity, but collateral security. Likewise, the basis of expanding loans is collateral security, regardless of investment opportunities. This helps explain the otherwise mysterious and frustrating phenomenon, which sometimes occurs, of excess reserves and low interest rates failing to stimulate lending at a time when many businesses desperately need credit and want to expand. That was true in 1991, and it is occurring again in 2009.

Money is never easy for those lacking bankable assets on which to borrow. This is especially true in the aftermath of a boom and crash, when banks lack liquidity, and they demand more collateral to make loans. In November 2008, CNN reported that "[t]he Federal Reserve's recent Senior Loan Officer Opinion Survey found that 75 percent of the banks surveyed had tightened their lending standards for small-business loans" (Cowley 2008). As a result of the credit crunch, small business failures have risen. In 2008, the small business failure rate was 12 percent, up from 2.4 percent in 2004 and 8.4 percent in 2007 (Maltby 2009).

Another such time, more notorious and aggravated, was after the collapse of collateral values in the Great Crash, 1930 and thereafter. The few "creditworthy" borrowers were swamped with lenders, so recorded interest rates were very low. But the majority of ineligible borrowers could not borrow, even at high rates. (Another cause of credit rationing is the drop of bank capital, discussed later.)

During the Great Depression, when the real interest rate on Treasury bills was as low as −1 percent, Joseph Nicholson (1938: 31–34) sought to explain the source of the complaint by small business that the cost of capital for expansion of plant and equipment was "prohibitive." Although banks provided U.S. Steel with a three-year, $50 million loan, banks had become so concerned about liquidity that they were unwilling to provide such financing to small business at any price. Small companies were forced sell securities, paying registration fees, legal fees, and other costs amounting to 9–10 percent for bonds and 15–20 percent for stocks (Nicholson 1938: 32).

The most eligible borrower in the 1930s was the U.S. Treasury. Treasury debts are "nondefaultable" because they are backed by the ability of the Treasury to raise taxes *and* to borrow from the Federal

Reserve Bank. The Fed can lend simply by printing money that is legal tender for the payment of taxes and other debts, and that no one can force it to redeem in anything but more money that it can also print. The Treasury moved into the breach, slowly at first and then rapidly during World War II. It issued new debt that the banks seized and "monetized."

During the 1980s and from 2002 to 2007, private collateral values moved back up, way back up. Almost anyone could borrow on his or her home, for almost any purpose, including personal consumption. The banks monetized those new collateral values and allowed real estate to displace federal debt as the major backing of our money supply. Repeating the mistakes of the 1930s led to the current wave of defaults on the loans that backed our money supply and the subsequent fragility of the banking structure.

The logic of economic contraction is built into the cycle from the start. There is direct conflict between the high land values of the boom phase and the rate of return on productive, job-making real investments. High land values may mean low rates of return on new investments. The high land values are supported by siphoning off part of cash flow to income payments to those who own the land, or to those who lend entrepreneurs funds to buy it. The combination of high creditworthiness with low returns on newly created capital can only spell trouble: banks expand as real investment falls. At the same time, rising land values discourage saving and encourage consumption, for example, by using home equity loans.

When land is so overpriced as to cut deeply into rates of return on job-making new investment, banks turn to taking land itself as collateral. When land gets so overpriced that the borrowers cannot pay the loans, banks panic, freeze up, and stop originating new loans. Then as old debts are paid, the money goes into the bank and never comes out again. What banks have created they can destroy. Just as expanding banks issue new money, contracting banks swallow it up again.

This is a major source of the notions of oversaving and cash hoarding, notions so common in depressions. "Where has all the money gone?" people ask, and look under the mattresses of misers. Most of it has simply been retired by banks that collect old debts without originating new ones.

2. Major Kinds of Loan Collateral; Basis of Valuation
The following are major kinds of collateral, and factors determining their volume and valuation.

 a. U.S. Treasury securities, determined by the U.S. government.
 b. Volume of trade times the mean period that inventories are in stock, or that accounts are receivable (this is the basis of "real bills").
 c. Amount of durable capital and its valuation. There is an upper limit on valuation—the cost of reproduction. There is no floor under values of durable capital, however. Once capital has been produced, value depends on discounting expected future cash flows. When expected flows fall, and discount rates rise, present values fall.
 d. Valuation of land. This depends at all times only on discounting expected future cash flows, and never has any anchor or basis in cost of production. It is highly subject to changes in expectations, and hypersensitive to discount rates.

The financial system is most vulnerable to collapse when an unexpected sharp rise of interest rates pulls the plug on "c" and "d" above. Land values are especially sensitive to interest rates; and doubly so in a rising market, such as that that prevailed in farming in the 1970s, and throughout the United States from 1984 to 1988 and 2002 to 2007. In a rising market, land values are based on this formula:

$$L = a/(i - g), \tag{1}$$

where *L* is value, *a* is current cash flow, *i* is nominal interest rate, and *g* is anticipated annual rate of growth of cash flow. (Both *i* and *g* are expressed as decimals, such as 0.04 or 0.07.) Cash flow is measured in current dollars, to be consistent with the use of nominal interest rates.

Equation (1) applies literally only to land. However, during the recent real estate frenzy, most income properties were trading based on that valuation formula, and with little equity contributed by the buyer. The result was "negative cash flow." Negative cash flow is what you get when your debt service is greater than your operating cash flow (*a* in Equation (1)). (On a long-term debt, debt service is 97 percent interest in the first few years.) To get negative cash flow from Equation (1), solve Equation (1) for a − Li:

$$a - Li = -Lg. \tag{2}$$

Equation (2) shows that if you finance your purchase 100 percent at the bank, the interest exceeds the operating cash flow by *Lg*. That is, the hypothecated (mortgaged) real estate does not yield enough cash to pay interest on the debt each year. That difference is "negative cash flow." The borrower has to get that cash from some other source.

In practice, borrowers seldom get 100 percent financing. But values during land booms have gone so high relative to cash flows that one could get 70 percent financing and still suffer negative cash flow. That is, cash flow (*a* in Equation (2)) was less than 70 percent of *Li*. Making it worse, in 2003–2007, a period of "irrational exuberance," many lenders financed buyers up to 100 percent, or even more. Nor was it just buyers whom the lenders financed. Many existing owners borrowed on the rise of their land values in homes, businesses, pure speculations, or income properties to live beyond their means.

The debt service therefore comes only partly from the mortgaged real estate. The difference has to come from the other incomes of the borrower. Many borrowers assumed that values would continue to rise, so that soon they could borrow more on the same real estate, using a second deed of trust, to pay the negative cash flow. And they assumed that rents would continue to rise, so in a few years the operating cash flow would exceed 0.7*Li*. Many of the early buyers lucked out. Others, especially later buyers, did not. The entire economy is now suffering the consequences of that behavior.

The same factors that freeze up the circulation of capital also act to pull the plug on valuations of land and durable capital. Thus a banking contraction or collapse is caused by the same real factors that make macroeconomic trouble anyway. It can be a fearful combination.

The trick, when the economy gets caught out too long, is to segue from collaterals *c* and *d* to *a* and *b*. However, with too high a share of capital frozen in *c*, alternative *b* takes a while to redevelop. That leaves *a*, U.S. Treasuries. It is a way to solve the banking crisis.

But in terms of reviving the market economy and producing private goods, we need to restimulate *b*, real bills.

3. Bank Capital or Net Worth

Bank expansion is limited also by bank capital. The capital ratio is used to evaluate the stability or health of a bank. It is equal to the bank's equity or net worth divided by a sum of the assets, weighted by the risk that they will not perform. The primary capital ratio is based only on "Tier 1" assets in the numerator. (The assets counted in Tier 1 are cash and government securities; common stock, valued at issue price, not market value; and accumulated net retained earnings.) In those evaluations, government securities are generally given a 0 percent risk weighting, and mortgage-backed assets are given a 50 percent risk weighting, while loans to individuals or companies are given a 100 percent risk weighting. (That means the loans in those three categories are multiplied by 0, 0.5, and 1.0, respectively, in calculating the denominator.) By this means, the Federal Reserve Bank encourages member banks to hold government securities and mortgage-backed assets.

When a bank creates a deposit to fund a loan, its assets and liabilities increase equally, with no increase in equity. That causes its capital ratio to drop and increases the risk of insolvency.[9]

The Federal Reserve defines a capital ratio of 4 to 6 percent as "adequately capitalized" and over 6 percent as "well capitalized." In practice, the Federal Reserve Bank begins monitoring banks if the capital ratio falls below 8 percent. Discussing the possibility that the same sort of discipline might be imposed on investment banks that is now imposed on commercial banks, Prudent Speculations (2008) observed:

> Based on my rough calculations Goldman Sachs has a tier one capital ratio of between 10.5 percent and 11 percent, Lehman a ratio of between 7.8 percent and 8.3 percent, Morgan Stanley a ratio of between 7.1 percent and 7.6 percent and Merrill Lynch a ratio somewhere between 7.75 percent and 8.25 percent. As you can see, Morgan Stanley, Lehman and Merrill Lynch would all be of concern to Federal Reserve regulators, if they were commercial banks instead of investment banks.

That commentary was written in the wake of the bankruptcy of Bear Stearns in April 2008. By the end of September 2008, Lehman Brothers and Merrill Lynch, plus AIG, Fannie Mae, and Freddie Mac, had all become insolvent and were acquired by other entities. This is an indication that the market failed to send the right signals to investment bankers, who imagined they were not subject to the same risks as commercial banks.

Why were the investment banks so vulnerable to a change in market conditions? A few major defaults cut deeply into their net worth and forced them to contract. If a bank had $20 billion in assets, $19 billion in liabilities, and $1 million in equity (5 percent of assets), the bank would become insolvent if only 5 percent of its assets become nonperforming. Being highly leveraged is the normal condition of banks, both commercial and investment banks. It is the feature that makes them vulnerable to economic changes that affect the marginal value of the collateral that backs their assets, such as sudden declines in the value of land. These declines do happen, and are continuing to happen as we write.

The necessity of maintaining a sufficient capital ratio helps explain the "mystery" of why commercial banks would not expand after the banking collapse of 1929–1933, even though they had excess reserves. The same pressure reappeared in 1991 and again today in 2009, when banks had to raise more capital to maintain liquidity.The problem faced by banks with bad assets is that the numerator (equities) must rise in a crisis to compensate for all of the high-risk (mortgage-based) assets in the denominator. To the extent that banks cannot raise new capital (increase the numerator), they must contract (reduce the denominator) by reducing their balance sheets.

After a crash, if banks hold mortgages of individual properties, foreclosure and seizure of collateral (real estate) leaves banks with more real property and fewer nonperforming mortgages. The bank now has a physical asset carried on the books. A house that exchanged for $600,000 in 2006 (the original collateral value) might be worth only $400,000 in 2009. Banks would prefer to avoid marking the value of that home down to its current market value ("mark to market") because the markdown reduces the equity of the bank by the difference between the 2006 collateral value and the 2009 market value. Banks hold on to houses in hopes of selling them for a price closer to the 2006 price. According to Rick Sharga of RealtyTrac (cited in Olick 2009): "The lenders are simply trying to defer the losses to a later date, because having to recognize the losses short term might pose severe risks to the banks in question." Banks are valuing repossessed homes on their books for the value of the mortgage on the property. But in many cases, the property is worth far less than the mortgage on it. "Untold numbers of these properties [are] sitting on banks' accounting ledgers where, the imputed value is considerably higher than the market value," says Sharga (qtd. in Olick 2009). (By contrast: "The Federal Deposit Insurance Corp. has said that it encourages banks to sell REOs [real estate owned—by banks] as quickly as feasible, because they are non-earning assets. FDIC rules permit banks to hold REOs for up to 10 years" (Condo Vultures 2008).)

The issue has been made more complex because of the growing practice of bundling mortgages into derivatives called "mortgage-backed securities" (MBSs) or "collateralized mortgage obligations" (CMOs) that were then traded by investment banks. That process mixed together sound and unsound mortgages. When the unsound mortgages are in default, an entire package declines in value, but the amount of its new value is hard to determine. The good apples were supposed to hide the bad, but now the bad ones spoil the barrel: it all becomes "toxic." Forced sales of CMOs in 2008 to meet margin calls and raise capital-adequacy ratios lowered their price below the capitalized value of expected cash flow from the mortgages within the bundle. On that basis, investment banks that hold large amounts of derivatives as collateral have argued for lifting the mark-to-market rule on those derivatives. An April 2009 ruling by the Federal Accounting Standards Board allowed banks to value securitized property at a value different from current market value (Applebaum and Goldfarb 2009: A15).

By failing to mark to market, the banks are failing formally to recognize what everyone knows: their equity has declined because of toxic assets. Their equity has been reduced by the amount of the loss, but they do not record it until the assets are sold. In this way, foreclosure and repossession improve the *visible* capital ratio of a bank, but since its net worth and capital ratio have actually declined to a dangerous level, it is less able to make loans. In addition, the bank now holds assets that do not turn over at all (i.e., they provide little or no payback that can be used as working capital for new loans).

This matter tends to be shrouded in secrecy because banks avoid disclosing the volume of defaulted loans. RealtyTrac's U.S. Foreclosure Market Report (http://www.realtytrac.com) now logs information on the total number of "foreclosure events" and properties affected by foreclosure. But after the foreclosure process, it is difficult to determine what happens to the property that served as collateral. Banks repossess the property and eventually sell it or otherwise transfer ownership, but there is no readily available database of those transactions. By comparing its own database of foreclosures with the Multiple Listing Service of the National Association of Realtors, RealtyTrac discovered that as many as two-thirds of the foreclosed properties are not being sold (Said 2009; Boomershine 2009). The FDIC maintains some information about bank-owned real estate (known as REOs or real-estate owned), but that information is released sporadically, with no assurance of completeness. RealtyTrac listed 190,543 REOs as of the first quarter of 2009 (RealtyTrac Staff 2009). At an average of $200,000 per house (the mean national house price before the bubble (U.S. Bureau of the Census 2009)), that would equal $381 billion. The FDIC reports only $23 billion in REOs at the end of the third quarter of 2008. That would suggest that, as of the middle of 2009, banks hold over $300 billion in residential foreclosed property that they have not yet put on the market.

In the Great Depression, banks deferred accounting "recognition" of losses by hanging on to foreclosed real estate for years and years. They took advantage of a form of mythology allowed by generally accepted accounting principles (GAAP) whereby capital gains and losses do not occur until they are "recognized" by some overt act like a sale, or formal ceremony like a "write-down." This mythology is taken much more seriously than its intrinsic credibility warrants.

During a previous real estate downswing, powerful interests pushed for a return to the same kind of deception. Paul Craig Roberts (1991), former Assistant Secretary of the Treasury in the Reagan Administration, wrote: "Depressed real estate prices are not only an important reason why we are in recession but they are likely to make it all but impossible for us to spend our way out of it." He proposed to "breathe life back into real estate values" with a capital gains tax cut, to:

save many financial institutions from failure, and save the government—or taxpayers—billions of dollars in bailout costs. . . . The downward spiral will have a long way to go if regulators succeed in forcing financial institutions to "mark-to-market," or value at current market prices their long-term investments.

The practice by banks of deferring the mark-down in value is obvious nonsense. Losses are actually taken when assets lose value, regardless of formal recognition. The banks knew then (in 1932 or 1991, to name but two years of crisis), as they know now in 2009, that their net worth was much too low. They chose to give the public other reasons to explain their low enthusiasm for expanding. The public and the banking professors let them get away with it: the clout of organized bankers is awesome; the eagerness of the public to be deceived and gulled is frightening.

Note in passing here a vital distinction between the volume of loans outstanding, and the volume of new loans. The first is a static economic "fund," a store of value. The second is a "flow" of new investment. The fund of M1 depends on the volume of loans outstanding, but the flow of real investing—the net income-creating investment (represented by I in standard macro equations)—depends on the volume of new loans, and on equity reinvested from the cash flows of self-financed businesses, mostly corporations, that do not depend on commercial loans.

A bank that lends long gets repaid only slowly, and can therefore originate only a small volume of new loans each year, relative to its assets. A bank whose borrowers default is in the same pickle, only worse. And their pickle becomes everyone's pickle to the extent that we depend on them to finance the flow of investment that keeps the Great Wheel of economic life turning.

D. Limit #4: The Limited Liquidity of M2

Do money substitutes increase net liquidity? As with demand deposits, there is a flip side to savings accounts, time deposits, CDs, S&L deposits, cash management accounts, money market funds, and so forth, and that is the liability of some debtor. All of those sorts of deposits are included in the category of "M2." As with M1, there is some net increase in liquidity that is manufactured by the intermediaries. That is how they earn their spread, and persuade their depositors to accept less interest than they could get by lending directly.

The intermediaries borrow short and lend long. It is just that they do not borrow quite so short as when they create demand deposits. Their deposits are not transferable on demand, and do not serve as media of exchange. They do, however, serve as stores of liquidity.

How important this is depends on how seriously you take demand-side economics. Economics texts take it seriously, and therefore emphasize the benefits that stem from this sense of liquidity created by M2. M2 lets individuals hold less M1, which causes money to circulate faster (increased "velocity") and raise aggregate demand.

Does M2 create net wealth? No, obviously, the flip side totally counterbalances the top side.

Money market funds (MMFs) are now included in M2. You can transfer them by check, like demand deposits, so they are a means of payment. These funds held $3.83 trillion at the end of 2008, 23 percent more than at the end of 2007 (Henriques 2009). MMFs do not create new deposits by expanding, as banks can. They can only lend money they have previously received from depositors. They still monetize the collateral they lend on, as banks do. However, what the MMFs monetize, the banks cannot. One asset can only be monetized by one lender at one time. MMFs compete for both depositors and borrowers, but they do not create new money. Their significance is that they are less regulated than bank loans and are uninsured. They lend only short, which is a selective control on the lines of the real bills doctrine. The fact that they spotted opportunities in the money market may suggest that regular commercial banks were neglecting it—a bad sign about the banks.

Two final forms of liquidity that do not show up as part of M2 are (1) credit card balances and (2) lines of credit that have been extended to some firms and individuals. The first form of credit at least shows up on the balance sheets of banks. The second category does not. These are a contingent liability of the banks, but do not appear on the books as demand deposit liabilities. Nevertheless, the firms that have them are certainly made more liquid, and access to such lines of credit dries up during periods of economic contraction.

IV

The Lorelei that Lure Banks Onto the Rocks of Illiquidity

A. Short-Term Gains

Confidence in banks is something of a collective good: it depends on collective behavior more than individual behavior. Thus, each individual bank is tempted to expand more than is good for banks collectively. To cut costs and increase profits, banks are lured into taking actions that provide them with short-term gains, but that collectively lure the financial system into illiquidity:

- Long-term loans. One loan agreement lasts for many years, and it costs staff time to evaluate and make loans. As we saw in the previous chapter, the ability of an economy to sustain full employment is more a function of how often capital turns over than the total stock of capital. Each bank has an incentive to make long-term loans. Rather than trying directly to regulate the average length of a bank's loans, regulators could more easily control the type of collateral that is accepted.

- Large loans. In the wake of potential insolvency among large investment banks and automobile manufacturers, Americans have become accustomed to the rationale that some entities are "too big to fail." When banks make large loans, such as loans made to foreign governments in the 1970s, a default by just a few debtors could wipe out the bank's capital (which is just 5 percent or so of the bank's total assets). Large banks may rely on the "too big to fail" principle in taking those risks, knowing that their collapse could damage the entire economy. When there are only a few extremely large banks, they take their cues about risk from each other rather than from any market signals.

- Excessive leveraging. For every dollar of capital, banks want to lend the maximum possible because that is how they make money. But that imposes risks on the whole financial system if every bank becomes excessively leveraged and if some loans become nonperforming. When regulators try to restrict lending with quantitative controls (such as the capital ratio), banks are able to circumvent those rules by granting "credit lines" to businesses. Since these are open-ended, they do not appear as liabilities in the accounts of the banks on which they are drawn. (The bank does not actually create a demand deposit. It simply allows a business to spend in excess of its immediate cash, on the expectation that revenue will soon cover the expenditures.)

• False savings on employees. It might seem to banks that they can save money in the short run by increasing the volume of loans faster than personnel are hired to oversee the loans. At the same time, overworked and often unrecognized loan officers are asked to issue an increasing number of loans. Should it come as a surprise then if banks are uncertain about the quality of their loan portfolios? When Continental Illinois went bankrupt in 1984 (the largest in U.S. history at that time), it seems that loan officers were so overworked that they did not keep accurate records on all of their loans.

All of the actions that cut costs and raise profits for the bank endanger its liquidity and reduce its service to the community. What makes them think they can get away with it? Banks can take comfort in recalling that if they get into deep trouble there is a history of federal aid. In the 1930s, the Home Owners' Loan Corporation and Reconstruction Finance Corporation and farm credit agencies took over billions of defaulted mortgages. In the 1980s, the savings and loans were rescued after they invested directly in real estate, using funds raised from federally insured accounts. Taxpayers eventually paid $124 billion to rectify those errors.

The banks might feel with some justice that the federal government is devoted to supporting real estate values by continually pumping in credit. It is one of those short-run solutions that keeps inflating the problem it is designed to correct: a vicious spiral, or positive feedback loop, with no good end in view.

B. Periodic Land Booms

Bankers, like other humans, tend to follow fashions. When some banks begin lending on the rising value of real estate, others feel safe in following suit. So banks compete with each other in lending money for real estate that can reach "irrationally exuberant" levels before it levels off and collapses, leaving banks holding assets of declining value and a highly illiquid portfolio. Thus, indirect land speculation is one of the most important ways banks are led into actions that result in low levels of liquidity.

The starting point of this irresponsible behavior lies in the confusion of land and capital. There is a tendency in modern parlance and theory to conflate the two and to treat lending for land on a par with lending for capital.

1. The Difference Between Land and Capital

Land and capital are mutually exclusive categories. Between them, they include all assets with intrinsic value. Some of each is needed for all production (each is "limitational"), so both are always relevant. As to formation, land (by definition) is what nature gives. It is only capital that humans form, by producing in excess of consuming. Propositions relevant to capital formation must always distinguish land from capital. Capital formation involves spurts of sacrifice, self-restraint, self-discipline, and self-control. Capital maintenance, and avoiding dissaving, calls for *continuous* self-restraint, generation after generation, and throughout life cycles, not "eating the seed-corn." Land (other than exhaustible natural resources) cannot be consumed, but capital must be maintained and replaced.[10]

Capital formation is not aided by, and may be deterred by, raising returns to land. All relevant analysis must carefully distinguish the two. Land and capital are not mutually convertible.[11] Capital is convertible into any other kind of capital each time it turns over. With each turnover it is 100 percent *fungible*. Land is not convertible even into other land, and certainly not into capital.

2. Interest Rates and Asset Values

Both land and durable capital are highly sensitive to interest rates. Rising interest rates lower the market value of each, with falling interest rates having the opposite effect. The value of every asset is affected by interest rates according to the expected life of the asset. Land is most strongly affected, then durable capital. Capital that turns over quickly is hardly affected. That is because, as we saw in the previous chapter, the longer the life of the capital, the larger the proportion of the cash flow from it that goes to interest instead of capital replacement. Since land does not depreciate at all, it is even more sensitive to interest rate fluctuations than any capital. As a result, when interest rates fall, the price of land rises more rapidly than the value of durable capital, which rises faster than the value of capital of short maturity.

A boom (period of rapid asset price appreciation) may be set off by any number of events, alone or together: a drop in interest rates, an expectation of increasing personal income (nominal or real), or a major "peace dividend," meaning a tax cut without loss of public services. Almost any such event will translate into higher land prices more fully and quickly than a rise in the value of capital. Once the price of land starts to rise, that may create the expectation of a further rise, which becomes a self-fulfilling prophecy up to a manic peak, unsustainable, to be followed by a depression.

3. The Role of Banks in Fueling Booms

Although binges of easy credit have fueled boom-bust cycles in the past, even bankers have short memories. (So do some economists, it seems.) Instead of remaining cautious about lending against an asset that can fall in price as readily as it rises, banks jump on the bandwagon and give increasingly risky loans on the expectation that land prices will continue to rise. As a result, banks accept land as collateral even when the ratio of price to annual lease value (similar to the price/earnings ratio for common stock) rises to an absurd level.

When the boom is in full swing, as it was in 1925, 1955, 1972, 1988, or 2005, and there is easy money to be made "flipping" properties, banks expand their balance sheets and allow their capital ratios to decline to a precarious level, which becomes the proximate cause of the ensuing recession or depression (Norris 2007).[12] Since everyone participates in the euphoria, it is difficult for loan officers to cast doubt on the premise that the good times will last forever.

When asset prices (particularly land prices) stop rising, they cannot simply level off. The only thing sustaining the inflated price of land ("property values") is the expectation of future rising prices. As soon as that expectation starts to evaporate, as soon as it becomes evident that there is not another buyer willing to pay an extra percentage point over the last sale price, then prices fall. They do not fall gradually; they come down in an avalanche, returning to a level that can be sustained from annual leases. Banks are not passive in the process. They accelerate the fall in land prices by refusing to lend against inflated collateral values.

Many or most banks cannot save themselves by prudence at the final stage in the cycle. Their balance sheets have been overextended by making loans on real estate with inflated land prices. When prices fall far enough, many owners find themselves "under water": they have negative equity (real estate worth less than the mortgage), and abandon their holdings. Or, they cannot make the payments, and the lenders foreclose. Either way, banks end up with large amounts of property that yield no income. Instead of working assets, banks have frozen assets. Their capital is effectively depleted because of the losses they have sustained by lending on land that has declined in value. Because of their low capital ratios, banks cannot expand their balance sheets by lending again. They are unable to perform their basic service of creating liquidity.

4. How Capital is Destroyed During a Speculative Boom

While credit is being extended during the upswing, a second process is also occurring that will put an additional restriction on bank lending after the land price bubble has burst. Saving, capital formation, and capital replacement all decline during the upswing. Thus, the personal saving rate (ratio of saving to disposable income) dropped precipitously on three occasions: by 25 percent from 1992 to 1993; by 44 percent from 1998 to 1999; and by 81 percent from 2004 to 2005 (U.S. Council of Economic Advisers 2009: Table B-30). These were all during periods when the economy was recovering or surging, either from real economic growth or from a bubble.

The loss of savings during the upswing reduces the capacity for capital formation. That is particularly a problem for small businesses that need working capital. The decline of personal saving pales in comparison, however, with the loss of value from the existing stock of capital.

The loss of value of existing capital during the period of rapidly rising asset prices stems from two sources:

1. Equity withdrawal. Rapidly rising residential and commercial land values create the illusion of increased wealth, even though there is no corresponding increase in real goods. Nevertheless, homeowners and other property owners treat the rise of land value as an increase in real wealth and increase their consumption accordingly. The capital in existing buildings is "consumed" economically because building owners treat land value increases as income and consume their depreciation allowances rather than reinvesting them.[13]

2. Misallocation of capital. When land values rise rapidly, there is a corresponding increase in construction of houses, offices, and commercial buildings to take advantage of the rise in demand for land. Much of this new construction represents a misallocation or waste of capital, which becomes evident in the downswing. The loss of the economic value of capital that occurs during a contraction as a result of misallocation has much the same economic effect as lowering the aggregate supply. The misallocation of capital takes three forms: (a) building in locations of low productivity, not ripe for development; (b) excessive building to economize on overpriced land during upswings; and (c) overinvestment in durable capital with long payout. All three categories lead to an unrecoverable loss of capital value during the downswing of the cycle, at which point there is excess capacity, locational obsolescence, and a very limited supply of working capital because so much capital is now frozen in durable structures.

As John Stuart Mill (1872: BK. I, Ch. V, §6: 47) said: "Capital is kept in existence from age to age, not by preservation, but by continual reproduction." Capital reproduces itself by yielding a capital consumption allowance. When rising land prices create the illusion of increased income, building owners consume that allowance instead of saving it, so capital stops reproducing itself. This is how rising land prices drive capital out of production and create so much unemployment and suffering during the downturn.

V

Lessons from the 1920s and 1930s

FOR THE PAST YEAR OR SO, we have heard many examples of how banks become overextended by lending on real estate and construction during periods of rapid expansion, only to find themselves unable to provide liquidity in the following downturn. "Subprime" loans (i.e., mortgages for borrowers who did not meet normal loan criteria) and financial pyramids of derivatives built on bundled mortgages of varying quality have been blamed for the crash. But those are the particulars, and we need to be looking for the general cause of economic failure, if we are to prevent it from recurring.

The general cause we have been examining in this essay is the tendency of banks periodically to break loose of regulatory moorings and to lend recklessly on overpriced land and speculative buildings that are being developed during a manic bubble. At the end of each round of that cycle, banks have been left holding large, unwieldy, low-value assets, and the economy has suffered from the inability of banks to extend credit, even to healthy businesses. By tying up capital in land and long-term projects that cannot be liquidated, banks allow the assets of the nation to become frozen and partially unusable.

The clearest example of that process of tying misallocation of capital to bank failures is the Great Depression of the 1930s. Yet economists have largely ignored that feature of the 1930s because of their focus on monetary causes of economic ills. According to this conventional view, the financial system is largely autonomous from the real economy and can be manipulated (well or badly) without reference to actual events. Here, rather, we provide evidence from the depression of the 1930s that land speculation is the chief cause of periodic booms and busts.[14]

A. Nationwide Perspectives

One way to understand the relationship between the land boom of the 1920s and the Great Depression of the 1930s is by viewing these events in terms of the national economy.

Simpson (1933) diagnosed the central cause of the economic contraction as "real estate speculation." Noting that speculation in western lands and railroad lands had caused previous boom-bust cycles in the 19th century, he observed that the 1930s cycle was the first one caused by *urban* land speculation, brought on in part by the massive migration from depressed rural areas to cities.[15] He provided as an example the speculation that took place around Chicago, where approximately half a million lots were subdivided in the 1920s and left vacant as of 1928 (Simpson 1933: 164). Banks and other financial institutions throughout the nation played a major role in the inflating of land values by their lending practices:

> [A]ll the financial resources of existing banking and financial institutions were utilized to the full in financing this speculative movement. . . . Real estate interests dominated the policies of many banks, and thousands of new banks were organized and chartered [to provide] the credit facilities for proposed real estate promotions. [Most were] located in the outlying sections of the larger cities or in suburban regions not fully occupied by older and more established banking institutions. . . . [C]ommercial banks . . . [were placed in a] highly over-extended position. . . . [A] large . . . portion of this loan structure depended for its solvency upon . . . a continued advance of real estate values. When [those real estate values stopped rising] . . . the banks found themselves loaded with frozen assets, which we have been trying ever since to thaw out. . . . [R]eal estate, real estate securities, and real estate affiliations in some form have been the largest single factor in the failure of the 4,800 banks that have closed their doors during the past three years and in the "frozen" condition of a large proportion of the banks whose doors are still open. . . . [I]t becomes increasingly apparent that our banking collapse during the present depression has been largely a real estate collapse. (Simpson 1933: 164–165).

Based on this broad-brushed analysis by Simpson, it should be possible to find evidence of the problem he describes in national statistics. However, since bank failures caused by real estate bubbles are localized, national banking statistics give only limited evidence of how real estate lending leads to the contraction of bank balances. Nevertheless, some national statistics from the 1920s and 1930s may be instructive.

Data on construction reveal something about the pattern of over-extended investment in real estate. Housing construction was the largest factor in the boom of the 1920s (U.S. Bureau of the Census:

Series N106, N115). Housing starts from 1922 through 1928 averaged 833,000 per year, almost exactly twice the average from 1910 to 1916. In the peak year, 1925, there were 937,000 starts, a level not reached again until 1949, when the number of families had grown by more than 30 percent. This figure declined by 20 percent from 1925 to 1928, and then by an average of 26 percent per year from 1929 to 1933.

Since housing construction began to decline after 1925, it might seem that the building boom of the 1920s was only peripherally related to the depression starting in 1930. The factor that explains the gap is the high level of nonresidential building construction from 1926 through 1929, which was 48 percent higher (in constant dollars) than the years 1922–1925 (U.S. Bureau of the Census 1960: Series N5, E133). In 1929, the peak year, investment in nonresidential building construction was 80 percent higher than in the base year of 1922. Then, in the downturn, from 1929 to 1932, investment in nonresidential buildings fell by 77 percent. By 1929, it would seem that banks had exhausted their liquidity and could no longer support construction loans.

The banking problems of the 1930s were not created by averages but by differences. For example, the ratio of real estate loans to all loans differed dramatically between nationally chartered banks and other banks (state-chartered banks, trusts, and other institutions). In national banks, the ratio averaged 6 percent in the 1920s. By contrast, the ratio in nonnational banks averaged 38 percent (U.S. Bureau of the Census 1960: Series X44, X45, X66, X67). In both cases, the ratio continued to rise in the 1930s as other types of loans were liquidated while real estate loans remained frozen on the balance sheets. State banks faced serious problems of liquidity because such a large portion of their portfolios was tied to real estate. Between 1930 and 1933, national banks liquidated 50 percent of their non–real estate loans, but nonnational banks had to liquidate 65 percent of the same loans (U.S. Bureau of the Census 1960: Series X42, X68). That left the state banks, on average, far less liquid than national banks. In 1931, state commercial banks outnumbered national banks by a factor of 2.2, but state banks were suspended 4.6 times as often as national banks (U.S. Bureau of the Census 1960: Series X42, X91, X166–168).

These national data hide the fact that real estate lending by a small number of banks in each region created liquidity problems for the entire banking system. Thus, it is necessary to look beyond national data to understand how overextended real estate investment damaged the banking system.

The regional nature of economic contractions can be observed in 2009. There is currently an obvious state-level relationship between recent real estate transactions and current economic difficulties. Of the 10 states with the highest foreclosure rates in the first quarter of 2009, eight had higher than average rates of unemployment, with Michigan, California, Oregon, and Nevada all facing double-digit joblessness, largely as a result of the "mortgage meltdown" in those states (U.S. Department of Labor, Bureau of Labor Statistics 2009; RealtyTrac Staff 2009). The integration of financial markets has spread the losses over every region and even to other countries, but the hardest-hit areas in the United States are still the epicenters of real estate speculation.

The best way to see how real estate speculation causes monetary problems is to examine how these relationships develop at the local level. To that end, we now turn to case studies of Florida and Detroit (with a brief reference to New York City).

B. Florida and New York City in the 1920s

The Florida land boom of the 1920s is well-known as an object of historical curiosity. Only a few contemporary observers recognized its economic significance. In his 1931 book *Only Yesterday*, Frederick Lewis Allen journalistically described at length the real estate frenzy that overtook Florida from 1922 to 1925 ([1931] 1959: Chap. 11). He said only a little about the connection with banking, but it was highly suggestive of the economic meaning of the land boom:

> In 1928 there were thirty-one bank failures in Florida; in 1929 there were fifty-seven; in both of these years the liabilities of the failed banks reached greater totals than were recorded for any other state in the Union. . . . Bank clearings for Miami, which had climbed sensationally to over a billion dollars in 1925, marched sadly downhill again:
>
> 1925............................$1,066,528,000
> 1926.............................632,867,000
> 1927.............................260,039,000
> 1928.............................143,364,000
> 1929.............................142,316,000 (Allen [1931] 1959: 199–200)

The previous rise of bank clearances had been equally rapid.[16] The bank-clearance data reveal the extreme local effects of the land boom on the banking system, and they hint at the severity of the banking contraction that occurred during the downswing of the cycle.

Homer B. Vanderblue (1927b) explained the way in which real estate lending in Florida drove down the capital ratio of the banks and how that led to their failure in 1926:

> At the end of December, 1925, many of the Florida banks had deposits 20 and 30 times their combined capital and surplus; as these abnormally large deposits were drawn down, such banks as had become involved in the real estate speculation through heavy loans to "operators" and "developers" found themselves unable to meet the demands made upon them. (1927b: 266)

It is instructive, however, that only one Florida bank that was a member of the Federal Reserve system failed in 1926 (Vanderblue 1927b: 268). The Federal Reserve Bank insisted that its member banks follow the discipline of the "real bills" doctrine. As one observer noted in 1927:

> The Federal Reserve System is properly given a great deal of credit for our present prosperity. The business world is now so well organized that any tendency towards trouble is quickly stopped before becoming general. As an example, the deflation of the Florida boom in the old days would have caused a country-wide panic, but now it made only a ripple on the surface. (*Credit Digest* 1927, qtd. in Holland 1972: 57)

It seems doubtful that the boom and crash in Florida real estate created only a "ripple on the surface," since many independent banks in Florida failed, and banks outside of Florida were also involved in real estate loans. Their loss of liquidity almost certainly contributed to the weakening of the national banking system. Nevertheless, the Florida experience did demonstrate that if all banks had stayed within the bounds of the real bills doctrine, that sort of prudence would have avoided the instability that followed.

Florida was only the most sensational case of the 1920s. Because of journalistic accounts at the time, it seemed to be in a class by itself. But it was not. Allen ([1931] 1959) touched on the effects of the real estate bubble of the 1920s elsewhere. He mentions the many skyscrapers built in Manhattan (among other cities) during this period, which ultimately ended up creating excess capacity:

The final phase of the real-estate boom of the nineteen-twenties centered in the cities themselves. . . . There is scarcely a city which does not show a bright new cluster of skyscrapers at its center. The tower building mania reached its climax in New York . . . coming to its peak of intensity in 1928. . . . [B]etween 1918 and 1930 . . . [office space] was multiplied approximately by ten. . . . The confidence [was] excessive. Skyscrapers [were] overproduced. In the spring of 1931 . . . some 17 percent of the space in the big office buildings of the Grand Central district, and some 40 percent . . . [in] the Plaza district farther uptown, were not bringing in a return. . . . [F]inanciers were shaking their heads over the precarious condition of many realty investments in New York. ([1931] 1959: 203–204)

Those financiers were shaking their heads because their investments were causing serious problems as nonperforming assets on their balance sheets. Yet, because these effects were localized, the financial damage caused by the excessive building of the 1920s is seldom mentioned by economists seeking the causes of the Depression.

C. Real Estate Speculation and the Detroit Bank Failure of 1933

Perhaps the most exhaustive case study of the origins of financial distress in real estate bubbles is the analysis by John Joseph Holland (1972), who explains the failure of banks in Detroit in 1933 in connection with land speculation in that city during the 1920s.

Although the case study by Holland deals with a single city, that city was of national significance in 1933. To begin with, Detroit grew much faster, by a wide margin, than any other American city from 1900–1930, rising from nowhere to become our fourth biggest city. It was boomtown U.S.A., the symbol of our successful industrialization and the nerve center of a mighty new economic empire. According to Holland (1972: ii), "the banking collapse in Detroit in 1933 touched off a national panic" that led President Roosevelt to declare a national bank holiday on March 6, 1933. That banking crisis "interrupted an economic recovery that had begun in mid 1932" (Holland 1972: ii). Thus, the events he examines are not merely of local interest. The experience of Detroit banks was symptomatic of the general causes of the Depression, and it was of particular importance in one distinctive phase of the national crisis.

Growth, of course, feeds speculation. One characteristic that made Detroit banks vulnerable to insolvency was the growth of real estate loans.[17] As banks expanded their balance sheets with a large increase in loan volume in the 1920s, the proportion of loans for real estate grew from 33 percent in 1921 to 41 percent in 1926, then fell to 36 percent in 1930 (Holland 1972: 45). This was particularly true of lending of money held by the banks in the form of time deposits (saving accounts). Throughout the 1920s, Detroit banks committed a larger proportion of their time deposits to real estate loans than did banks elsewhere. In 1929, real estate loans loans were 56 percent of time deposits in Detroit, as compared to 26 percent for Federal Reserve member banks in other cities (Holland 1972: 45).

The problems with this form of lending were better understood in the 1920s than they are today. The Federal Reserve Act was originally based on the real bills doctrine that requires lending to be self-liquidating (Holland 1972: 57). The problem was that banking was no longer organized along those principles. A report by the Federal Reserve Board said:

> the cause of banking difficulties in recent years has been the extension of activities of banks beyond the traditional field of commercial banking and into the field of capital financing and real estate loans. (Board of Governors of the Federal Reserve 1931: 53)

Detroit banks were unable to follow the principles of the real bills doctrine as strictly as Chicago and New York banks because the opportunities for commercial lending in Detroit were so limited. The automobile companies were mostly self-financed, and there was little trade-related commerce there.[18] Thus the proportion of loans in Detroit eligible for Federal Reserve backing fell from 12.3 percent in 1925 to 6.4 percent in 1929. This gave the Federal Reserve little basis for lending to Detroit banks in the event of a liquidity crisis. Holland (1972: 59) concludes that "[t]he gap between the Detroit banks and the Federal Reserve as a potential source of liquidity grew wider as the [1920s] progressed." In any event, trust companies, which were not part of the Federal Reserve system, were the instititutions most heavily engaged in real estate lending. As Holland (1972: 95) says: "The banking collapse in Detroit was triggered by the illiquidity of the Union Guardian Trust Company. The problems . . . originated with a predecessor, the Union Trust Company."

After World War I, there was considerable latent demand for housing in Detroit, particularly in the suburbs.[19] For example, Dearborn grew by almost 2,000 percent and Ferndale by 750 percent in the 1920s (Holland 1972: 112). The postwar recession of 1921 delayed construction. The following were boom years:

> From 1922 to 1929, real estate activity in Detroit went through three phases. First, was the boom in residential construction, which ran from 1922 to 1926. The second phase was the speculation in lots, subdivisions and improved farmland, which had its peak from 1924 to 1926. The final phase was the construction of large office buildings and apartment complexes, which reached peak activity from 1927 through 1929, when most of Detroit's skyscrapers were built. This was a "lagged" type of construction activity, which had its roots in the 1922–1926 boom when many of the plans for these buildings were made. But unlike residential construction built on subdivided farmland, these large buildings required considerable time between planning and construction. (Holland 1972: 102–103)

In the first few years of the residential building boom (phase 1), the new housing was filling an unmet demand. However, by 1925, that demand was met, but building continued, and created excess capacity. Construction of residences declined after 1925, but construction of large office buildings (phase 3) doubled from 1926 to 1928. In the interim, the growth in construction of suburban housing set off the speculation in new subdivisions (phase 2). About 91 percent of all lot subdivision in Detroit took place between 1915 and 1935, and 60 percent of that took place in 1924–1926. Although demand by builders for lots began to decline in 1925, speculative trading of lots continued into 1926. Lot prices in residential subdivisions rose in a speculative fever, far beyond their value for houses, to 10 or more times assessed value (Holland 1972: 115–117).

Builders who invested in large subdivisions after 1922 were constantly in danger of insolvency. They borrowed to buy the land, then had to borrow more to finance public improvements (streets, sidewalks, trees, etc.). They were "land poor." To assist them with their financing problems, the Union Trust Company invented "land contract bonds," which enabled it to lend money against entire subdivisions, despite the existence of previous liens on the property, with almost half of the bonds issued against the property of two subdividers as the security. The highly cyclical nature of employment in Detroit (tied to the automobile industry) made such loans highly risky, and by 1926, defaults began to accumulate (Holland 1972: 121).

The Union Trust Company actually increased its mortgage lending during the years following the initial crash of the residential housing market, from $6 million in 1925 to $18 million in 1928, mostly because of its relationship with large contractors. In addition, whereas most state banks financed real estate in established parts of Detroit and older suburbs, the Union Trust Company lent money in new suburbs, where subdivision and construction were highly speculative (Holland 1972: 123–124).

As a result of its lending against real estate in the extensive margins of Detroit, the value of the collateral held by Union Trust fell rapidly after 1926. "Well before the full force of the depression was felt, the frozen nature of its assets and the company's basic illiquidity was apparent" (Holland 1972: 127). Bills payable rose tenfold from 1927 to 1929, and real estate in foreclosure increased sevenfold. More than half of its assets were held in the form of mortgages or collateral loans. An exceptionally large proportion of mortgages were for low-cost houses ($3,000 to $5,000), which was the category of housing most hurt by the depression (Holland 1972: 127–130). (These were the sorts of houses bought by middle-income households most affected by unemployment, who were only marginally able to meet payment obligations during the best years, and the first to be foreclosed during the downturn.)

From 1929 to 1932, bank deposits shrank throughout the nation, as households feared the insolvency of banks and created the very condition they feared by withdrawing deposits. Since bank assets were largely in the form of real estate holdings, they could not be liquidated easily, and those that were liquidated through foreclosure lost much of their value. (The same process is occurring now, in 2009.) Thousands of banks closed during this period, as their capital proved insufficient to cover the drain on deposits (Holland 1972: 147).[20]

In 1931, weak banks borrowed from more liquid banks locally, and some banks borrowed from Federal Reserve banks to maintain liquidity. Fearing that depositors might start a run on the banks, every bank sought to increase its liquidity, but doing so meant selling off assets at a loss. Since everyone was trying to sell simultaneously, the price of assets fell, which further reduced the value of each bank's capital and assets, but not its liabilities. Underlying the general problem of liquidity (and the resulting deflation of asset values) was the frozen character of real estate loans. Banks held assets that could not be used to pay off nervous depositors, which is is precisely why the depositors were nervous.

Bank failures (as measured by aggregate deposits) were only half as severe in 1932 as 1931 (Holland 1972: 147). During the second half of 1932 (after a run on the banks in Chicago in June), the banking system began a recovery. At the end of 1932, the banking system as a whole had excess reserves, and withdrawals were slowing. However, while New York and Chicago banks were glutted with over $500 million in free reserves, the banks in the rest of the country had negative reserves of $200 million (meaning they had borrowed that much to shore up their capital) (Board of Governors of the Federal Reserve 1943: 397–399). The general decline of economic activity still prevented many borrowers from paying their debts—because banks were unable to provide working capital to businesses. Without repayments, the Great Revolving Fund had slowed almost to a standstill. Many banks remained illiquid, even if they were technically solvent. The Federal Reserve Bank was able to pump money into the banking system, but it could not make the money move. The problem was not the quantity of money or reserves. The problem was the immobility or illiquidity of the assets that prevented them from being recycled. Under those conditions, "[a]ny sharp jar to confidence could topple the entire structure. The storm broke in Detroit with the failure of the Union Guardian Trust Company" (Holland 1972: 196, citing Chandler 1959: 405).

The loss of liquidity of a single finance company (Union Guardian Trust) in a single city (Detroit) certainly could not have "caused" the bank run in 1933 entirely on its own. However, once hundreds of banks around the country became vulnerable because of their own real estate lending, the mutual reliance of banks within and between cities to provide liquidity to each other created the conditions for a domino effect. The failure of one major lender could then easily lead to the failure of many others. During January 1933, the withdrawal of $1 million in deposits from Union Guardian made it insolvent, not just illiquid. Despite efforts on February 9 by President Hoover and his advisors to persuade Henry Ford to salvage it, the Union Guardian Trust became insolvent. The governor of Michigan declared a bank holiday on February 14, 1933, because of the threat to the entire Michigan banking system posed by the public knowledge of the failure of the Union Guardian Trust (Holland 1972: 192–194). The fear of panic, as evidenced by a national surge in demand for currency (more than twentyfold increase in Chicago, for example) during the last week of February and the first week of March, persuaded governors in Maryland, Ohio, Illinois, and New York to suspend bank operations in their states as well. On March 6, 1933, President Roosevelt declared a one-week national bank holiday, and the panic subsided by April (Holland 1972: 196–198).

In the aftermath of the 1933 banking crisis, Detroit bankers became overly cautious, investing primarily in government and corporate securities, rather than making loans to local businesses (Holland 1972: 251). This was the wrong lesson to learn. While the bankers were wise to shy away from real estate lending, which tied up assets and reduced bank liquidity, they could easily have shifted into lending for accounts receivable and installment loans for consumer durables. These self-liquidating loans would not have left banks vulnerable to illiquidity. Even when household and business income dropped during a depression, these kinds of loans were still repaid (Holland 1972: 254, citing Board of Governors of the Federal Reserve 1957: 83). Because those sorts of loans turn over quickly, they not only benefit households and businesses, they also ensure the health of the banking system and the local economy.

In the 1930s and in later decades, some bank regulators drew the conclusion that branch banking was partially responsible for the insolvency of banks during the Depression. Those restrictions were lifted over time, but it is useful in retrospect to understand the partial validity of the original concern. The problem in Detroit was *not* branch banking per se. Instead, the connection between branch banking and instability was the creation of branches in new suburbs where the major form of lending was for subdivisions and other speculative real estate ventures. When the boom came to an end, the lending practices of those branches caused the banks or trusts to face a liquidity crisis or even insolvency. If branches had been set up merely to create convenience for households, in order to attract deposits, there is no reason to believe that branch banking would ever have been viewed as problematic.

VI

Conclusion

THE FINANCIAL SYSTEM of any nation is built on confidence. No amount of "backing" from gold or reserves or "too big to fail" plans can sustain a financial system in which participants have lost confidence. Trust is the greatest asset that any system of credit can have. It is what permits businesses to engage in exchange and allows an entire economy to succeed.

Periodically, trust and confidence recede, leaving an economy with very limited liquidity and the danger of shrinkage. Once that occurs, financial bailouts may succeed in preventing the complete collapse of the system, but they do not truly restore health. The soundness of an economy and its financial system must be based on the production of real goods and services, not merely the increase in financial transactions.

The aim of this essay has been to show that the trust created by banks is fragile and that it is a collective good. A relatively small number of banks can destroy the confidence that has been created as a collective good. They do so by lending against inflated real estate values and thereby losing their liquidity and their ability to issue short-term loans. Because banks are so interconnected, the high-risk behavior of a few banks can undermine liquidity not only in a small region, but now on a global basis.

Monetary authorities have tried with very limited success to prevent the creation of speculative bubbles by imposing quantitative controls on credit formation. There are too many ways to circumvent those controls. Thus, what I have proposed here is the establishment of rules that would implement the real bills doctrine, which favors short-term self-liquidating loans. That would entail curtailing real estate lending or at least limiting the proportion of any loan portfolio for that purpose. I have not tried to spell out in detail what sorts of rules might apply to banking. Until economists and the political leaders who follow their advice are convinced that the most serious problems in banking stem from real estate lending, any effort to provide a specific reform plan is premature.

This proposal to operate the banking system according to the principles of the real bills doctrine is in keeping also with the recommendations in previous chapters to (1) adopt land-value taxation (which would reduce the capital value of land and thus require less financing); (2) adopt improved and more frequent property assessment (to reduce the likelihood that bubbles will form); and (3) adopt labor-friendly tax policies that will have the effect of reducing demand for the kinds of durable capital that cause liquidity problems for banks.

I repeat the adage from John Stuart Mill (1872: BK. I, Ch. V, §6: 47): "Capital is kept in existence from age to age, not by preservation, but by continual reproduction." Most of the troubles of modern economies stem from failing to heed that message—by treating capital as a stock from which we can draw rather than as a revolving fund that must constantly be renewed. The taxation of land transforms the money loaned on it from a frozen capitalized lump to a flexible flow. As we saw in the previous chapter, the removal of taxes on labor will have the beneficial effect of increasing the turnover of capital and reducing unemployment while simultaneously reducing sprawl. Applying the same principle to turnover of capital in the financial system, we should seek to implement policies that preserve the liquidity of banks rather than waiting for crisis and then fruitlessly attempting to inject that liquidity.

The old lesson retaught by the financial crisis of 2008–2009 is that the liquidity of the financial system is endogenous. The kinds of loans that banks make affect the real economy and vice versa. By adopting a unified framework that encompasses land, capital renewal, and banking, economics could lead us out of the present morass and save us from the next. This next one is due in about 2026, based on the 18-year average period of past land cycles.

Notes

1. As a result of deregulation in the past two decades, many institutions now perform some of the services previously limited to banks. For the sake of simplicity, we will refer to all of them as banks, except when it is necessary to differentiate among them.

2. It is called a demand deposit because it amounts to redepositing the bank's loan in an account on which the borrower can write checks at any time ("on demand").

3. One of the conventions in telling the story of the origins of banking is to insist that it began with gold as the collateral for loans. This perpetuates the mythology that gold is somehow an inherent store of value and that monetary systems not backed by gold are weak. In fact, the real source of backing of any currency is the real economic activity that gives value to the assets held by banks.

4. A 100 percent reserve requirement would mean that banks could only lend the currency they received as deposits. This would mean that banks could not issue credit and that the money supply would remain constant unless the government increased it by issuing more currency. Whereas banks create credit only in response to economic demand, governments can create currency without limit, thereby risking inflation. On the other hand, if governments issue insufficient currency, they can stifle economic development. Thus, a fractional reserve system leaves flexibility in private markets, where it should remain. That does not preclude other forms of public regulation of banks, however.

5. One of the contributing factors to the current crisis was the repeal of Glass-Steagall in 1998.

6. In theory, this constraint applies to every country. However, since the U.S. dollar is the global currency of account, the United States has not been held accountable in international markets for continuously running a trade deficit for several decades. If the international currency switched to the euro (for example, if OPEC started demanding payment in euros, not dollars), the world market would be glutted with dollars that no one would want. The value of the dollar would collapse, and the United States would suddenly have to begin paying off its international debts, which would lower the standard of living of Americans drastically. The United States would face the stringent demands currently confronting many developing countries—how to increase productivity while interest rates are high.

7. For an empirical refutation of the Friedman-Schwartz thesis, see Calomiris and Mason (2003), who argue that bank failures from 1929 to 1933 were not primarily the result of "contagion" and "panic" (the Friedman-Schwartz thesis). Instead, those failures represented shocks to the banking system from real economic factors. They do not, however, examine real estate speculation and price collapse as significant factors contributing to the liquidity crisis that caused the failure of hundreds of banks.

8. One partial exception to this general rule is Gordon and Wilcox (1981: 77–79, 103 fn. 36). Gordon and Wilcox recognize that (a) endogenous factors help explain "the Great Contraction," (b) excessive residential construction from 1924 to 1927—at 8.6 percent of GDP—was an important precipitating

factor, and (c) the resulting decline in housing starts from 1926 to 1930 reduced GNP by 5.6 percent (over 40 percent of the total decline). However, they do not recognize that the expansion and contraction of bank lending was in any way related to the boom and bust in construction. In that respect, they continue to follow the Keynesian and monetarist view that financial factors are independent of real events.

9. If the risk associated with bank expansion is not self-evident, consider this. Liabilities divided by assets (L/A) is always less than 1 because assets equal liabilities plus equities. The higher that L/A ratio, the lower the percentage is left over as assets to cover nonperforming assets. Suppose L/A is initially 4/5 or 80 percent. The difference $(5 - 4 = 1)$ is the amount of equity. If the bank expands both assets and liabilities, the L/A ratio might become 9/10 or 90 percent. That still leaves 1 $(10 - 9)$ as the equity, but it must now cover a larger base of assets, which increases risk. In this simple way, expansion of bank assets (and corresponding liabilities) increases risk.

10. As John Stuart Mill (1872: 46–47) so ably expressed it: "When people talk of the ancient wealth of a country, of riches inherited from ancestors, and similar expressions, the idea suggested is, that the riches so transmitted were produced long ago, at the time when they are said to have been first acquired, and that no portion of the capital of the country was produced this year, except as much as may have been this year added to the total amount. The fact is far otherwise. The greater part, in value, of the wealth now existing in England has been produced by human hands within the last twelve months. . . . Capital is kept in existence from age to age not by preservation, but by perpetual reproduction: every part of it is used and destroyed, generally very soon after it is produced, but those who consume it are employed meanwhile in producing more."

11. The important case of exhaustible resources is not considered here. It is a subject in itself. For one of many analyses, see Gaffney (1967).

12. Norris (2007) cites 1974, 1980, and 1991 as recession years. In each case, the recession followed a decline of at least 33 percent in housing starts over two years. The 1958 recession was preceded by a similar pattern, with housing starts peaking in 1955 (U.S. Bureau of the Census 1960: Series N-106). The depression of the 1930s will be discussed at length below.

13. Under normal circumstances, the cash flow from an existing, middle-aged building that has largely paid off the interest on the original construction loan will mostly finance the owner's depreciation allowance or capital consumption allowance (CCA). The CCA is invested elsewhere, to conserve the owner's capital. When the building is finally torn down, the owner (and society) will have as much capital as ever. When the price of the land under the building rises during a speculative boom, the cash flow of the building

remains the same. However, the price of the land under the building rises so high it is now worth as much as the combined land and building were worth before. The owner no longer feels the same pressure to save in the form of a CCA to conserve his or her wealth. Instead, it seems that the rise of land price has accomplished that goal. The cash flow from the land plus building combination is now imputable to the land alone, to justify the land's higher price. The cash flow is all net income because land does not depreciate. The owner may spend it all on consumption, which many do.

14. In the first essay in this volume, we examined the periodic nature of the expansion and contraction of the economy based on real estate speculation, of which the Great Depression was only one example. For analysis of the history of this phenomenon, see Cole (1927), Hoyt (1933), Harrison (1983, 1997, 2005), Foldvary (1997, 1998, 2007), Kavanagh (2007), Anderson (2008), and Gaffney (2008).

15. "The agricultural depression [of the 1920s] in reality contributed substantially to the urban inflation [of land prices] by forcing the movement of millions of people" into the cities (Simpson 1933: 163).

16. The value of bank clearances in Miami was $202 million, according to Vanderblue (1927b: 262), the same as the 1927–1928 average. Similar figures on bank clearances for Tampa and Jacksonville, in Vanderblue (1927a: 118), show that the peak year in both of those cities was 1926, not 1925. The peak in Jacksonville was 57 percent higher than in Miami.

17. Detroit banks were also vulnerable because their capital ratio was lower than in many other cities: 12.7 percent in Detroit compared to 18.6 percent for banks in New York City and 19.5 percent in St. Louis and Pittsburgh (Holland 1972: 53). However, Holland points out that this weakness was actually a sign of strength in a way. Detroit banks had low capital ratios because their deposits grew so rapidly in the 1920s, compared to most other cities in the eastern United States. In San Francisco, which also experienced rapid growth in this period, the capital ratio of two major banks was around 9 percent (Holland 1972: 56).

18. On the problem of self-financing and the banks, see Currie (1931). Currie goes on to give this event a wrong spin, in my opinion, but the phenomenon he highlights was real enough

19. This did not include Highland Park and Hamtramck, where the Ford and Dodge plants had moved in 1910 and that were mostly built out by the 1920s, when speculative suburban development began on a large scale.

20. Bank failures by size of deposits almost doubled from $139 million in 1928 to $234 million in 1929, then rose by 250 percent to $865 million in 1930, and almost doubled to $1.7 billion in 1931 (Board of Governors of the Federal Reserve 1933: 220).

References

Allen, Frederick Lewis. ([1931] 1959). *Only Yesterday.* New York: Bantam.

Anderson, Phillip J. (2008). *The Secret Life of Real Estate.* London: Shepheard-Walwyn.

Appelbaum, Binyamin, and Zachary A. Goldfarb. (2009). "Under New Accounting Rule, Toxic Assets May Be Revalued." *Washington Post* (April 3): A15. Available online at: http://www.washingtonpost.com/wp-dyn/content/article/2009/04/02/AR2009040201264.html

Board of Governors of the Federal Reserve. (1931). *Report of the Branch, Chain, and Group Banking Committee, Vol. 2: Branch Banking in the United States.* Washington, DC: Federal Reserve.

———. (1933, April). *Federal Reserve Bulletin* (April). Washington, DC: Federal Reserve.

———. (1943). *Banking and Monetary Statistics.* Washington, DC: Federal Reserve.

———. (1957). *Consumer Installment Credit,* Washington, DC: Federal Reserve.

Boomershine, Gary. (2009, February 9). "Real Estate Investor Alert: Ghost Inventory in the REO Machine Haunts U.S. Housing Markets." Boomer's Blog. Available online at: http://www.garyboomershine.com/blog/2009/02/09/real-estate-investor-alert-ghost-inventory-in-the-reo-machine-haunts-us-housing-markets/

Calomiris, Charles W., and Joseph R. Mason. (2003). "Fundamentals, Panics, and Bank Distress During the Depression." *American Economic Review* 93(5): 1615–1647.

Chandler, Lester V. (1959). *The Economics of Money and Banking.* New York: Harper and Row.

CNBC.com. (2008, September 15). "Lehman Is in Advanced Talks to Sell Key Business." Available online at: http://www.cnbc.com/id/26708143/

Cole, Arthur H. (1927). "Cyclical and Sectional Variations in the Sale of Public Lands." *Review of Economics and Statistics* 9(1): 41–53.

Condo Vultures. (2008, April 17). "Lenders Reposses 52 South Florida Properties a Day in First Quarter of 2008." Available online at: http://www.condo.com/Community/UserBlogPost.aspx?ID=1689

Cowley, Stacy. (2008, November 16). "Message to Obama: Send Loans Fast." CNNMoney.com. Available online at: http://money.cnn.com/2008/11/14/smallbusiness/loans_needed_asap.smb/index.htm?postversion=2008111608

Currie, Lauchlin. (1931). "Bank Assets and Banking Theory." PhD diss., Harvard University.

Curry, Timothy, and Lynn Shibut. (2000). "The Cost of the Savings and Loan Crisis: Truth and Consequences." *FDIC Banking Review* December:

26–35. Available online at: http://www.fdic.gov/bank/analytical/banking/2000dec/brv13n2_2.pdf

Foldvary, Fred. (1997). "The Business Cycle: A Georgist-Austrian Synthesis." *American Journal of Economics and Sociology* 56(4): 521–541.

——. (1998). "Market-Hampering Land Speculation: Fiscal and Monetary Origins and Remedies." *American Journal of Economics and Sociology* 57(4): 615–637.

——. (2007). *The Depression of 2008.* Berkeley, CA: Gutenberg Press.

Friedman, Milton, and Anna Jacobson Schwartz. (1963). *A Monetary History of the United States, 1867–1960.* Princeton: Princeton University Press.

Gaffney, Mason. (1967). "Editor's Conclusion." In *Extractive Resources and Taxation.* Ed. Mason, Gaffney. Madison: University of Wisconsin Press. Available online at: http://www.masongaffney.org/publications/B1Extractive_Resources_Conclusion.CV.pdf

——. (2008) "The Great Crash of 2008." Unpublished ms. Available online at: http://www.masongaffney.org/essays/Great_Crash_of_2008.pdf

Goldfarb, Zachary A., David, Cho, and Binyamin Appelbaum. (2008). "Treasury to Rescue Fannie and Freddie: Regulators Seek to Keep Firms' Troubles from Setting Off Wave of Bank Failures." *Washington Post* (September 6): A01. Available online at: http://www.washingtonpost.com/wp-dyn/content/article/2008/09/06/AR2008090602540.html?hpid=topnews

Gordon, Robert J., and James A. Wilcox. (1981). "Monetarist Interpretations of the Great Depression: An Evaluation and Critique." In *The Great Depression Revisited.* Ed. Karl Brunner. Boston: Martinus Nijhoff Publishing.

Harrison, Fred. (1983). *The Power in the Land.* New York: Universe Books.

——. (1997). "The Coming 'Housing' Crash." In *The Chaos Makers.* Eds. F. J. Jones and Fred Harrison. London: Othila Press.

——. (2005). *Boom Bust.* London: Shepheard-Walwyn.

Henriques, Diana B. (2009). "Money Market Funds Are a Refuge, Right?" *New York Times* (January 10). Available online at: http://www.nytimes.com/2009/01/11/business/mutfund/11money.html

Holland, John Joseph Jr. (1972). *The Detroit Banking Collapse of 1933.* PhD diss. New York University. ProQuest Document ID: 759633141.

Hoyt, Homer. (1933). *100 Years of Land Values in Chicago.* Chicago: University of Chicago Press.

Kavanagh, Bryan. (2007). *Unlocking the Riches of Oz.* Melbourne, Australia: Land Values Research Group.

Maltby, Emily. (2009, February 25). "Small Biz Loan Failure Rate Hits 12 Percent: A Report on the Small Business Administration's Loan Guarantee Program Shows a Sharp Jump in the Default Rate." CNNMoney.com. Available online at: http://money.cnn.com/2009/02/25/smallbusiness/smallbiz_loan_defaults_soar.smb/

Mill, John Stuart. (1872). *Principles of Political Economy with Some of Their Applications to Social Philosophy*, 7ᵗʰ ed. Boston: Lee and Shepard. Available online at: http://books.google.com/books?id=48BNoKxhD90C

Mints, Lloyd W. (1945). *A History of Banking Theory in Great Britain and the United States*. Chicago, IL: University of Chicago Press.

Nicholson, Joseph L. (1938). "The Fallacy of Easy Money for the Small Business." *Harvard Business Review* 17(1): 31–34.

Norris, Floyd. (2007). "Housing History Sends Recession Warning." *New York Times* November 24.

Olick, Diana. (2009, January 28). "Banks Sitting on an Inventory Time Bomb." CNBC, Inc. Available online at: http://www.cnbc.com/id/28898377

Prudent Speculations. (2008, July 9). "Will the Fed Mandate Capital Ratios for Investment Banks?" Available online at: http://seekingalpha.com/article/84295-will-the-fed-mandate-capital-ratios-for-investment-banks

RealtyTrac Staff. (2009, April 16). "Foreclosure Activity Increases 9% in First Quarter." Press release. Available online at: http://www.realtytrac.com/ContentManagement/PressRelease.aspx?channelid=9&ItemID=6180

Roberts, Paul Craig. (1991, February 18). "Rescuing Real Estate Will Save Banks and the Economy, Too." *Business Week*. Available online at: http://www.businessweek.com/archives/1991/b32004.arc.htm

Said, Carolyn. (2009). "Banks Aren't Reselling Many Foreclosed Homes." *San Francisco Chronicle* (April 8). Available online at: http://www.sfgate.com/cgi-bin/article.cgi?f=/c/a/2009/04/08/MNL516UG90.DTL

Seidman, L. William. (1996). "The World Financial System: Lessons Learned and Challenges Ahead." In *History of the Eighties: Lessons for the Future*. Washington, DC: FDIC, Division of Research and Statistics. Available online at: http://www.fdic.gov/bank/historical/history/vol2/panel3.pdf

Simpson, Herbert D. (1933). "Real Estate Speculation and the Depression." *American Economic Review* 23(1): 163–171.

U.S. Bureau of the Census. (1960). *Historical Statistics of the United States, Colonial Times to 1957*. Washington, DC: Government Printing Office.

——. (2009, April). "Median and Average Sales Prices of New Homes Sold in United States." Available online at: http://www.census.gov/const/uspricemon.pdf

U.S. Council of Economic Advisers. (2009). *Economic Report of the President, 2009 Spreadsheet Tables*. Available online at: http://www.gpoaccess.gov/eop/tables09.html

U.S. Department of Labor, Bureau of Labor Statistics. (2009). "Table 3: Civilian Labor Force and Unemployment by State and Selected Area, Seasonally Adjusted." Available online at: http://www.bls.gov/news.release/laus.t03.htm

U.S. Department of the Treasury, Office of Thrift Services. (2008, September 25). "Washington Mutual Acquired by JPMorgan Chase." Press

release. Available online at: http://www.ots.treas.gov/?p=PressReleases&
ContentRecord_id=9c306c81-1e0b-8562-eb0c-fed5429a3a56

U.S. Federal Deposit Insurance Corporation. (2002). "The S&L Crisis: A
Chrono-Bibliography." Available online at: http://www.fdic.gov/bank/
historical/s&l/

———. (2008). *FDIC Failed Bank List.* Available online at: http://www.fdic.gov/
bank/individual/failed/banklist.html. Accessed April 20, 2009.

Vanderblue, Homer B. (1927a). "The Florida Land Boom (Part 1)." *Journal
of Land & Public Utility Economics* 3(2).

Vanderblue, Homer B. (1927b). "The Florida Land Boom (Part 2)." *Journal
of Land & Public Utility Economics* 3(3).

Index

for

A

Afghanistan, 112
AIG, 5, 180
Alabama, 54
Allen, Frederick Lewis, 194, 195
Allianz, 28
Angkor Wat, 136
Argentina, 85
Arizona, 7, 54
Arkansas, 54
ARMs (adjustable rate mortgages), 5
Army Corps of Engineers, 138
Asian financial crisis, 11, 12
Assessment
  Accuracy, 51–53
  Frequency, 53–54
  Importance of, 50–54
Asset values and interest rates,
  187–188
Austrian cycle theory, 33, 37
Austrian economic tradition, 2, 81,
  82, 101
  Basis of new macroeconomics,
  as, 81–82
Averch-Johnson effect, 121
Aztecs, 136

B

Banks
  Booms, role of in, 188–189
  Capital, 179–183
  Detroit bank failure of 1933,
    196–202
  Illiquidity of, causes of, 185–190
  Lending by, qualitative controls
    on as limit to bank
    expansion, 169–174
  Net worth, 179–183
Barzel, Yoram, 138
Bear Sterns, 6, 179

Bell Telephone Company, 128
Berlin, 139
Bernanke, Ben, 32
Berndt, Ernst R., 87
Berry, R. Albert, 93
Blue Book, 117
Board of Works, 136
Boom and bust cycles, real estate,
  27–29, 186–190
Borrowers, creditworthiness of,
  174–176
Boulding, 138
Brasilia, 137
Brazil, 10
  Brasilia, 137
Britain, *see* England
Buildings, taxes on, 39–43,
  45–48, 50
Business Cycle Dating Committee
  (NBER), 4
Business Week, 4

C

California, 7, 53, 54, 85, 88, 91, 137,
  139, 194
  California Water Plan, 137
  Friant-Kern Canal Service Area,
    88, 89
  Los Angeles, 156
  Proposition 13, 54
  Sacramento Valley, 85
  San Francisco, 30, 94
  San Joaquin Valley, 88
  Tulare County, 85
California Water Plan, 137
Canada, 85
Capital
  Bank, 179–183
  Destruction of during speculative
    boom, 189–190

Faster recovery of, 134–136
Growing and flowing, 100–103
Income tax treatment of, 113–119
Investment, 122–124
Labor and, 69–77, 82–134
Land and, 82–132, 187
Longevity of, effect on labor,
    95–100
Monuments as capital sinks,
    136–140
Property tax treatment of,
    112–113
Replacement of as source of
    national income, 130–132
Shortages of, 63–65
Taxation of, 85–86, 106–122
Turnover
    Achieving full employment via,
        61–154
    Activating capital by faster,
        103–106
    Historic recognition of,
        125–126
    Investment and, 122–124
    Valence of, increasing, 77–79
Capital gains, 72, 76, 109–111, 115,
    117, 119–121, 142, 182
CDs, 183
Census of Governments, 51
Chicago, 30, 55, 192, 197, 200, 201
Chicago Real Estate Cycle, 29
Chicago School of economics, 164,
    170–173
China, 160
Chile, 11
Civil expansionism, 94–95
Cleveland, 30
Cline, William R., 93
CNN, 175
Collateralized mortgage obligation
    (CMO), 181
Collateral, loan, types of, 177–179
Computerized mass appraisal
    (CMA), 51
Consumer Price Index (CPI), 54
Continental Illinois, 186
Corporate income tax, 120–122
Council of Economic Advisers, 4
Credit, money and crisis and,
    155–210

Creditworthiness of borrowers,
    174–176
Crisis, money and credit and,
    155–210

D
Dearborn, 198
Demolition and renewal, timing of,
    42–44
    Long-run effects, 43–44
    Short-run effects, 42–43
Depression, *see* Great Depression
Destabilizing effects, technical limits
    on, 164–165
Detroit, 30, 194, 196–201
    Speculation and bank failure of
        1933, 196–202
Domar, Evsey D., 77

E
Earth, 64, 79, 133, 144
East Asia, 10
Eckstein, Otto, 67
Economic crisis, land market role
    in, 27–60
Egypt, 136
Eisner v. Macomber, 117
Employment
    Capital and, 133–134
    Full, achieving with capital
        turnover, 61–154
    Land use intensity and,
        88–92
Employment Act of 1946, 65
England, 7, 33, 77, 142, 170
English colonies, 84
Environment, benefits to of new
    macroeconomics, 79–81
Equilibrium, sources of,
    165–184
Euler Hermes, 28
Europe, 85, 86, 142, 160
    See also specific countries by
        name
Excise tax, 40, 108, 121, 141
Expansionism
    Civil, 94–95
    Counterproductive, 86–88
    Military, 94–95

F

Faisal, King, 140
Federal Accounting Standards
    Board, 181
Federal Deposit Insurance
    Corporation (FDIC), 155, 172,
    181, 182
Federal Home Loan Bank, 116,
    172
Federal Home Loan Mortgage
    Association (Freddie Mac),
    6, 7, 156, 168, 180
Federal Housing Finance Agency
    (FHFA), 156
Federal National Mortgage
    Association (Fannie Mae), 6,
    156, 168, 180
Federal Reserve, 4, 166, 167–169,
    171, 174–176, 179, 195, 197,
    199, 200
  Deposits, 167
  Member banks, 197
  Notes, 166, 167
  Regulations, 174
  System, 166, 168, 195
Federal Reserve Act of 1913, 166,
    197
Federal Reserve Bank, 166–169, 174,
    179, 195, 200
  Expansion, 168
  Lending to member banks by,
    168–169
Federal Reserve Board, 167–169,
    171, 197
  Controls as limit on bank
    expansion, 167–174
  Policy, 167
Ferndale, 198
FHA, 166
Fisher, Ernest, 29, 30, 110
Florida, 7, 53, 54, 194, 195
  1920s situation of, 194–196
  Miami, 194
Foldvary, Fred, 33
Ford, Henry, 201
Forest Service, 94
Fortune magazine, 93
France, 71
Friant-Kern Canal Service Area,
    88, 89

Friedman, Milton, 66, 164,
    170–172
Frontiers as capital sinks, 136–140

G

Gaffney, Mason, 1, 2, 15–18
GDP, 69, 156
Generally accepted accounting
    principles (GAAP), 182
General Motors, 1
George, Henry, 9, 15, 33, 55, 62,
    65, 81, 82, 84, 137
Georgia, 54
Georgist economic tradition, 2, 72,
    73, 81
  Basis of new macroeconomics,
    as, 81–82
Germany, 7, 71
Glass-Steagall, 166
GNP, 156, 158, 159
Goldman Sachs, 179
Grand Rapids, 30
Great Crash, 175
Great Depression, 7, 9, 17, 155,
    175, 182, 191, 196, 201
Great Revolving Fund, 126,
    129–130, 200
Greece, 136

H

Haig, Robert M., 118
Haig-Simons logic, 142
Hansen, Alvin, 86
Harrison, Fred, 33
Harrod, Roy, 77
Harrod-Domar model, 86
Harvard's Joint Center for Housing
    Studies, 5
Hawaii, 139
Heller, Walter, 111
Highway Trust Fund, 110, 122
Holland, John Joseph, 196, 197
Home Owners' Loan Corporation,
    186
Hoover, Herbert, 200
Houthakker, Hendrik, 116
Hoyt, Homer, 29–31, 33, 55
  Land cycle research of, 29–33
Hutterites, 116

I

Illinois, 54, 201
  Chicago, 30, 55, 192, 197, 200,
    201
Incan canals, 136
Income tax, 38, 52, 73, 104,
    106–109, 112–119, 121,
    141–143
  Corporate, 120–122
  Treatment of capital, 113–119
IndyMac Federal Bank, 155, 156
Inflation as tax, 119–120
Initial public offering (IPO), 111
Interest
  Asset values and rates of,
    187–188
  Deduction of and property tax,
    116
  Rationale for, 161–163
Internal Revenue Service (IRS), 52,
    117–119
Internet, 34
Investment, capital, 122–124
Investment tax credit, 72, 116, 132,
    142
Iowa, 54
Iran, 140
Iraq, 64, 79, 112, 139
Ireland, 7, 14, 136
  Irish potato famine, 136
Irish potato famine, 136
Israel, 139

J

Jacobs, Jane, 105
Japan, 7, 10, 13, 71, 85, 130, 139
Jews, 160
JPMorgan, 6

K

Kahn, Alfred, 112
Kahn, Harry, 106
Kellerman, David, 7
Kendrick, John, 70
Keynesian economics, 2, 55, 61,
    65–67, 72, 73, 77, 78, 82, 86,
    111, 130, 157, 165, 167, 171,
    172
  Misleading nature of, 157–158

Keynes, John Maynard, 55, 62, 78,
    82
Korea, 139
Krugman, Paul, 10–14, 78

L

Labor
  Capital and, 69–77, 82–132
  Displacement of
    Longevity of capital and,
      95–100
    Taxation and, 106–122
  Idle, 63–65
  Land and, 82–132
  Land use intensity, effect of on,
    92–94
Laffer Curve, 67
Lampman, Robert J., 120
Land
  Engrossment, historical
    observations on, 84–85
  Labor and, 82–132
  Capital and, 82–132, 187
  Cycle, 29–38, 186–190
  Markets, economic crisis and,
    27–60
  Ownership, concentrated, effect
    on labor, 92–94
  Property tax treatment of,
    108–112
  Taxation of, 41–44, 48–50, 88–92,
    108, 141
  Use, factors affecting, 38–49,
    88–92
Lehman Brothers, 6, 156, 179
Lending, bank, controls on as limit
    to bank expansion, 169–174
Lereah, David, 9
LIFO accounting, 117
Liquidity
  Cost of creating, 163–164
  Creation of, 159–161, 163–164
  Real economy and, 158–165
  Sources of, 165–184
Loan collateral, kinds of, 177–179
Logging, *see* Timber, trees, and
    logging
Los Angeles, 156
Losing Ground, 65
Lovins, Amory, 80

M
Macroeconomics
    Failure of, recent history, 65–67
    Half-truths of, 69–77
    Health, how to restore, 82–132
    Microeconomic basis for,
        124–132
    New framework for, 61–154
        Austrian-Georgist roots of,
            81–82
        Environmental benefits of,
            79–81
        Valence of capital and,
            77–79
    Origins of, 67–69
Malaysia, 11
Mandel, Michael J., 4
Manhattan, 195
Market, as limit on bank expansion,
    174–183
Marshall, Alfred, 52
Marxism, 68, 77, 95
Maryland, 54, 201
Mennonites, 116
Merrill Lynch, 6, 179, 180
Mexico, 10–12
Miami, 194
Michigan, 54, 194, 201
    Dearborn, 198
    Detroit, 30, 194, 196–202
    Grand Rapids, 30
Military expansionism, 94–95
Mill, John Stuart, 125, 130, 190,
    203
    Capital turnover and, 125–126
Milne, Richard, 28
Milwaukee, 30, 51, 52
Mints, Lloyd, 170
Monetarist orthodoxy, 157–158
Money
    Amount of, 158–159
    Credit and crisis and, 155–210
Money market fund (MMF), 184
Monuments as capital sinks,
    136–140
Morgan Stanley, 179
Mortgage-backed security (MBS),
    4, 5, 181
Mortgage Bankers Association,
    5, 7, 28

Multiple Listing Service of the
    National Association of
    Realtors, 182
Mumbai, 14
Muth, Richard, 94

N
National Association of Realtors,
    9, 182
National Bureau of Economic
    Research, 4
National income, capital
    replacement as true source
    of, 130–132
Nevada, 7, 54, 194
New Economics, 65, 66, 78, 130
New Jersey, 54
New York, 54, 143, 196, 197, 200,
    201
    Manhattan, 195
    New York City, 121, 194–196
New York City, 121, 194
    1920s situation of, 194–196
Nicholson, Joseph, 175
Non-accelerating-inflation rate of
    unemployment (NAIRU),
    66, 67
North America, 84, 86

O
Obama, Barack, 76, 77
Office of Thrift Services, 166
Ohio, 201
    Cleveland, 30
    Toledo, 30
Oklahoma, 54
Only Yesterday, 194
OPEC, 71
Oregon, 54, 194

P
Pacific region, 4
Pahlevi, Mohammed Reza, 140
Palma, Gabriel, 11, 12
Payroll tax, 90, 91, 104, 106, 107,
    113, 141, 142
Pennsylvania, 53
Peoria, 96
Phelps, Edmund, 66
Phillips Curve, 66, 67

Portugal, 84
Progress and Poverty, 82
Property tax, 16, 27, 37–42, 45,
    49–51, 53, 73, 76, 81, 82,
    102, 108–116, 119, 122,
    140–143
Proposition 13 (California), 54
Prudent Speculations, 179
Public confidence, loss of as limit
    on bank expansion, 165–167
Puritan ethics, 66

R
Reaganomics, 2, 171, 182
Read economy, liquidity and,
    158–165
Real estate, *see also* Land
    Avoiding cycle of, 49–54
    Booms and busts, 27–29
    Chicago Real Estate Cycle, 29
    Speculation in and Detroit bank
        failure of 1933, 196–202
Real estate owned (by banks)
    (REO), 181, 182
RealtyTrac, 180, 182
Reconstruction Finance Corporation,
    186
Ricardo effect, 104
Ripening of land for higher use,
    47–49
Risner, Marc, 91
Roberts, Paul Craig, 182
Roosevelt, Theodore, 196, 201
Roman Empire, 115, 136
Romer, Christina, 4

S
Sacramento Valley, 85
Sakoui, Anousha, 28
Samuelson, Paul, 65, 66
San Francisco, 30, 94
San Joaquin Valley, 88
Savings and loan (S&L) fiasco,
    171, 172
Say's Law, 130
Schwartz, Anna, 171, 172
Securities and Exchange
    Commission, 6
Seidman, L. William, 172

Senior Loan Officer Opinion Survey,
    175
Sharga, Rick, 180, 181
Shiller, Robert, 8–10, 14
Short-term gains, as leading to bank
    illiquidity, 185–186
Simons, Henry, 118
Simpson, Herbert D., 192
Singapore, 130
Smith, Adam, 84, 124, 125, 130,
    170, 173
    Capital turnover and, 125–126
Solow model, 86
South Carolina, 54
Southeast Asia, 10, 160
Spain, 14, 84
Speculation
    Detroit bank failure of 1933 and,
        196–202
    Effect of property tax on, 49–50
Standard metropolitan statistical
    areas (SMSAs), 51
Stiglitz, Joseph, 10, 11, 14
Stockfisch, Jack, 73

T
Tax
    Buildings, 39–43, 45–48, 50
    Capital gains, 72, 76, 109–111,
        115, 117, 119–121, 142, 182
    Corporate income, 120–122
    Excise, 40, 108, 121, 141
    Income, 38, 52, 73, 104, 106–109,
        112–119, 121, 141–143
    Inflation as, 119–120
    Labor displacement as result of,
        106–122
    Land, 41–44, 48–50, 88–92, 108,
        141
    Land and capital combinations,
        biases affecting, 85–86
    Land value, 14, 203
    Payroll, 90, 91, 104, 106, 107,
        113, 141, 142
    Property, 16, 27, 37–42, 45,
        49–51, 53, 73, 76, 81, 82,
        102, 108–116, 119, 122,
        140–143
    Role of, 140–144
    Sales, 108

Tax Reform Act of 1981, 171
Tax Reform Act of 1986, 172
Texas, 54, 116
Thailand, 10, 12
Timber, trees, and logging, 75–77,
    94, 100–102, 113, 117–119,
    121, 124, 133, 135, 136, 141,
    198
Toledo, 30
Trees, *see* Timber, trees and logging
Troubled Asset Rescue Plan, 1
Tulare County (California), 85

U
Udell, Jon, 94
Union Guardian Trust Company,
    197–201
United States, 7, 12, 13, 52, 54, 62,
    64, 70, 71, 79, 123, 156, 177,
    194, 196
    See also specific states, entities,
    and agencies by name
University of Chicago, 170
U.S. Bureau of Reclamation, 88, 129
U.S. Census of Agriculture, 92
U.S. Foreclosure Market Report, 182
U.S. Interstate Highway System, 137

U.S. Steel, 175
U.S. Treasury, 167, 175, 177, 178
Uy, Marilou, 10

V
Vanderblue, Homer B., 195
Volcker recession, 86

W
Wages, capital and, 69–72
Wales, 7
Wall Street, 5, 132, 137
Washington, D.C., 94
Washington Mutual Bank (WaMu),
    155, 156, 166
Washington State, 54
Wealth of Nations, The, 170
Weeks, David, 95
West, Charles, 95
Wicksell, Knut, 16, 77, 78, 101, 125,
    126, 138
    Capital turnover and, 125–126
Williams, Ellis, 113
Wisconsin, 94
    Milwaukee, 30, 51, 52
World War I, 198
World War II, 79, 86, 176